The
Journey
to Wholeness
in Christ

If you would like to contact the Rev. Conlee and Signa Bodishbaugh, or would like to receive a newsletter from one of the
organizations listed below, please write or fax:

The Journey to Wholeness in Christ
P.O. Box 50635
Mobile, AL 36605
Fax: (251) 443–6937
e-mail: JourneyPress@aol.com
www.ChristAnglican.com

Pastoral Care Ministries
Leanne Payne
P.O. Box 1313
Wheaton, IL 60189
www.leannepayne.org

The Marriage Retreat
The Rev. Forrest and Nancy Mobley
4421 Commons Drive East - PMB 404
Destin, FL 32541
Fax: (850) 650-8001
fmobley@earthlink.net

Desert Stream Ministries (healing
  ministry to the sexually and
  relationally broken)
Andy Comiskey
P.O. Box 17635
Anaheim Hills, CA 92817-7635
Fax: (714) 701-1880

Redeemed Life Ministries (healing
  ministry for sexuality and identity)
The Rev. Mario Bergner
P.O. Box 1211
Wheaton, IL 60189

The Journey

to Wholeness in Christ

A Devotional Adventure to Becoming Whole

Signa Bodishbaugh

Journey Press

Published by Journey Press
P.O. Box 50635
Mobile, AL 36605

Second printing, May 2000
Third printing, December 2002
Fourth printing, December 2004

Printed in the United States of America

Library of Congress Cataloging-in-Publication Data
Bodishbaugh, Signa, 1940–
    The journey to wholeness in Christ : a devotional adventure to becoming whole / Signa Bodishbaugh.
    p. cm.
    ISBN 1-887650-39-3
    1. Spiritual life—Christianity—Prayer books and devotions—
English. 2. Devotional calendars. I. Title.
    BV4811.B55 1997
    242'.2—dc21   97-1684

To Leanne

who always called me into wholeness,
who saw through God's eyes the woman I could be
and who gave me the language to write this book

"For I will take you out of the nations; I will gather you from all the countries and bring you back into your own land. I will sprinkle clean water on you, and you will be clean; I will cleanse you from all your impurities and from all your idols. I will give you a new heart and put a new spirit in you; I will remove from you your heart of stone and give you a heart of flesh. And I will put my Spirit in you and move you to follow my decrees and be careful to keep my laws. You will live in the land I gave your forefathers; you will be my people, and I will be your God. I will save you from all your uncleanness."

Ezekiel 36:24–29

Contents

Preface

THE SCRIPTURAL PRINCIPLES UPON WHICH THIS BOOK IS BASED ARE ONES I first encountered in my friendship with Leanne Payne. Her place in my life has been significant. She was the Christ-bearer to me; she is my mentor, my prayer partner, a fellow minister and continues to be a dear friend.

Through Pastoral Care Ministries (worldwide seminars led by Leanne and her team) we are given a biblical model for effective ministry to those who choose to become whole. Her many books, which include the wisdom of great minds of theology and psychology, provide the world with an understanding of God's healing of the human soul.

My book contains many of the concepts about Christian wholeness that Leanne has taught the world. Much of the terminology and many of the definitions I use are taken directly from her teachings and writings. They have been applied to personal situations but not re-interpreted. For an in-depth study and theological comprehension of what is presented in this book, the reader is strongly encouraged to absorb the foundational and effectual truths of our Judeo-Christian heritage in the works of Leanne Payne.

From her first book, *Real Presence* (Baker, 1991), based on the works of C. S. Lewis, we are given a vital exposition of Incarnational Reality, the basis of all Christian wholeness. It is upon this same foundation that my book is constructed.

In her books *The Healing Presence* (Baker, 1991) and *Restoring the Christian Soul* (Baker, 1991) one can find a rich presentation of the following subjects presented in this book: Practicing the Presence of God, Finding My True Self, Seeing My Heart as a Garden of the Lord, Identifying the Desire of My Heart, Valuing and Apprehending the True Masculine and the True Feminine, Cleansing the Imagination, the Healing of Memories, and Renouncing the Idols of the World.

In my book, one will encounter the importance of Taking in God's Word, Discerning His Voice in a Sea of Many Voices, and Keeping a Listening Prayer Journal, all presented in great detail in Leanne's book *Listening Prayer* (Baker, 1994).

Her other books, *Crisis in Masculinity* (Baker, 1996) and *The Broken Image* (Baker, 1996), illumine a biblical understanding of gender and sexuality.

Further information on Pastoral Care Ministries is presented at the front of this book.

Acknowledging My Partners on the Journey

Since the first printing of *The Journey to Wholeness in Christ* in 1997, I have received hundreds of letters, e-mails, phone calls and had personal conversations with men and women who have shared with me their stories of what God is doing in their lives as they read and use this book. For many years I have worshiped in awe the God who has made me whole through the principles I write about, but it is quite another thing to comprehend the vast scope of what God has done with so many others who have been encouraged to follow the same path to wholeness. I have always known that these principles work; they are scriptural and they have been tested for hundreds of years by faithful Christians. However, the vastness of personal experiences and deprivations to which these truths have been applied successfully is surprising to me. But why should I be surprised? After all, our stories, backgrounds, and circumstances do not need to be the same — our Lord is the same!

While writing this book I always felt that I was conversing very personally with someone sitting on the other side of my desk. I have been so encouraged to have many people tell me that they sensed that; they felt as though it was a one-on-one conversation. I am grateful that objective was realized.

From the time I first started writing, several years ago, my husband, Conlee, has continually encouraged and blessed me. He continues to be my best cheerleader and best friend. Next to Jesus, Conlee has been the rock in my life. With his high standards for truth and integrity, and his genuine enthusiasm for creative gifts, he has stood with Jesus to be the firm foundation upon which I have the freedom to minister and be real.

My association and friendship with Leanne Payne continues to give me guidance and joy as we minister together in her Pastoral Care Ministries seminars throughout the world. European

11

prayer partners I have met through PCM have been a particular blessing and encouragement: in England, the Rev. Norman and Jackie Arnold, Ron and Lin Button and Dr. Andrew and Ruth Miller; in Germany, Christiane Mack, Christa and Pastor Hartmut Bernitz, and our excellent German translator, Manfred Schmidt.

The ministry of *"The Journey to Wholeness in Christ"* seminars has grown beyond our dreams. God has expanded our outreach beyond America and translated the ministry into other cultures without a flaw. The experience of taking our team to Israel, Germany, Canada, and Great Britain has been a joy. The daily, intimate relationships I have with these team members is a constant source of strength to me. We worship, pray, play, rejoice and weep together. The miracles we have seen as we minister together are too large for any book to contain.

Particularly I wish to thank those on the *"Journey"* team: Kellie and Alan Armstrong, Susan and F.G. Baldwin, Kathy Maitre, Richard Weavil, Becky Patrick, Pris and Bert Milling, Judy Oschwald, Carolyn and Bernard Hogan, Sue and John Webster, Marie Nickerson, Jacque Drane, Nancy and Bob Gordon, Claire Cloninger, Diana and Frank Parker, and our excellent worship leaders, Deby and Kirk Dearman and John Chisum.

The need for wholeness only increases in our fragile world. I am so grateful for each of you who has shared your story with me. Not one was too horrific (and some were exceedingly difficult for you to share and me to hear) for our Lord Jesus to enter, forgive, cleanse and make whole. The courage it took for many of you to face your pasts is incredible. It stands above some of our bravest heros and heroines. But as you faced pain with the Cross always before you, you found hope. And when there is hope there is always redemption and then wholeness.

This is a book for those who are being redeemed from the sin and pain that either you have chosen, or that which was imposed upon you by others, or that which this sinful world flings upon you. Use it with the assurance that many have gone this way before you and many will come after you. As you begin your "Journey" with Jesus, know that before long, you will be encouraging someone else along the way. That's the way it works!

Signa Bodishbaugh
Hamewith Cottage, 2002

Introduction

The Vision for the Journey

A VIGOROUS, GOLDEN-TANNED YOUNG MAN WALKED TOWARD ME ALONG THE river bank through the verdant orchard of fruit trees. He saw me lying on the grassy bank of the river in the cool shade of a large tree. He did not speak to me, yet clearly communicated his concern. As he approached he pulled leaves from each tree under which he passed and handed them to me one at a time. In ways apart from language this young man made me aware of exactly how each leaf could minister to me in places I had not even realized were hurting.

Slowly and deliberately, knowing the incredible gravity of what I was doing, I ate one leaf, let another dissolve in my mouth, applied another to a wounded place on my body, placed one over my heart, placed one on my forehead, one over my mouth, another over my ears, on my hands, my feet. Then I drank tea brewed from the leaves and, crushing some into a paste, applied it to deep scars that had never completely healed. When the pain went away I could not imagine how I had lived with it for so long and yet survived.

Before he left, the young man scattered some of the leaves down into the water and I watched the current carry them far beyond my sight of vision. When I looked back he was gone, but I knew he had given me a mission—to pick leaves as he had done and give them to others.

I opened my eyes and began to write in my prayer journal the vision God had just given to me. I had recently read Ezekiel 47:12:

> Fruit trees of all kinds will grow on both banks of the river. Their leaves will not wither, nor will their fruit fail. Every month they

will bear, because the water from the sanctuary flows to them. Their fruit will serve for food and their leaves for healing.

Where else had I read about the leaves for healing? Whenever I receive a *rhema,* or personal word from God to me for my particular situation, I run immediately to the Scripture for further understanding. Now, with the help of my concordance I quickly found Revelation 22:1–2:

Then the angel showed me the river of the water of life, as clear as crystal, flowing from the throne of God and of the Lamb down the middle of the great street of the city. On each side of the river stood the tree of life, bearing twelve crops of fruit, yielding its fruit every month. And the leaves of the tree are for the healing of the nations.

I thought about these two amazingly similar visions given seven hundred years apart, first to Ezekiel and then to John. John saw the river of the water of Life flowing from the throne of God and of the Lamb. This river runs right down the middle of the main street of the city of God, through the heart of where God's people dwell, where I will live one day. The banks on both sides of this great river of Life provide the fertile soil for the great tree of life to grow. *Is this the same tree of life that grew in the Garden of Eden for Adam and Eve?* I wondered.

Ezekiel's vision seems to suggest that rather than one huge tree, there is a whole orchard of everbearing fruit trees with roots running deep to the lifegiving water. The fruit provides real sustenance for whatever needs God's children have, and even the leaves themselves have healing properties.

I let the imagery of the two Scripture passages wash over me.

Lord, I prayed, *show me Your truth today through these visions. Speak to me, Lord, as I sit in Your presence.*

And He did.

The Mission

Pondering the vision, I thought of many ways in which healing leaves have been given to me by obedient children of God. What wholeness I have experienced in my life by applying them where I hurt! I realized that the ways in which leaves of healing can be applied are uncountable and often surprising.

All through my life, the messengers who brought me leaves have been varied and often unlikely bearers of such important gifts. Now, with God's Word and the vision vividly before me, I had a strong sense of being presented with a mission to take healing leaves to others.

How awesome for such an ordinary woman to be asked to do such an extraordinary task! But I joyfully accepted the invitation from my Lord to set out on His mission, because I had His full assurance that He would go with me every step of the way.

I am aware that I will not always know exactly how the leaves are to be applied in someone else's life, but my job is to offer them as gifts from God to whomever needs them. Somehow I, like the young man, will become a messenger, a delivery person.

This book is one way of fulfilling my mission. Through it I long to deliver healing leaves to you. I invite you to commit yourself to seeking God's face and His continued healing for you.

Perhaps you have already been to a healing conference, received healing prayer, read books or heard tapes, and have experienced the first joys of hope for your wholeness. Like most of us, you may need a support group, a prayer partner or a spiritual director to help you continue whatever wonderful freedom you have tasted.

Perhaps you have never had specific prayer for the healing of your soul, but have asked God to bring you peace within. Maybe you are searching for the next step.

As my husband, Conlee, and I lead "The Journey to Wholeness in Christ" seminars we are often approached by participants who beg us for a book to take home, one that will keep them on course, refresh them with the truths they have received and help discipline them in prayer, Bible study and intimacy with Jesus. With these requests in mind I felt the voice of the Spirit urging me to write such a book. It is an invitation from the Holy Spirit to you and me. He is urging us to keep on. He wants us to know that the struggle is worth the effort!

Your choice to explore *The Journey to Wholeness in Christ* probably means you are searching for "something more." Perhaps your need is obvious to you and to everyone who knows you, or perhaps only you are aware of the nagging yearnings to make something right or different on the inside.

Whatever the case, congratulations! The first step to becoming whole is to recognize your brokenness. The fact that you are reading a book on wholeness marks that recognition and launches you on your journey to find all the potential God has for you.

As we go on this journey together, our Lord will show you what to do with each day's offering, with each healing leaf from the tree of life. He will show you how to apply it where you need it. I may never know how He uses the leaves in your life (although I welcome your letters), but I offer them to you with prayer and joy.

Not one of us alive today has attained the goal of wholeness yet, and we will not until we join our God in heaven—His "city of wholeness" where He will bring us all to completion.

Meanwhile, He has made available wonderful helps in our quest toward wholeness so that every day we can become more like the persons He created us to be than we were yesterday. The purpose of this book is to encourage you toward faithful use of these spiritual helps so you can begin to shake off the obstacles that keep you from being all you should and can be.

On the journey to wholeness we will read God's Word every day. We will open our hearts to Him in prayer in a quiet place. We will listen for His healing personal word to us. We will each keep a listening prayer journal. (More about that later.) Finally, we will try to obey what He tells us to do, knowing that He will empower us to do far more than we are able to do in our own strength.

Wholeness Means Becoming the "Real You"

Do you know that God sees you as perfect? He has *always* seen you as perfect. Oh, He knows all your faults and sins and soulish warts, but He has a true image of the real "you" firmly established in His heart—the image that embodies all the potential He created for you.

- When you were being conceived in your mother's womb, your Creator God had His hand on you, calling you forth into wholeness (Psalm 139:13).
- If you have asked His Son, Jesus, to be the Lord of your life you have willingly collaborated with His plan for your wholeness.

- If you have yielded your life to the power of the Holy Spirit you have given Him further access into the depths of your being to empower you for the journey.
- Each time you pray and enter into His presence you are coming closer to the image of "you" that God has seen since creation. He wants you to be whole more than you want to draw your next breath.

And to that goal of perfection He constantly calls you, nudges you, draws you and woos you.

Do you ever wonder why you are miserable in certain situations that seem fairly tolerable to others in the world? Your loving Father is too faithful to you and too committed to your perfection to allow you temporary happiness in a situation that fails to advance your well-being. He sees things in your life that He knows could destroy the goal the two of you have in common—your wholeness. Often your very misery prompts you to reach for something better.

Remember, He can see way, way down the road on the journey. He can even see the final destination. We cannot see much past the immediate stretch of highway in front of us. Are there curves ahead? Roadblocks? Detours? Bridges washed out? Uncharted waters? Storms, tornadoes or hurricanes? We need an experienced Guide!

The Time Frame for the Journey

This book comprises a forty-day journey we will take together on the path toward the wholeness God has already begun in our lives. But why forty days?

On my fortieth birthday I took time to reflect on the solemnity of the occasion. Several years have passed since then, but I recall that it seemed serious indeed to have finished my fourth decade of life. I had spent the same amount of time on this earth as the Hebrew survivors of the great exodus out of Egypt had wandered through the wilderness of the Arabian Desert. For the same length of time that I had been alive they had drifted, searching for the realization of God's promise to them.

A complete generation had lived, loved, lusted and eventually missed their goal. Yet the wandering time had served a purpose. God had ordained its length and He had used it to bring wholeness to the life of an entire family of believers. At the end of forty years God let new eyes see its fruit.

Forty. It is a significant number in our spiritual history. Important judges like Deborah and Gideon and powerful kings like Saul, David and Solomon each governed for forty years.

Forty seems to have been a round number ascribed to a generation, a number denoting the completion of a lifetime or of an ordeal which, when accomplished, marked the beginning of a promise.

Periods of forty days appear frequently in the Old and New Testaments as times used to accomplish God's purposes in His people. A period of forty days is very nearly a tithe of the total number of days we are each allotted in one year's time. Just as immeasurable blessings become ours when we cheerfully give Him our monetary tithes as the firstfruits of what He has given us, so it is with the tithe of our time.

For many believers in sacramental churches the observance of Lent, a forty-day period of penitence and intimacy with God preceding Easter Sunday, is a special opportunity to discover what is in one's own heart. As our spirits become fine-tuned to His voice we learn to achieve an intimacy with Him that we will never want to be without.

This particular journey, then, is scheduled to last for forty days, although it may take you a longer or shorter period of time, depending on God's dealings in your spirit. Remember, too, that you probably will take subsequent journeys to go deeper yet into the wholeness God has for you.

As we approach God through the reading of this book and the incorporation of its healing leaves, God is asking:
"Are you willing to give Me forty days to speak to you?"

A Look at the Itinerary

The Bible contains several accounts of forty-day periods when God accomplished extraordinary things with ordinary people. Each account helps us to map out a region we need to visit on our journey.

- After enlisting Noah to help carry out His plan to salvage a remnant of the human race, God sent rain upon the earth for forty days to *purify* His people.
- Moses, when he was forty years old, fled Egypt. He was in Midian for forty years, and stayed on the holy mountain for forty days to hear God's plan to *free* His people.
- The leaders of the Israelites spent forty days exploring Canaan to see for themselves what God's *Promised Land* held for them.
- Elijah fasted and traveled for forty days in order to reach the mountain of God to *hear the word* of the Lord.
- Jonah preached God's message of repentance to the Ninevites, who then fasted for forty days to *repent and stand before God* so they would not be destroyed.
- Jesus stayed in the desert for forty days, *fasting and overcoming temptation* in preparation for ministry. He also remained on the earth for forty days after His resurrection.

1. Purification
2. Finding freedom from bondages to my past
3. Finding God's promised land for me
4. Fulfilling the yearning to hear His word
5. Acknowledging the need to repent and stand before God
6. Learning how to overcome temptations in my life

Each of us must visit these six regions if we are to enter into wholeness. While they have distinct themes, all six are interrelated. Exploring all six will move us toward the same destination—personal wholeness in Jesus!

As we enter each region we will look at the life of at least one individual to see how God worked in his life as he traveled. Seeing our connection with other travelers throughout history and identifying with God's healing power in their lives will give us courage as we ask Him to heal our own.

I hope you are committed to traveling toward wholeness with the Healer of your soul. It is the ultimate journey, one that will take your whole life and will continue even beyond this lifetime into eternity. View these forty days as a sacrificial beginning. Give yourself fully to Jesus and let Him anoint your mind, your imagination and your spirit to receive all He wants to give you.

In the next section I will offer some pre-journey instructions to help you get ready for our departure.

Prayer

Lord Jesus, I pray for the one you have led to read this book. Come, Holy Spirit, anoint Your child to receive all the wholeness God the Father gives to His loved ones. Please stir up excitement in our hearts for Your Word and the joy of being in Your presence. May Your healing gifts be present on this divine journey and may Your Word take root in the hungry heart.

Thank You, Lord. Amen.

Pre-Journey Instructions

TRAVELERS USUALLY FALL INTO ONE OF TWO CATEGORIES. THE FIRST IS MADE up of planners: men and women who arm themselves with lists of items to pack, maps, airplane and train schedules, pre-routed itineraries, regional guidebooks and advance accommodation reservations. Planners like to know when, where and how they are going, and they do not like surprises!

The second category consists of the more spontaneous types. They decide tonight to take a jaunt tomorrow, throw a few things in a bag and hope for the best. They view surprises as assets!

Most of us lean toward one category or another. I fall in the middle and tend to take the kitchen sink, just in case! So here are a few pre-journey instructions I feel are critical if our time together is to be spiritually productive.

What to Take Along

If you are like me you are wondering what to take on this journey. We want to be prepared for any occasion. Most of us will take a lot of baggage we would be better off without, baggage that will only slow us down. Let's not worry about that right now. Jesus will carry it for us when He knows we are ready to give it up to Him. What can be an incredibly heavy burden for you or for me is extremely light for our Lord.

It may make you feel more secure to make a list. Before I started traveling as frequently as I do now, I used to make very complete lists so I would not forget some obvious item, like my hairdryer. I have learned by now to keep a suitcase packed with the essentials so the journey is much easier and less stressful.

What essentials will you need for our forty days with God? Here is a checklist:

___ Certainty that God the Father is real.
___ Belief that Jesus Christ is His Son and your Savior, the Lord of your life.
___ Secure knowledge that the Holy Spirit is working in your life.
___ An open heart to receive whatever Jesus has for you. (Remember, there may be some surprises!)
___ Permission for God to do whatever He desires in your life.
___ Freedom to go wherever He leads you.

These essentials are not just for this trip, but for every step you will take with Him for the rest of your life.

Our list, however, still lacks one very important item.

Be Sure to Bring Your Camera!

Every journey evokes memories. We bring home remembrances of our adventures through souvenirs we buy or rolls of film we take at each stopping place, as well as through the images we store up in our hearts.

God, who invited us on this journey to wholeness, wants us to have the most meaningful time possible. He wants us to preserve each memory, each word, each breakthrough. He advises us to

Remember the wonders he has done, his miracles, and the judgments he pronounced.

1 Chronicles 16:12

On this journey God's healing words to us will be so important that we will want to keep them in a safe place where they will not be stolen, tarnished or perverted by the world, our flesh or the devil. Time and circumstances will attempt to rob us of the power of the godly word for us in the moment it is given and received. Oh, to have a "spiritual camera" to record every healing word from God!

We do have a "camera"! It is one I believe has been inspired by God for His people's use. It is a listening prayer journal.

God has always encouraged His people to keep the story of their relationship with Him alive in their hearts, to tell it to their children, to share it through oral tradition, and later to record it on tablets, scrolls, books, tapes and disks. Some of these records of His relationships with His loved ones were so powerfully inspired by the Holy Spirit that they were considered sacred enough to be canonized into Holy Scripture. Those Scriptures are our foundation. In the Hebrew *shema* God's people are told to take His commandments, the Word of God, and let them:

> be upon your hearts. Impress them on your children. Talk about them when you sit at home and when you walk along the road, when you lie down and when you get up. Tie them as symbols on your hands and bind them on your foreheads. Write them on the doorframes of your houses and on your gates.
>
> Deuteronomy 6:6–9

The Word of God is to be connected intimately to everything we do!

Both Deuteronomy 30:14 and Romans 10:8 tell us that God gives words to every seeking heart who listens:

> The word is very near you; it is in your mouth and in your heart so you may obey it.

God constantly speaks His healing words to our hearts. It is His desire that we have such a personal relationship with Him that we are like sheep, hearing our Shepherd's voice clearly in the chaotic noise of all the voices that vie for our attention. Jeremiah received the following word from God to his heart while he was imprisoned:

> This is what the LORD says, he who made the earth, the LORD who formed it and established it—the LORD is his name: "Call to me and I will answer you and tell you great and unsearchable things you do not know."
>
> Jeremiah 33:2–3

Any way in which we can successfully bind God's written or personal word to our hearts is a true gift from God. For centuries

Christian men and women have employed the gift of keeping listening prayer journals. The words God spoke to saints of old can bless us today because those words were recorded in their journals. The words God will speak to our hearts along this journey can continue to bless us as we ponder them in our hearts, pray them with our spirits and keep them safely recorded in our prayer journals for those times when we are tempted to forget, doubt or disbelieve.

The psalmist willed to do just that:

I will remember the deeds of the LORD; yes, I will remember your miracles of long ago. I will meditate on all your works and consider all your mighty deeds.

Psalm 77:11–12

Of course, concentrating on our relationship with God is the most important focus of our journey, but some tried and true suggestions for keeping an effective, meaningful, listening prayer journal will help us keep that focus. These are so important to our journey together that we will spend the rest of this section discussing them.

First, though, let me tell you how keeping a prayer journal has affected my relationship with God.

Patterns—and Progress

About 25 years ago, as I first began to seek God in a more personal way, my spiritual godmother said to me daily, "Now be sure to write in your prayer journal! Write every word God gives you in your prayer journal."

But what *was* a prayer journal? I knew it was more than an intercessory prayer list, more than a spiritual diary, although it included some of each. I eventually learned that a true prayer journal contains both the intensely personal words my heart pours out to God as well as His personal words spoken back to me in a variety of ways.

Learning to keep a prayer journal enabled me to make hearing God's voice a reality. I learned how to be still and listen with my heart. It was difficult at first—actually more difficult to learn to be still than to listen. But I practiced, alone and together with prayer partners. And as I began to know that God was yearning to speak to me, I, too, began to long more and more to hear His healing words and to expect to receive them.

Every word I received through Scripture, through a prayer partner or directly from His heart to my heart, I faithfully recorded in my prayer journal. What a pattern of my spiritual growth I can see as I look back over 25 years! God was calling me to be a woman whom I did not yet know. Although I am still very much a person in process, it is good to know that I am becoming the woman He created me to be, moving down His road toward wholeness.

There were times when I had no idea who I was supposed to be, when I imitated first one role model and then another, thinking that in imitation I could discover who I was. For long periods I would "watch myself" to hear how I spoke and see how I looked, judging the reactions of others to determine my own responses. I attempted to "find myself" in my roles as wife, mother, daughter and friend, rather than as a child of God. I begged my husband to give me my identity, mistakenly thinking this was his responsibility. In so doing I put an undue strain on our marriage. Learning to hear God's voice began to define for me the person *He* had created me to be.

Part of my journey has been a terrific struggle. There are long gaps in my prayer journal indicating times when I quit listening and went my own way. There are pages blurred with my tears. Some entries contain many question marks. But one thing is sure: Whenever I quieted my soul and listened for His voice, He always spoke His healing word to me, calling me to be the person He longed for me to be.

Words God has spoken to me have pierced my heart and changed me in miraculous ways. Some have been so poignant I have wept; many were so powerful I thought I would never lose their impact. Yet the busyness of our lives, the voices of the world, the flesh and the devil and the passage of time can rob us of the richness of gifts from God. I am constantly grateful to have the content of God's messages to me through revelation, dream, parable, metaphor, picture, song, word, Scripture or intuition recorded in my prayer journal.

You will benefit greatly from the small amount of time it takes each day to record the experiences we will share together on this journey. I guarantee that there will be something worth writing each day as we go where our Guide leads us. Just as you are thankful for photographs and diaries you have kept from family holidays that recall each experience and enable you to share them with others, so you will rejoice in years to come that you preserved the record of the eventful journey on which God led you to bring you into wholeness.

You will quickly discover that the more you discipline yourself to write in your journal each day, the easier it will become to hear God's voice speaking to you as you write.

Beginning Your Prayer Journal

I now offer several tips for developing a practical, effective prayer journal.

1. Master the Mechanics: What to Use and How to Organize It

If you have never kept a prayer journal before, or if you have filled one with expressions and descriptions of your own negative thoughts, depressing introspection, pain and doubt, start over. Treat yourself to a fresh, clean book, ripe for a new beginning of listening to and receiving healing words from Jesus.

Most of us choose something lovely to begin with—a flowered, unlined book of blank pages or a handsome, leather, desk-quality notebook. But after a while nearly all seasoned "prayer journalists" opt for the old, reliable loose-leaf binder, so comfortable and well-worn that it becomes as familiar a friend as your Bible. I like a loose-leaf binder because when it is full I can file a year's pages in a folder and refill my old friend for a new season.

Another advantage to the loose-leaf binder is the ease with which you can compartmentalize your prayer journal using index tabs, as you will probably want to do after a time. In my journal, for instance, I have sections for "Creative Ideas and Things God Is Urging Me to Do," "Books, Authors and Favorite Passages," "Notes for the Next Book" and "Notes from Other Speakers." I find it helpful to have these categories at hand when I am being quiet before the Lord. When my mind wanders over a mental "to-do" list, or when an amazing inspiration pops into my mind and I am afraid I will lose it, I can easily flip to that section of my journal and jot it down, knowing it will be there as a reminder when the appropriate time comes. This has helped me to stay focused, a goal I struggled with for years.

By far the most important section in my prayer journal, however, is the one labeled "Prayer." Under this heading are spaces for "Words to and from God," "Intercession" and "Dreams." In these sections I write my heart out freely before the Lord and record His precious words to me. I can copy Scripture verses that have particular meaning and, seeing them in my own hand, ask Him to personalize them for me.

As I interceded for others (an activity I have always found difficult), I became aware that I needed a system of some sort to keep on track. So my section labeled "Intercession" contains subsections. One is labeled "Church," and covers not just my local church, but other ministry teams worldwide that I know and love. Other sub-sections are labeled "Family" (with each by name), "Friends" (many with pictures) and "Ministry" (which includes names of persons I minister to or individuals who have requested prayer).

The last sub-section in my prayer journal under "Intercession" is labeled "Beloved Enemies." Praying for my beloved enemies is vital if I am to obey God and be free from the wounds others inflict upon me. I first listen to God and then with fresh, creative insight from His words to me, especially about the difficult people in my life, I am able to pray more powerfully, objectively and honestly for each person or situation. Instead of the exhausting, rote repetition so many of us associate with intercession, I find myself praying "more than I know" as I collaborate with God's Spirit. Instead of a task I ought to do, intercession becomes a joy, an act of love and gift-giving.

The section where I record dreams has been of particular value as I have allowed God to uncover patterns revealed out of the deeper recesses of my heart. The most insignificant-appearing dream can become an integral part of a series of dreams that, when seen as a whole, may be the revelation of a block about which I have been crying out to God.

I find that if I write out even particularly confusing or silly dreams without analyzing or attempting to interpret them, I can go back in a few weeks and God will show me definite patterns running through all of them. Many times He will show me these patterns as important keys to unlock something in my heart, and will interpret them for me. Dreams are symbolic, the language of the heart, and we must not assume them to be literal. God, not a book on dream interpretation, will show me the meaning of the symbols in my heart as I listen to Him. With this knowledge come true understanding and healing.

2. Decide Where to Have Your Quiet Time

Ask God to lead you to a special "holy space" in your home where you can spend time with Him in listening prayer. It should be comfortable and quiet, a place where you can keep your Bible, your prayer journal and perhaps a symbol that is meaningful to you—a cross or crucifix, a picture, flowers or maybe a view of a garden or water.

When we moved into our present home I had a spot all picked out for my quiet time, but it soon became obvious that God had consecrated another place to be my listening post. Now I look forward to going into my study to pray. My desk sits in the bay window area overlooking a calming, pastoral setting: a camellia orchard, a barn and water. A crucifix and an angel are nearby. I have a tiny hot plate for my cup of tea, because I often forget it for a half hour or so. My study also houses a bookcase, clock, telephone and computer, but I choose to let the answering machine take any calls that come during my special time with God.

Once you have found your "holy space," you may want to pray this prayer:

> Lord, please make this a sacred place for Your heart and mine to come together. Let me hear and receive the word You have for me as I sit here in Your presence. Amen.

3. Decide When to Have Your Quiet Time

Coordinate your quiet time with the rhythm of your day. This will not be easy! But try to be consistent. It is an act of the will:

You choose to have a quiet time, and then you incorporate it into whatever goes on in your busy schedule. If you are persistent, it will become *part of the rhythm* of your daily life.

Putting this "appointment with God" on your calendar or in your daytimer will help you to form the habit and stick to it. If you have a daily appointment with the Creator of the universe every day at ____ o'clock, what could be a higher priority?

When you miss a day or two, however, do not heap guilt upon yourself. It is much better simply to tell God you have missed being with Him and to begin immediately to enjoy His fellowship, than it is to wallow in remorse and shame over your lack of discipline. Remember, discipline takes practice!

4. Begin the Dialogue of Listening Prayer

First, quiet yourself with deep, cleansing breaths. Then, begin to read God's Word. Remember, the Bible is God's love letter to you. Reading it is one of the surest ways we have to hear His heart.

Here are several suggestions to make your listening prayer time enjoyable and healing:

1. *Use a Bible you can write in, take notes in and underline.* Your Bible will become as personalized as your prayer journal.
2. *Ask God to lead you to the Scripture He wants you to read today, or use a daily lectionary or devotional.* Although I do read Scripture and meditate on it in His presence at this time, I prefer to do Bible *study* at another time. Study engages our *head* energy and I want to engage my *heart* with God in responsive listening prayer.
3. *Write out in your prayer journal whatever Scripture God gives you that particularly speaks to your heart each day.* The very act of writing links the words to your being.
4. *Personalize the Scripture.* Insert personal pronouns and your name when appropriate. When I read 1 Peter 2:9 recently, for example, I wrote,
    "*I* am a chosen person, a royal priest, a holy nation; *I* belong to God so that *I* may declare the praises of Him who called *me* out of darkness into His wonderful light."
5. *Once you have personalized a Scripture verse, ask God how it applies to you today.* Let the Word soak into your mind and

heart. One of my conversations with Him about 1 Peter 2:9 went something like this:

> "Lord, how can I meaningfully declare praises of You?"
> "My child, just say to Me what is on your heart," He replied in my spirit.
> "O Lord, You are too wonderful for me to put into words. What You have done for me is indescribable. When I think back to how I was stumbling in the darkness and thinking it was the day, I remember that I was nearly blinded to see the light You possess. You truly called me and I never want to take for granted who You are and what You have done in my life."

6. *Pray what is in your heart.* If the demands of the day crowd your mind, write them down on your "to-do" list or in your daytimer, thus freeing your thoughts for dialogue with God. Empty your heart to Jesus as best you can.

If Jesus reveals sin in your life, confess it to Him and receive His forgiveness. Looking at a crucifix or a picture of Jesus on the cross may help you to grasp the reality of what He *continues to do,* having died for you on Calvary.

If negative thoughts and attitudes come up, write them out, giving them to Jesus. See Him receive them into His hands, into His body, into His heart. Ask Him for the healing word to come and replace any negative thoughts you have given up to Him.

If you have been overcome with resentment about a certain person or situation, confess it directly to Him and ask Him to forgive you. Tell Him you gratefully receive His forgiveness and take it into yourself. Offer words of forgiveness toward the other person in the power of the forgiveness He has extended to you.

Now make a divine transaction. For instance, in exchange for my resentment toward another, I might hear Him say, "You are acceptable in My sight. I give you the gift of contentment." Then I gladly receive this precious gift and write my new definition of myself straight from God's heart: "God sees me as acceptable to Him and contented in His presence."

7. *Listen with your heart, not your analytical mind.* This is difficult to describe, especially if you feel you have never heard

God's voice. You actually have: His voice called you to commit your life to Him. How did you know that was God? You learned to trust Him as you grew to know Him.

The way you hear God will be unique to you. Some call it a divine intuition, an inner knowing, a still, small voice, an impression or a spiritual sensing. So stop striving. Be still and listen. It will help you to join occasionally with a prayer partner with whom you can listen and share the words God speaks.

8. *Write in your prayer journal whatever God gives you.* It may be a picture, a dream, a vision, an idea or a single word. When I first began doing this years ago, no matter what I read or prayed or how hard I listened, I only heard or felt the phrase, "Be still and know that I am God."

Over and over I heard it, and over and over I wrote it in my journal. After several weeks I became frustrated, feeling I was not really hearing the phrase from God: I simply was repeating it to myself like a broken record. I wanted desperately to hear something else.

Finally I realized that I was indeed hearing from God and that He did want me to be still and know Him in an intimate way. When I learned how to do that, He began to speak to me in other ways.

9. *Obey whatever God tells you to do.* Remember, anything God speaks directly to your heart can be measured by the standard of the Scripture. He will not tell you anything that will contradict what He has given us in the Bible.

Bon Voyage! Vaya con Dios!

You have readied your sacred space and have your prayer journal and Bible at hand. Now it is time to move out!

I hope you are excited about what lies ahead. Yes, it will be exciting, and perhaps painful at times. There may even be days when we run out of energy. But our destination—the wholeness God has reserved for us—is firmly implanted in our hearts, and we will encourage each other to stay the course and complete the journey.

Your daily Scripture reading, meditation, listening prayer time and journaling may open up life-changing experiences with Jesus. Or He may affirm His ever-abiding presence in a quiet way. The time may also serve as a catalyst to take you wherever He wants to lead you.

Let me remind you again: It is important to take this journey at *God's pace for you*. The "forty days" may be more figurative than literal, since each of us needs intensive work in different areas. Never feel condemned or rushed if you and God need to continue with a certain day's leaf or experience for several days' time. Give yourself permission to move prayerfully and carefully, forsaking any goal-orientation that robs you of the ability to "smell the flowers" along the way. Know that when you and God are ready to move on, I will be waiting for you.

As we embark on Day 1 of our journey, you will hear how I began the journey to wholeness.

Day 1

Pre-Journey Jitters

A T THE BEGINNING OF EVERY JOURNEY MOST TRAVELERS EXPERIENCE A LIT-tle anxiety and uncertainty about how all their arrangements are going to work out. This is especially true if they will be with unfamiliar traveling companions.

I realize you are not familiar with me, although I am certain you will know me fairly well by the end of our forty days together. Let me assure you of one truth that will make you feel much more secure: I am not your guide. God the Father, Son and Holy Spirit is our Guide, so we are in very safe hands. I would never attempt this journey without knowing that He is in charge. He knows exactly where we are going. He has been there before.

Are you one of those people who absolutely hates to admit you are lost? Some people will go miles out of their way to avoid stopping to ask for directions. The old joke is their motto: "I'm not lost, I just don't know where I am."

We have friends who can laugh (now!) about a family vacation they were taking one summer years ago when their four children were little. They were driving across Kansas en route from the East Coast to Colorado, and the scenery looked much the same for miles and miles and miles.

On the second of two long days of travel, our friends decided to stop in mid-afternoon to let the children swim and eat an early supper so they could get a pre-dawn start the next day. All went according to plan, and at 3:30 a.m. the following morning the parents settled their little ones, still asleep, in the car and set off for Colorado.

33

It was a rainy night, and they drove for hours through deserted countryside with nothing but darkness to their right or their left.

At about 8:00 a.m. the children woke up ready to eat. Everyone began watching for a restaurant until, as if on cue, the children shouted, "Let's eat there. That's where we ate yesterday!"

Sure enough, the driver had turned east rather than west, and had retraced about five hours of the previous day's journey!

During our journey to wholeness we will stop to ask for directions at every opportunity. We will do all we can to avoid making wrong turns. Our Guide in all things, the Holy Spirit, will lead us each step of the way.

Getting Acquainted

In our ministry of wholeness we encourage men and women to write out their spiritual histories, the narratives of their introductions to Jesus Christ. You do not need to have a dramatic introduction to Him in order to do this; it may have been a gradual, deepening acquaintance. But you should be able to track a progression of growth in your life during the time you have been intimately acquainted with Him.

This is an important exercise to do whether or not anyone besides you will ever read it. It can be extremely therapeutic to write it out before the Lord. Telling our stories, even in our journals, helps us to understand our healing.

When each of us begins to be whole, we will be able to tell our stories objectively, without falling apart or being formed and shaped by them. And when we are ready, God will provide the opportunity for us to tell our stories to others who need to hear them.

Besides that, there is no better way for us to get acquainted at the beginning of this journey than to tell each other our spiritual histories. This is the beginning of a trusting relationship, when we both realize we are intimately linked to each other by a close relative—the Lord Jesus.

I will begin by telling you my story, how I came into relationship with Jesus Christ. I want you to tell your story later.

I first met Jesus face to face on February 27, 1972. The date and time are indelibly etched on my heart because meeting Him was the most remarkable experience I had ever had. It changed my life forever.

I knew a lot of things about Jesus Christ before I met Him because I had been active in our church, serving on lots of committees, attending worship services regularly and leading a "good, moral life." But I never even dreamed about meeting Him face to face. I did not think such a thing was possible and, to be honest, I was not terribly concerned about it.

Conlee and I were part of the early-seventies generation of liberated young adults coming right out of "Happy Days." We had the means to make things happen! We lived in a university town; Conlee's business was taking off; we were attaining career and social goals we had set for ourselves. We had two young sons, a new house we had designed with pride, plenty of income, fun trips, a respectable church, satisfying volunteer work and nice friends. Life was "lookin' good."

In the fall of 1971, Conlee was serving as convenor of the adult Christian Education class in our church. It was a secular, elitist, avant-garde group of about sixty intelligent adults who loved to argue, welcomed a challenge and did not want the class to last too long!

Midway through a six-week series on professional ethics a lovely young woman began attending the class regularly. She had a serenity and peace about her that intrigued us all, but she never stayed afterwards for coffee and no one seemed to know anything about her except her name—Leanne Payne. At the end of the six weeks it was announced that someone had volunteered to teach a series on C. S. Lewis' book *The Abolition of Man*. The teacher? Our "mystery woman."

As Leanne taught, the class discussions were animated, intellectual and controversial, but beyond her words we sensed a profound lesson. In her very demeanor I saw a calm assurance, peace and loveliness I had seen in no other human being. Conlee and I were so intrigued that after several weeks we issued a risky invitation to the whole class to come to our home on a Sunday night to hear Leanne tell some of her personal experiences. Everyone seemed interested, and we expected a crowd.

Three people came.

We had never seen the man before, and the two women were only faces we had seen at church: We did not know their names. One seemed to have her life in perfect order. The other appeared cynical, jaded.

Where were our friends?

It was an awkward two hours. Conlee was restless, stoking some damp wood in the fireplace in a fruitless effort to start a fire, pacing as Leanne spoke. Leanne shared many stories about knowing God personally, about healing and deliverance. I remember few specifics about what she said. No one else said anything. Conlee and I were relieved when everyone prepared to leave and we stood at the door, holding their coats and wearing gracious smiles. The evening had not gone as planned.

But as she said good-bye to Leanne, the woman who looked so perfect remarked, "Leanne, I've never heard of the things you talked about tonight, but if they're true I need to experience them in my life."

The other woman (who had seemed so cynical) said, "Then we can't leave until we pray for you." She took the first woman by the hand, led her back in front of the fireplace and knelt with her on the floor. The man followed. Leanne went after the three of them. Conlee and I stood dumbfounded at the door, still holding everyone's coats as our four guests knelt in our den.

I looked to Conlee for help, but he only shrugged and whispered, "Let's make this quick and get them out of here."

Reluctantly we knelt with them. Until then our only experience with prayer in our home was a standard blessing at dinner with the children. If anyone was going to pray that night it was going to have to be Leanne. She began to do so quietly. I have no idea what she said, for I was looking at the woman who had expressed her need and saw tears running down her face. The room was very still. *Something was happening.*

I became aware of a sound. It seemed faraway, like a roar somewhere over the roof of our house. It got louder and louder and I felt a moment of panic as I recalled descriptions I had heard of tornadoes approaching. The noise hovered over the chimney as we remained on our knees. I remember thinking how absurd the situation was, yet no one moved. It was as if we were paralyzed, in awe of the moment.

My left side was near the fireplace and I literally *felt* the roar descend the chimney and explode in a burst of flame on the still-wet logs. The resulting blaze had the intensity of a bonfire. My eyes flew open and I looked at the fireplace with amazement and fear.

Then the "intensity" or "energy" from the fire—I still do not have a name for it—went into our circle and danced among us, alighting on each one. I had a sense of being charged with a sudden burst of life and vitality that surpassed anything I had ever felt. Health and wholeness filled me in a way my body could barely contain; I thought I would burst.

No one spoke for a long time, and at some point everyone left. We who had been strangers only moments before parted as dear friends, as though we had known each other all our lives.

When everyone was gone, Conlee and I were both exhilarated and terrified. Still energized by the incredible phenomenon, we could not sit down, could not stand still. We walked around the house laughing, hugging each other, astounded that we had experienced the same wonderful manifestation of God's presence.

In the next moment we were confronted with the terrifying fact that we had no more excuses before God! Not only was He real, present and alive, He also knew our names, our address and had even been in our home that very night with an awesome invitation.

R.S.V.P.

Yes, we knew without doubt that when God came to us with fire from heaven, He was issuing an invitation to a lifetime of relationship and commitment to Him. He also expected an answer. I do not know if there was a time limit on the reply He expected or not, but I know He waited until we were sure. This was not something to be taken lightly.

Although our initial introduction to God's reality and presence was sudden and dramatic, our sober consideration of the seriousness of the commitment into which we entered took several days. A week later, on March 5, trusted friends witnessed our quiet and peaceful vow as we pledged our lives to the living Savior.

Whether you have had a dramatic introduction to the living God or a quiet, gradually dawning awareness of His presence, the invitation is the same. He says to you, "Will you allow Me to be the Lord of your life? Will you belong to Me and to no other as long as you shall live?"

If you have never given Him a definitive answer, this is the perfect time to do so. I hope you say yes! But it must be *your* choice. No one else can carry this relationship for you: It is between you and God. And it must be honest.

My Prayer from My Journal

Here is the prayer I wrote in my journal shortly after accepting God's invitation:

Lord Jesus Christ,
I acknowledge that I have gone my own way.
I have sinned in thought, word and deed.
I am sorry for the sin of trusting in myself and others more than in You.
I am sorry for the sin of not taking You at Your word and not delving into the depths of the commitment I am making.
Right now I want to alter that habit, that pattern, by letting You be in control of my life, and by entering fully into a covenant relationship with You.
I believe You died for me, to take all my sin and all my anxieties and all my depression and all my sickness into Your own body.
I thank You for Your great love for me.
Now I open the door to You.
Come in, Lord Jesus.
Come in as my Savior and cleanse me.
Come in as my Lord and take control of me.
I will serve You with all the strength You give me all the days of my life. Amen.

If you want to pray the same prayer I prayed, please do. Pray it from your heart. I am sure someone gave it to me many years ago when I wrote it in my journal, and it has continued to be my personal mission statement. I read it from time to time and always share it with any group I minister to, inviting them to pray it as well.

These are my spiritual roots. This is my story.

Beginning the Journey to Wholeness

They overcame him [the accuser, the devil] by the blood of the Lamb and by the word of their testimony.

Revelation 12:11

1. A good way to begin the journey to wholeness is to write out your prayer of commitment. Use mine, if you wish, or recall your own as closely as you can.
2. Now it is your turn to share your spiritual story with me. Write it out in your prayer journal. Do not feel it must be dramatic or "churchy." Just be honest. The only requirement is that it be *yours*. God draws each of us in unique ways.

   In addition to helping us begin to sense our own spiritual roots, writing "the word of our testimony" is, as the verse above indicates, a tool against the devil who would like to accuse us of never having made the commitment to life with Jesus. Knowing we are covered by the blood of Jesus the Lamb, and objectifying our experience through its narration, provides us with a beginning to which we can point when Satan comes against us.

   Once you have completed writing your story, you will be ready to move on to the first region on our itinerary.

Region 1
Practicing God's Presence
to Be Purified

BASED ON THE EXPERIENCES OF NOAH, AS FOUND IN GENESIS 6–9; OF JOB, AS FOUND IN THE BOOK OF JOB; AND OF MARY AND MARTHA, AS FOUND IN LUKE 10:38–41 AND MARK 14:3–10

Day 2

The Garden Security System

MY HUSBAND, CONLEE, AND I HAVE A LITTLE SAYING WE FREQUENTLY USE when we are about to take a chance on something risky. I do not mean risky as in buying a lottery ticket or riding the "Zipper" at the county fair. I am talking about risky living in the spiritual realm, as in practicing the presence of God by obeying His orders even when they seem the most unlikely course of action to the natural mind.

Our little saying comes from a folksy parable Conlee told me years ago about an elderly couple sitting on their front porch, sadly rocking away in their rocking chairs as they reminisce over the sixty years they have spent together. They remember all the missed opportunities, the times they opted for the security of this world rather than the excitement of following the desires of their hearts. They think about the boredom and monotony that finally set into their lives, the frustration of being locked into a no-win situation. Now in the sunset of their lives they have nothing to show for their choices but bitter regret.

The old man searches for just one thing he can say to his wife to make her feel better about the eternal grayness of their life. Finally he offers this gem: "Well, we could have. . . ."

That one statement sums up so well all the lost opportunities and the emptiness a person is left with at the end of a long life girded only with worldly security and earthly boundaries. To Conlee it symbolizes the frustration of living one's life without exploring every avenue God opens up for us. Whenever I hear him say,

"Well, I could have . . ." with a long pause, I know he is wrestling with God over something important.

Learning to Live in the Flow of the Spirit

Conlee and I have taken some risks in living our lives totally open to God, but the sense of risk was far more from our imagined fears than from any real dangers to us or to our children. More than anything we have attempted to turn to God's presence first to hear the Word from Him, and then to obey as best we can what we believe He is telling us to do. I am not speaking of reckless, irresponsible living, but of learning to live in the exciting flow of God's Spirit wherever He takes us.

I hope this does not read like we have mastered this way of life. I want to be completely honest with you and before God. We often struggle to take the time to listen to God and to wait if we do not hear from Him right away. Sometimes we are called to take unpopular stands (especially with our children when they were young). But I can assure you that the more we practice His presence and live in the flow of the Spirit, the easier it gets.

When Conlee and I sit on our front porch in our rocking chairs years from now, we will not say, "Well, we could have. . . ." Rather, we will say, "Remember when we did . . . ?" I am profoundly grateful for my husband's wisdom in leading our family into the godly adventure of practicing God's presence for the last two decades. And I am overwhelmed that God has proved His faithfulness time and time again as we have practiced His presence in our journey with Him. God's love and care and gentle nudgings to push us out of the nests of our own security never cease to amaze me.

As I shared in my story, the revelation of a living God through personal relationship with His Son, Jesus, came upon us suddenly. It was as though on February 26, 1972, we were living on one planet with our eyes focused on worldly gain, personal happiness and self. But on February 27, 1972, we seemed to be transported to a different galaxy, filled with prayer, miracles, Christians, the King of the universe Himself and the holiness of His Spirit. You can imagine what our old friends thought about this radical turnaround in our lives.

Leaving the comfortable confines of our well-established social structure in a small Arkansas city to become completely immersed in the world of prayer groups, Bible studies, spiritual retreats and church three times a week was a gigantic step for our family.

To raise three sons with biblical absolutes when other parents were being permissive felt risky to us. Would we promote rebellion in our children? Would we make them oddities to their peers? These were real fears for two young parents.

The most difficult step of all came twelve years later when we left friends, a prosperous business and the comfort of our beautiful home to follow God's call for Conlee to go to seminary. But it was also the most exciting step. It was certainly not without tears that we packed up to leave the place where our children had grown up, where we had met our Lord personally for the first time, where we had a loving support system of friends and family and where we knew we were accepted. But before we got halfway to our new destination we felt anticipation and excitement. Conlee says, and I agree, that it would have been a far harder thing to ignore the call from God than to leave the comfortable world we had known to set out on this new adventure.

We all live in a world where security is valued above all else. We seek social security, job security, health security, private security and the security of living under a stable government. For many, the attainment of these various securities becomes a full-time occupation, indeed, a religion. The goals of this "religion" are happiness and contentment, with lots of "stuff" to give us pleasure. But it does not take an astute mind to see that few in our society realize these goals. Never have so many people been so frustrated, so much in debt, so angry, so desperate and so insecure, while having more "benefits" than any previous generation has enjoyed.

An Early Risk-Taker

The Bible is full of stories about men and women who were called out of their security systems into risky places where they had to practice God's presence. One of the most interesting and courageous was Noah, and he will be the first "past traveler" we will study. If you have already read Genesis 6–9 you have a head start.

According to Babylonian tradition, Noah lived in a city called Fara, on the Euphrates River, about seventy miles from the site of the Garden of Eden. Boat-building and river traffic must have been familiar to him from childhood. The Bible tells us that he was the grandson of Methuselah and great-grandson of Enoch, both godly leaders in pre-flood civilization.

From early Babylonian writings we know that Noah was a city-king with influence and wealth. Henry H. Halley's *Bible Handbook* (Zondervan, 1965) tells how archaeologists have reconstructed an accurate picture of settled life in early Babylonia from relics of pre-flood cities, including Fara. They have unearthed painted pottery, flint implements, tools, turquoise vases, copper mirrors, fish hooks, models of boats, an underground kiln, cosmetics for darkening eyebrows and eyelids, brick ruins of temples, artwork, a chariot and architectural accomplishments indicating an astonishingly advanced civilization. They have also discovered a sophisticated written language and records of business transactions and libraries.

In spite of the immense wealth and prosperity that surrounded Noah, the inevitable encouragement from his peers to amass more wealth and, doubtless, pressure to preserve what he had accumulated, we are told in Genesis 6:9 that "Noah was a righteous man, blameless among the people of his time, and he walked with God."

Noah must have yearned to walk with God as his great-grandparents, Adam and Eve, had done nine generations back before they were driven from the Garden of Eden because of sin. Adam and Eve had known the joy and contentment of being in God's presence at all times. No barriers whatsoever existed between them and their Creator. They had satisfying work to do with their hands and the rewards of a good day's work in the Garden. They shared intimate companionship with each other. God provided for their every need and they sensed the completeness that comes from being one with Him.

Living in God's presence in such an intimate way was a natural part of their lives, as natural as breathing. God walked with them. He spoke to them. They listened, they responded, they obeyed. This was Garden living, the ultimate security system that each of us still craves today, no matter how twisted the path we often take to find it.

But it was not as easy for Noah to attain the same kind of security in his life that he had heard about through family stories, the Garden Security System his great-grandfather had enjoyed. Noah, genetically burdened by the sin of his ancestors, had to find that security in another way, since it was no longer a natural response: He had to learn to *practice* being in God's presence. He had to *practice* spending time with God, as Adam had spent time with Him. How? Noah had to *practice* listening to Him, as Adam had listened. He had to *practice* responding to Him, as Adam had responded. And he had to *practice* obeying Him, as Adam had learned to do through the hardest lesson of his life—the lesson that obedience to God is absolutely necessary if we humans want to maintain the Garden Security System.

The times in which Noah lived were not so different from our own. God saw that the earth was corrupt and full of violence. So is ours. Noah felt the constraints of that corruption. So do we. Yet in the midst of an unholy environment, Noah took time each day to practice God's presence and to listen to His personal word for him.

What Noah Heard

One day during Noah's quiet time God said,

"I am going to put an end to all people, for the earth is filled with violence because of them. I am surely going to destroy both them and the earth. So make yourself an ark. . . ."

Genesis 6:13–14

Because Noah had practiced God's presence, he was accustomed to listening to God's voice and recognized when God was speaking to him. That is why he took seriously the instructions for building an immense ship. His willingness to listen and obey what seemed like a radical word from God saved his life, his family members' lives, the lives of all species of animals that roamed the earth at that time and, ultimately, your life and mine, since all other humans were destroyed in the flood.

Noah obediently worked on this huge ship for the better part of 120 years, with no rain in sight. But the word God had spoken to him must have penetrated his heart daily. When God speaks directly to our hearts, no matter how hard we might run from Him or how often we might turn our backs to Him, we cannot "un-hear" His word.

Noah probably employed thousands of men to help build the ark. It was an immense undertaking. Perhaps his fellow citizens called it "Noah's Folly." Perhaps God was speaking to others, also, about being part of a divine escape route from judgment, but they were not listening. Even if they were, they certainly did not obey Him.

Did Noah know the implications of his obedience when he started drawing plans and cutting wood? Did he ever wonder if he had "mis-heard" God? Did he get so weary he wanted to quit? Did he have trouble persuading his wife, three sons and their wives to attempt this risky venture? Was he afraid he might die before it was completed? Since Noah was fully human, I imagine he experienced the same emotions we would have experienced were we in his place.

But Noah obeyed God in every detail. He completed the ship, stocked it with food and brought in a male and female of every species of animal and bird living on the earth at that time.

The rain did not fall.

Finally God directed Noah to take his whole family into the ship. According to God's timetable the rain would begin soon and last for forty days. Noah obeyed, and God shut them in. Sure enough, it began to rain and rain and rain. For nearly six weeks Noah and his family were tossed back and forth on a stormy sea. We will continue their story later, but let's look at its implications for us so far.

Our Escape Route

Practicing the presence of Jesus is not an option for Christians who want to live biblical, victorious lives. It is a necessity. We are living in the same kind of "city" Noah lived in. We are facing all the same obstacles to our faith that he faced. We have the same pressures and diversions. We have the same fears and sins.

But Jesus offers us something wonderful that Noah knew nothing about. He offers us a means of escape that does not have to be built with human labor or ingenuity. He offers us a clear path to achieving Garden-like security.

He offers us His Body.

As Jesus reveals to us our sins, fears and unholy desires He says, "Give them to Me. I AM the way out. I AM your ark. Come into Me and I will rescue you. But you must listen to Me and you must obey Me. To do that you must practice My presence so that you become familiar with My voice. In My presence you will find the wholeness you seek."

Practicing God's Presence

By faith Noah, when warned about things not yet seen, in holy fear built an ark to save his family. By his faith he condemned the world and became heir of the righteousness that comes by faith.
Hebrews 11:7

1. As you read the story of Noah (Genesis 6–9), what is God saying to you? Pause now and ask Him to be clear. Listen with your heart to His answer. Write in your prayer journal any word, idea or picture He may be giving you.
2. Ask God to show you any "Well, I could haves" in your life, any regrets. Ask Him to remind you of any sins of disobedience, any wasted years, any lost relationships. Pause to give each sin and regret deliberately to Jesus. Deal with each one separately, calling it by name. See what He does with each one as you hand it to Him.
3. Receive His forgiveness. Clothe yourself in it. Listen for His personal word to you right now. Be sure to write it in your prayer journal.

Day 3

Excuses, Excuses, Excuses

It's impossible for me to make myself take the time to sit down and be still. I barely get everything done each day that needs to be done as it is! How in the world can I allot even more time to practice God's presence? I'll just have to pray on the run. I think God understands."

Not only do I frequently hear the above statement from well-meaning Christians, but I have said it myself—many times! Believe me, I understand those sentiments all too well.

If our friend Noah had maintained this attitude for very long, how different the world would be today! You and I would not be alive, for one thing, since we are all descended from Noah through post-flood society.

Yet Noah, too, had work to do, businesses to run, payrolls to make, household duties to maintain, taxes to pay, important political decisions to make, social obligations to keep, children to father and a wife to love. His agenda was full enough to keep a man busy from daylight until dark. When did he find time away from all those legitimate activities to sit, pray and be quiet in God's presence?

Somehow he did it all, because Genesis 6:9 tells us "Noah was a righteous man, blameless among the people of his time, and he walked with God." Evidently he did not neglect his earthly relationships (no one who knew him blamed him for anything) or his heavenly relationship (God called him righteous, a man in right standing with his Creator).

To give the proper attention to our earthly responsibilities, our families and our friends, and at the same time keep up an intimate relationship with God requires a delicate balance. Each takes concentrated, intentional time. We have to practice working at each in order to achieve meaningful results. A slothful, undisciplined life will not yield meaningful relationships and accomplishments, either with God or with anyone or anything else.

Running from God

I have been trying hard to discipline myself to walk, jog or run every morning. I bought myself some nifty running shoes so I could "float" down the street, some cute running shorts and shirts and even a printed headband to keep my hair out of my eyes.

The first few days were great. I was proud of myself for "hitting the street" at 7:00 a.m. I felt healthier right away. I looked forward to getting up and out every morning.

But after a while conflicts arose. I had to be out of town for a week. An important phone call came at 6:50 a.m. A child was home, sick. I turned on the television to watch the news. It was too hot. It was raining. The dog threw up. You name it, it happened.

Where did all my enthusiasm go? Running no longer called me, no longer enticed me in the same way. I rationalized myself into putting it off for another day, another week. Pretty soon my new shoes were buried in the back of the closet. I got out of shape. I began to think, "Well, maybe I'm not meant to be a runner."

I know that *you* know exactly how this relates to your quiet time with God, your time to practice His presence. Check your reasons for not staying with your plan to spend more time with Him.

    ___ I want to get a new Bible.
    ___ I am looking for a good Bible study book.
    ___ I need a group to motivate me.
    ___ I will get to it after lunch,
    ___ . . . after school,
    ___ . . . after dinner,
    ___ . . . at bedtime,
    ___ . . . tomorrow.

___ I need my rest.
___ I have too much to do.
___ I cannot seem to get my thoughts organized.
___ It is just not my gift.

I hear you! I hear you!

God hears you, too.

What can we do to make our special time with God more inviting, more meaningful? No, let's go even further: What would make it *irresistible?*

The Holy Imagination

Have you ever used your imagination to enhance your time with God? Let's try it together using a powerful passage of Scripture, but first, let's pray:

> Lord, You made us with imaginations to contain images from you. I ask that You sanctify, protect and anoint our imaginations. Expand and make holy these picture-making faculties of our hearts and minds so we may grasp more completely some larger images of who You really are. Thank You. Amen.

Now, stop and read Revelation, chapter four. Read it aloud if possible, and *really* get into it! Hear, feel and see the drama. Go on, do it now. I promise you will like it. Then come back and we will explore it together using our sanctified imaginations.

————⊷◆⊶————

The imagery in this fourth chapter of John's revelation is so large and awesome that we can barely grasp a fraction of the holiness portrayed. Immerse yourself in any one of many incredible images—the vibrant colors, the powerful booming voice, the elders, the furniture, the clothing, the jewels and crowns, all the symbols of authority, the lightning and thunder, the light, the water, the creatures. Let any or all of these images soak into your soul!

There is majesty here, and power and the converging stimulation of all the senses. Any one of these revelations would cause us to fall on our knees in fear and trembling. But imagine yourself as John, in the vicinity of a throne room where a storm is issuing forth, where a rainbow encircles the main throne, where two dozen crowned royal priests are seated, where four creatures with many wings and eyes surround the throne!

In spite of the incredible grandeur of the vision, the one overwhelming sense we have is the presence of holiness everywhere. One cannot be anywhere near that kind of holiness without being totally humbled, without falling down to worship the Holy God. Even those creatures who might inspire us to worship them are themselves on their faces before the Holy One. His holiness, in fact, is so tremendous that they never stop singing, "Holy, holy, holy is the Lord God Almighty, who was, and is, and is to come."

John was actually allowed to witness this holy presence. And in this kind of holy presence we will one day permanently dwell. There is no sin in God's holy presence, and it is in this presence that we are able to become all we were created to be.

Even now this presence beckons us from our daily routine. In God's presence, a sin-free environment, we can receive nurturing, strength, peace, guidance and wisdom. We can learn who we really are. It is a place where we can be real.

Our Prayer for Holiness

We have used our holy imaginations to picture God's holiness, the way in which He is now being worshiped in heaven and the way He will be worshiped there for all eternity.

What does this say to us today about holiness and worship? Let's tell God.

> O Lord, I realize now that I frequently worship You too casually. Sometimes I am only thinking my thanksgiving, rather than offering it to You. Sometimes I am grateful only for what You do for me and those close to me, rather than for who You are. My world has become a microcosm of my own interests and needs. Forgive me, Lord.
>
> But today, Lord God, I choose to fall down before You, literally and symbolically. You are grand in a way I cannot even comprehend. I cannot understand "forever past" and "forever future," but I believe that is who You are—the eternal One.

I thank You for what You have given to me and restored in me.
I thank You for the ways in which You are using me. I see all that
You have given me as a jeweled crown of love and I willingly lift
it from my head where You have lovingly placed it. With my fee-
ble hands I want to place this symbol of all Your blessings for me
at Your feet.

As I lie prostrate before You with my gift in my extended hands,
I slowly loosen each finger, knowing I am giving You all I have,
my identity, my life. I gently push the crown toward You, not daring to look, until finally I feel it totally freed from my grasp—no
longer mine, but Yours.

"You are worthy, our Lord and God, to receive glory and honor
and power, for you created all things, and by your will they were
created and have their being" (Revelation 4:11).

Practicing God's Presence

1. As you pray the prayer above, what crown are you giving
   to God? Name each jewel in it. In your journal list the
   things, people, gifts and blessings you are willing to surrender to Him.
2. What image of God's holiness is speaking to you at this
   moment? In your journal write out that image in your own
   words.
3. How did allowing God to sanctify your imagination give
   life to the Scripture and excitement to your quiet time? Try
   it again with another Scripture to which He leads you.

Day 4

At the End of the Rainbow

As I shared with you on Day 1 of our journey, I had the most remarkable experience on the evening of February 27, 1972, an experience that totally changed my life. I had an encounter with the living God that I could not deny, could not explain away and could not forget. This encounter soon caused me to fall on my knees before Him and say, "I am Yours, Lord. Please be mine!"

For weeks afterward I felt as though I was walking through a holy cloud. Everything was God-centered. Colors were brighter, sounds more harmonious, people more beautiful and prayers more meaningful. I just knew I had entered into "happily-ever-after" land.

But on the morning of May 2, 1972, I had barely awakened from a deep sleep when I knew something was terribly wrong. Before I even opened my eyes I knew I was surrounded by a dark cloud. Heaviness penetrated every breath I took. A sense of "not-being" filled my heart. Simultaneously I was lonely, afraid, empty, hurt, rejected, sad, angry and bitter. I felt . . . dead. I wondered if my worst fear had materialized: *Had God abandoned me?*

I feigned illness so Conlee would get the children off to school. He prayed healing prayers for me, kissed me and went to work. I felt worse. I lay in bed with the covers over my head as if I was in a tomb. I felt as if I could never recover.

For the next five hours I prayed aloud for deliverance from this dreadful state. I read my Bible and cried out to God. Finally, exhausted, I let myself become very still. Somewhere down deep inside my heart stirred a tiny thought, a still voice. I was almost afraid to trust it. A big part of me did not want to. I literally commanded myself to obey the minute nudging I was sensing: "Get out of bed; get in the shower and sing to Jesus."

Sing to Jesus! That was the last thing I wanted to do. He had left me! It took every ounce of courage and strength I had to obey this simple impression, but I did.

With the stinging water spraying over me I turned my face upward, closed my eyes and, making a well-known praise song personal, began to sing:

> I will praise You, I will praise You,
> I'll praise the Lamb for sinners slain.
> I give You glory, I Your servant,
> For Your blood will wash away my stain.

As my heart turned to the One I was singing about, and as I entered into praise for the Lamb, it was as though the shower became a fountain of baptismal waters over me. His presence washed me, saturated me, cleansed me, purified me. I came out of my "baptismal stall" a new person with a new set of spiritual truths to hang on to.

One truth that became very clear to me was that I did not have to have warm fuzzy feelings about Jesus for Him to be with me. I needed no manifestations of the spectacular to be certain that I was in His presence. He had not abandoned me whenever I could not sense His presence. I was learning to relate to Him in a mature faith walk. I was to practice His *real* presence, not a *sense* of His presence.

I opened my Bible to passages that suddenly came alive for me.

"Be strong and courageous. Do not be afraid or terrified . . . for the LORD your God goes with you; he will never leave you nor forsake you."

Deuteronomy 31:6

"As I was with Moses, so I will be with you; I will never leave you nor forsake you."

Joshua 1:5

Though my father and mother forsake me, the LORD will receive me.

Psalm 27:10

56

"Surely [says Jesus] I am with you always, to the very end of the age."
Matthew 28:20

Incarnational Reality

This was to be my single most important spiritual lesson: Jesus is truly *Emmanuel*—"God with us." He never leaves us alone—never!

Even when we *feel* as if He has left, He is there. Even if we sin so terribly we think He *ought* to leave, He is there. Even if we turn our backs on Him, He is there . . . waiting.

This is the incarnation. Practicing this fact is vital to our healing and to our remaining whole.

Jesus became incarnate within Mary as she submitted her will to God's will and allowed the Holy Spirit to bring the actual presence of God into her inmost being. She became pregnant with God (Luke 1:26–56).

In like manner, when we give our wills to God, we allow Him to come upon us, to dwell within us. We become "in-Godded," pregnant with His presence. He is incarnate within us.

Saint Paul called this the greatest mystery of the universe, now revealed: ". . . Christ *in* you, the hope of glory" (Colossians 1:27, italics mine).

Twenty-five years after discovering the reality of the incarnation, I do not have warm fuzzy feelings about Christ all the time. These days, in fact, I seldom focus on relating to Him in that heady, sensate way. Certainly there are many times when I am keenly aware of His presence with me, some times when I am so aware of Him I cannot stand, but depending on that awareness has not become the focus of my relationship with Him. Never, ever, for even one second do I doubt that He is with me, in me, surrounding me. I have learned that lesson! The evidence of His presence is apparent to me in too many other ways.

In "The Journey to Wholeness in Christ" seminars, I always begin by inviting each person to make his or her own affirmation of Jesus' Lordship. I ask everyone present to place a hand over his or her heart. Then we all proclaim aloud:

"Another lives within me. His name is Jesus. Jesus lives in me!"

Some have never before made this affirmation; they have taken this awesome fact for granted. Even worse, some have never grasped this truth at all.

I invite you, right now, to place your hand on your heart and say those words aloud. Say them several times, acknowledging with each statement another area of your life that you are purposefully giving to God.

Next, still keeping one hand over your heart, raise the other hand high to connect you with the Father. Here is the divine incarnation—the mystery of the universe revealed in you right now: Jesus lives within you. His presence connects you to the Father and the Holy Spirit binds you together.

You may need to proclaim this truth repeatedly so its reality takes firm root within your spirit. This, too, is part of practicing the presence of God.

Let me say it again: No other truth will be more important to your continued, growing wholeness than a firm grasp of this fact: Jesus lives in you!

Waiting on the Lord

Our friend Noah was aware of God's presence continuing with him during more than a century of building a rescue vehicle for his family. After God's primary command, we know of no other words God spoke directly to Noah until just before He indicated that it was time to enter the ark. We do know that Noah maintained a constant relationship with God during the construction time, because when God was ready for the dramatic events of the flood to unfold, Noah heard His voice clearly once again: "Go into the ark, you and your whole family, because I have found you righteous in this generation" (Genesis 7:1). The sure knowledge of God's presence had kept Noah faithful to his commission.

Noah had heard God's voice; he had proven himself faithful by trusting God's presence through a long period of silence. Now he would learn another lesson.

Noah, his family and the animals he had been commanded to load waited in the ark for seven days before God sent the rain.

Imagine the restlessness those eight people experienced, not to mention a whole raft of nervous animals who had never been caged before!

God's word, however, was true. When they finally came, the rains fell for forty days and forty nights, just as God had told Noah they would.

But even at the end of forty days of rain, the ordeal was not over. For five months the flood waters continued to rise. There was no sign of land. Yet Noah's faith in an unseen God remained. He had heard the voice of His Creator. He did not "un-hear" it because of the circumstances.

When the storm finally ceased, things did not improve right away. After the little group of flood survivors felt the "thud" of the ship coming to rest on a solid base, they had to wait two and a half more months before the tops of some mountains became visible.

And still the wait was not over. Another forty-day period passed during which they were unable to leave the ship. Finally Noah began to send out birds to scout out the possibility of dry land. He sent a raven and it returned. No dry land. More waiting. He sent a dove and it, too, returned. More waiting. On the third try he sent another dove—and it returned to the ship that evening with a freshly picked olive leaf in its beak!

How Noah's family must have rejoiced! Yet again they waited a week, then released the dove once more. This time it did not return. At that point Noah felt God's permission to open up the hatches and look around. He saw dry ground!

How is your addition? No matter how you figure it, even give or take a few weeks, we are talking about a family of eight (with in-laws mixed in) tossing and turning for a whole year in a boat, sealed up with numerous animals and not knowing when or if the situation would ever resolve itself. It was not a pretty picture.

But Noah was a righteous man, remember? He knew God was with him. This whole ordeal had lasted much longer than the initial forty days God had told him about in the beginning, yet Noah could not forget God's reassuring presence, His voice or the affirmation God had given him.

The ordeal of coming into personal wholeness may last a lot longer than we would hope. It is vital, therefore, that we, like Noah, clearly hear God's reassuring word that He wills for us to be whole. We need to know that He is affirming His will in us, that even in the midst of our impatience and discomfort and despair, His will is being accomplished.

The Sign of the Rainbow

The very first thing Noah did after he stepped out onto dry land was to build an altar. He wanted to sacrifice a thank offering to the God who had sustained him and his family. During that sacrifice of praise and thanksgiving God made a covenant with Noah. It was a covenant with promises and a sign that God would keep His promises for ever—the sign of the rainbow.

Are you ever able to look at a rainbow without feeling even a little bit of joy? Even those who do not see it as a sign of God's covenant with His people do view rainbows as symbols of hope, beauty, freshness and new beginnings.

But you and I are His people—and we are "rainbow people." We are the ones at the end of the promise, the recipients of an everlasting covenant promising that, no matter how we feel or however long the wait, God is eternally with us.

Let me share with you these words, impressed on my heart by the Lord Jesus, recorded in my prayer journal:

> If only you could know for just a moment how very much I desire total intimacy with you. You have never experienced from anyone on this earth more than a tiny glimpse of the kind of love that I have to give you. You even have a fear of expecting the kind of love I want to give you.
>
> When you are immersed in My love, however, that fear will disappear and you will begin to understand that I did die for *you,* and that I am calling you to be more than you ever thought you could be.

Practicing God's Presence

> And God said, "This is the sign of the covenant I am making between me and you and every living creature with you, a covenant for all generations to come: I have set my rainbow in the clouds, and it will be the sign of the covenant between me and the earth."
>
> Genesis 9:12–13

1. In your prayer journal, write brief descriptions of two or three times when you have *felt* deserted by God. As you allow each memory to come into your consciousness, ask Jesus to allow you to see Him in that scene. What is He doing? What is He saying to you? Enter this revelation of His presence in your journal.

2. In what ways is the evidence of Christ's presence real to you now? Can you begin to believe that you, like Mary, are pregnant with His presence? What provisions has He made for your wholeness?

3. See yourself as a Noah, after a storm in your life, stepping out from your fragile boat onto solid land. In what ways can your thanksgivings and praises to Him be a true sacrifice? Be sure to write these out in your prayer journal. Spiritually erect an altar during your quiet time today, and offer your thanks and praise to Him.

Day 5

Only the Lonely

I AM AN ONLY CHILD. SO IS MY HUSBAND. SO WAS MY MOTHER. YET NOT ONE of us has suffered from chronic loneliness.

Why? I have realized that even though I did not know God personally until I was an adult, and even though my childhood home was far from perfect, I had a sense of belonging to someone, of being loved and cared for by my family that eliminated me from the ranks of those who are desperate for companionship. Being in right relationships with others does produce a security that excludes loneliness, even when we are by ourselves.

I have prayed with many precious individuals whose reserves of inner strength have been taxed to the limits by just trying to "keep it together" until someone comes to be with them. Counselor-counselee or pastor-parishioner relationships of this type can be trying when the needy one literally feels death would be preferable to being left alone.

I have witnessed firsthand the misery of those who think they will die if they have to spend more than a few hours at a time by themselves. Anxiety surfaces, panic sets in, good judgment and common sense may be thrown to the wind and inappropriate behavior may follow if the individual feels it will alleviate the fear of being alone.

The Need for Identity

The sixties, when I attended college, were years when, unfortunately, a lot of young women enrolled in school to earn their

"Mrs." degrees. Many a bright, lovely young woman felt desperation as she neared graduation with no prospects of a husband. Altogether too many peer-pressured, lonely females made near-fatal mistakes as they reached out to the nearest available men to ensure their dreams of lifelong security in a relationship—any relationship.

I was amazed at the intelligent young women with outgoing personalities, women who appeared to have everything going for them, who would date the most undesirable men just so they would not have to stay in the dorm on a weekend. Some of these women actually married men they knew would abuse them, men who already treated them with cruel disrespect.

Even in my most unspiritual state at that time I failed to understand why these women would not prefer a good television movie or a stimulating book to being with just "anybody." But I was not in their shoes and I did not understand then the underlying lack of personal identity and affirmation a person can feel when no one validates or affirms his or her significance.

Times have changed a great deal since my college days and singleness seems to evoke less panic. Humankind's basic fear of loneliness, however, has not changed at all. Indeed, the frustration level may be higher than ever for those who have many options available and still experience a deep-seated sense of not belonging.

A Sense of Being

Henri Nouwen once said, "With God, the desert of loneliness is turned into a garden of solitude." His comment has nothing to do with being an introvert or an extrovert. It has everything to do with relationship.

Just as a good parental-familial relationship gives the only child—or any child—a sense of belonging, of being a part of a larger whole, so the relationship into which we enter when we join God's family gives us the same sense of being part of something far greater than ourselves.

Even more, when we enthusiastically take our places in God's family, we receive a presence within ourselves that surpasses any relationship we can have on this earth. We receive the Holy One. Another Being truly lives within us!

When I pray for those who seem to have no sense of identity apart from others, I am often led to ask God to set in their hearts a "sense of being." I might place one hand on a person's chest and the other on his back to demonstrate physically the completeness of healing God wants to bring—indeed, a filling of the very center of his being with God's own presence.

I then ask God to affirm him as His own, with the unconditional love that He has for each of His children, that he might be the person God intended him to be. Perhaps he has a deep need to hear the Father's voice of affirmation saying, "You are My beloved child. You please Me greatly" (just as He said to His Son, Jesus). If an earthly father was unable to say these words, that lack of paternal affirmation can cause children to flee into the arms of one partner after another, yearning for that deep-seated need to be met. The lifelong deprivation of a father's affirmation and affection devastates children regardless of gender.

Other men and women may need to bond aright with their own mothers or with a feminine presence. For whatever reason, be it illness, extreme poverty, death, ignorance, birth practices or evil, some human beings are deprived almost from birth of the loving, affirming touch of "mother." This touch (bonding) is essential for each of us to develop a primary sense of identity. If bonding does not occur, the results are tragic: In addition to the neurotic gravitation toward a woman's arms in order to fill this deprivation, children (of all ages and both sexes) may also feel an intensely difficult ambivalence toward "woman." Desperately desiring woman's love, they may still hate women in general because they have not been able, for whatever reason, to appropriate the mother love they needed.

Only in the awareness of the presence of God Himself within our hearts will we begin to feel secure as the persons we were created to be.

Entwined with God

When Noah and his family were isolated from all other human contact for a long period of time, Noah lost all evidence of the identity he had gained as a city-king in Fara. All of his wealth, prestige, social standing, reputation and business experience lost its worth. He was stripped of everything that had mattered in a materialistic world. Locked up in a ship, Noah's identity was totally dependent upon and defined by the hand of God.

When your identity is so entwined with God's that your very *being* (who you are and how you relate to others) is defined, affirmed and called forth by Him, you will truly dwell in a garden, even if it is a solitary one. Let's read together Psalm 68:5–6:

A father to the fatherless, a defender of widows, is God in his holy dwelling. God sets the lonely in families, he leads forth the prisoners with singing; but the rebellious live in a sun-scorched land.

Only as our sense of being—who we really are, and *whose* we really are—is secure in our heavenly Father, will the lonely be set in families and those needy ones who have been imprisoned be led forth with song. Conversely, when we refuse to be centered in Jesus, our hearts and emotions will become dry and parched. Then we will find ourselves in a sun-scorched land, overcome by the desert of loneliness. Here, from my prayer journal, is what the Lord Jesus said to me:

Do you know how much I want you to be comforted? I never want you to sense loneliness. It is not good for you to be alone, and it has never been in My plan for men and women to be isolated. The holy Comforter will provide the security you crave. My very presence is the powerful source of completeness you yearn for in your deep heart. Allow Me to come into you and make you whole.

Practicing God's Presence

"I will be a Father to you, and you will be my sons and daughters, says the Lord Almighty."

2 Corinthians 6:18

1. Place your hand on your heart and affirm aloud, once again, "Another lives in me. Jesus lives within. I acknowledge Your presence, Jesus." Allow His presence to become more apparent to all your senses. Breathe in His presence deeply. Whenever you think of it, continue to affirm that Another truly is within you.

2. With the awareness of His presence within, let the memory of a lonely time in your life begin to surface. Allow yourself to see the scene and feel the emotions. Let Jesus speak directly to your heart as you sense His presence in the midst of your lonely desert.

3. In your prayer journal write out as many evidences as you can recall of a desert in your life being turned into a garden in Jesus' presence.

4. What or who has determined your identity? How would you describe yourself in a letter to someone who has never met you? What if you, like Noah, were in a situation where all outward vestiges of personhood were stripped away? Who would you be then?

Day 6
Only One Thing Is Needed

Over the long, tedious years while Noah worked obediently on the ark he must have recalled, methodically and faithfully, those moments when he had been in God's holy presence and had heard Him speak so clearly. His recollection of the divine Word stored in his heart gave him the spiritual, emotional and physical energy he needed to complete the seemingly insurmountable task God had directed.

Noah's example of long-suffering perseverance and discipline is a godly model for all of us. But what about those times when we need to respond *spontaneously* to God? Where do we find a scriptural model for the virtue of living *in the moment* in our daily relationship with Jesus?

As part of today's journey, pause and read one such model from the story of Mary and Martha in Luke 10:38–42. Then let's take a look at the distinct ways in which these women responded to Jesus and His Word.

Mary, Martha and their brother, Lazarus, all spent a lot of time getting to know Jesus, listening to Him and being in His presence. They frequently had "open house" when Jesus was in their village of Bethany, inviting friends and neighbors into their home to sit around the table, share a meal and listen to His teachings.

Martha's Story

Martha must have been the older sister, because the Bible tells us she actually owned the family home. She willingly opened it

67

to Jesus any time He was in the vicinity. Apparently all three siblings had been greatly blessed by the teachings of Jesus, and we can assume He had brought much healing to each of them because of the way they all adored Him as Master.

Although Martha loved opening her home to Jesus and all who wished to sit at His feet and learn from Him, she felt the full weight of the responsibility of caring for her honored guest and the others who came. Shopping, planning menus, arranging service, having laundry done, overseeing the servants as they did most of the physical work, clearing the table and making sure each guest was comfortable so he or she could best absorb whatever truths Jesus would share—it all made for an immense undertaking. And being the accomplished hostess she was, no one knew better than Martha how important it was to make the effort appear effortless to her guests!

When we strive to be perfectionists and no one else seems to care, the stage is set for the lid to blow off the pot. And that is exactly what happened. According to Martha, all Mary wanted to do was to sit in the dining room with the rest of the guests and let Martha do all the work. Martha's frustration level peaked and she erupted to Jesus, "Lord, don't you care that my sister has left me to do the work by myself? Tell her to help me!" (Luke 10:40).

Yes, Mary was sitting as close as possible to Jesus that day, hanging on His every word. But Martha was harried. Perhaps she felt her renowned identity as a good hostess was endangered because her sister ignored her subtle messages to get up and help with the preparations. I really believe Martha felt that her ultimate expression of love, respect and honor to Jesus was all bound up in her ability to serve Him and His friends properly.

To give to the utmost of the talents you have been given is an honorable goal. For a consummate hostess like Martha, a perfect dinner, impeccable service and an efficient household would have been a love offering to Jesus.

Jesus in no way put down Martha's gifts. He recognized them, in fact, and acknowledged that she was worried and upset about many things. He did her the honor of understanding all that had gone into her love gift. But then He said lovingly to her, "Martha, Martha, you are worried and upset about many things, but *only one thing is needed. Mary has chosen what is better, and it will not be taken away from her"* (Luke 10:41–42, italics mine).

Mary's Story

Mary loved to sit at Jesus' feet and listen to Him talk. He told stories that came alive for her. He brought the glories of God right into her ordinary world. Some things He said puzzled her, but she felt such peace being near Him that it did not matter. Being in His presence meant more to her than anything in the world.

Mary probably sensed that Martha was out of sorts and wanted her to get up from her favorite spot on the floor near Jesus. She knew Martha needed help in the kitchen, but it did not seem to bother Jesus or anyone else that the dishes were not taken away quickly, or that the coffee was not poured immediately. Everyone else at the table seemed as intent on every word He said as Mary was. Mary knew the dishes could be done tomorrow, but Jesus was here right now and she did not want to miss a moment or a word of anything He said or did.

Undoubtedly Mary saw Martha call Jesus over to the side of the room and ask Him to scold Mary for being lazy. Being a "Mary" myself, I can understand the complete astonishment Mary must have felt when Martha blew up over something Mary thought to be totally insignificant in the whole scheme of things. She was probably steeling herself to leave her favorite spot and be sent to the kitchen when she heard Him tell her sister that she—Mary!—had "chosen what (was) better."

And what was that one thing, that better thing, never to be taken away, that Mary chose? The presence of Jesus Himself!

More Precious than Gold

Mary sat at Jesus' feet at another dinner party in Bethany in His honor, this one held in the home of a man named Simon. She had brought with her a gift for Jesus,

> an alabaster jar of very expensive perfume, made of pure nard. She broke the jar and poured the perfume on his head.
>
> Some of those present were saying indignantly to one another, "Why this waste of perfume? It could have been sold for more than a year's wages and the money given to the poor." And they rebuked her harshly.

"Leave her alone," said Jesus. "Why are you bothering her? She has done a beautiful thing to me. The poor you will always have with you, and you can help them any time you want. But you will not always have me. She did what she could. She poured perfume on my body beforehand to prepare for my burial. I tell you the truth, wherever the gospel is preached throughout the world, what she has done will also be told, in memory of her."

Mark 14:3–9

A very expensive jar of perfume made of pure nard, or spikenard, was a treasure in a family like Mary's. It was an extremely sweet-fragranced, durable ointment, thick like honey, with a reddish color. Because it was so valuable, it was usually given to a woman as part of her dowry or as a loving gift from her father when she became a woman.

But the purpose of nard was not cosmetic. Rather, nard was a tool for a job belonging exclusively to women—that of anointing or preparing a body for burial. Because a Jewish man was considered unclean if he touched a dead body, and had to remain outside the temple or synagogue until a ritual of cleansing could occur, this job was solely a woman's. It was considered not a duty but a privilege to perform this last, loving ritual of anointing a loved one's body with the best ointment a family could afford, and respectfully dressing the body in appropriate clothes.

A woman's bottle of perfume might have been her most valued material possession. It was a very concentrated substance and a little went a long way. A very small amount of it would be used on each of her closest and dearest family members.

At the time Mary went to Simon's house, her parents were dead and her only brother, Lazarus, had already died and been raised to life again by this Man at whose feet she sat. Mary and Martha had probably used some of their precious nard to anoint all three loved ones' bodies.

A Gift from the Heart

Apparently at some point Mary's understanding had awakened to what Jesus had been telling His friends for days. He had said repeatedly in various ways that He was going away. He seemed so sure, though His disciples and friends argued with Him. Talk among them about what He "really meant" had become their chief preoccupation, and they had discussed many theories in Mary's presence.

Suddenly all His words made sense in her heart, falling upon her like a weight. Most likely she had wanted desperately to cling to a more popular interpretation of His words, but now she quit trying to argue logically or plead with Him.

So Mary came to the dinner party at Simon's with her perfume bottle in hand. Hers was no spur-of-the-moment decision: Jesus had become the single most important Person in her life and she wanted to honor Him in the most meaningful way she knew. Her whole identity was wrapped up in Him and that night she knew in her heart that He was going to die. Perhaps she would not even be able to go on living without Him. She had given Him her heart completely and He had made it come alive in a way she had never dreamed possible.

Instead of giving Jesus the gift she had brought, as perhaps she had at first intended, she broke the whole jar and spontaneously poured its contents over His head. For a Jew, it was the ultimate, symbolic gesture of anointing.

The dinner guests were stunned. The expensive, potent fragrance of nard filled the air lingeringly, cloyingly, excessively sweet. Perhaps some around the table were embarrassed by this flagrant outpouring of affection. As soon as they recovered from their astonishment they began to berate Mary, reducing her gift from the heart to its monetary value.

Jesus Sees the Heart

Unlike the other guests, Jesus saw the value of Mary's heart-gift, her love. He not only found what she had done "acceptable," He called it a "beautiful thing," one that would be talked about and remembered as long as people remembered Him.

I wonder: *Would Mary have caught on to the real meaning of Jesus' words about "going away" if she had not been willing to sit at His feet?*

And what a reminder her story is that our heart-motivated ministry, spontaneous or planned, is precious to Jesus! Here, from my prayer journal, is what the Lord Jesus said:

My beloved, obligations and responsibilities are with you all the time and you can spend a large part of each day tending to them.

But the special time of quiet intimacy with Me cannot be postponed. When you wait until all else is done before making time for us to commune together, you are going to find much frustration in your attempts to have intimate union with Me.

My response:

Lord Jesus, a precious ointment in my possession that I can pour over Your head is time. I choose to open that gift and anoint You with it just by being in Your presence.

Practicing God's Presence

You prepare a table before me in the presence of my enemies. You anoint my head with oil; my cup overflows.

Psalm 23:5

1. Do you feel that your identity is wrapped up in anything or anyone other than Jesus? If so, does the thought of losing that thing grieve you at times, so much so that you cling to it neurotically? Are you willing, as Mary was, to release that grief to Jesus and be filled with His life?
2. Can you choose this day the one thing that is needed in your life, the better choice, the one thing that will not be taken away from you—time in His presence?
3. In what ways can you, like Mary, minister to Jesus? What precious ointments do you possess (besides time) that you can give lovingly to Him? Write out your ideas in your prayer journal.
4. Would you be willing to write a "Statement of Choice" in your journal today? Perhaps you could purpose to choose Jesus' presence over a time-consuming habit or pastime for a definite period of intimacy with Him each day.

Day 7

At the End of the Rope

I RECENTLY REREAD THE BOOK OF JOB. THEY SAY THAT MISERY LOVES COM-pany, and I was in the center of a very trying time. My trials were nothing compared to what poor Job went through; nevertheless my anxiety, frustration and stress levels were so real they were beginning to manifest in physical symptoms.

As stress increases and our natural immune systems begin to shut down, all sorts of things start to go haywire. One unfortunate result is that we begin to give as much, if not more, attention to our churning emotions, physical symptoms and friends' advice as we do to God's voice and the comfort of being in His presence.

My friend Becky was kind enough to let me use her condominium at the beach for a few days so I could separate myself from everyone and everything else and hibernate with Jesus. In other similar situations Conlee has gone along to pray for me, but this was one of those times when I needed nothing but God's presence.

The temptation, of course, was to sleep, read or even watch old movies on television. Instead, I literally willed myself to sit down with my prayer journal and pour my heart out to God—not to friends, counselor or husband, but to God.

As I asked for His presence to be real to me and acknowledged Him as my only source of wholeness, I began to dialogue with Him in my journal in a way that turned out to look like a script. The objectivity of this form of holy conversation was divinely therapeutic in allowing the release of what was in my heart so I could receive what was in His heart. In my journal, it looked something like this:

God-Talk—Act I

Signa: O God, I feel so upset, so sick at heart inside. . . . I cannot imagine either of the alternatives I see before me. *Please* speak to my heart.

God: Listen to Me. I am preparing a place for you. It will be the perfect place—the place where you need to be!

After several pages of intimate conversation with Him along these lines I felt as though we had indeed had a face-to-face encounter. With every word from Him my stress level decreased slightly and the anxiety began to diminish. After several hours (which seemed to pass quickly) I stood up, stretched and walked to the large wall of glass where I could look out on God's beautiful creation with newly child-like eyes, eagerly awaiting what He and I were going to do out there—together! No concrete answers had come from our dialogue, but in the intimacy of His presence I felt a calm assurance that all would be well.

I had just read Job 42:5: "My ears had heard of you but now my eyes have seen you." I knew how Job felt. All that I had thought about, heard about, discussed with others and feared diminished in value as I "saw" God during our dialogue. My situation was not resolved right away but my spirit was quieter and I had an enlarged ability to see the bigger picture.

Job had come to the end of a long ordeal in which he thought he had understood God. Then he realized he did not understand Him at all. He listened to a lot of advice from well-intentioned friends who were speaking out of their own understanding, not God's. Then finally, finally, in the storm of chaos around him he received God's voice directly to his heart.

Why do we, like Job, wait until things are in turmoil and life seems nearly impossible, until we are spiritually, mentally and physically depleted, before we go to our knees, crying out for His presence to comfort us?

God Knows Where You Are

I would like you to read a psalm with me now. It is long, 43 verses of Psalm 107, but please take the time to do it. Using a New

International Version of the Bible, please mark four distinct sections so you will see them clearly as you read:

Part 1 begins at verse 4;
Part 2 begins at verse 10;
Part 3 begins at verse 17; and
Part 4 begins at verse 23 and ends with verse 43.

Read now, with an open heart.

Did you catch the refrain of this song? "Then they cried out to the LORD in their trouble, and he delivered them from their distress" (verse 6; see also verses 13, 19, 28). It spoke to me clearly because this is what I did at Becky's condominium. This is what Job did in his agony. Maybe you have done it, too. It is part of a great opportunity we have as God's children: We have a place to cry and One who hears us.

Notice that in Part 1 some people are crying from the desert wastelands, unable to find a city. I know some of these wanderers intimately; perhaps you are one of them. You have been unsettled all your life, probably from birth, never finding the affirmation, security, love and protection of home or family that you long for with all your heart. Your desperate attempts to find what you need have led you down one wrong path after another, dying a little inside with each unfulfilled attempt.

Part 2 pictures the prisoners, bound, rebellious and living in darkness. I know these inmates, also, for they are often our neighbors, friends and family. Perhaps they represent you. You wear your prison chains with pride, and pride has been your undoing. You have refused to accept the Lordship of Jesus, for this would make you appear weak and helpless. Instead man and creation have become your lord, and you have laughed at piety and pitied the devout.

Part 3 describes the fools, those who rebelled against God, not through ignorance, but because they have deliberately chosen to pursue their selfish interests and vices. Is this what you have done? Are you the one who knew God and yet purposely chose to do what He forbade? Did you suffer, knowing what would heal you but refusing to accept it until it was nearly too late?

75

Part 4 relates to the family of God. We can all identify too clearly with this predicament. We are believers, doing "good things," aware of God and His work in our lives, yet little by little taking Him for granted, forgetting His awesome power, forgetting that He is holy. Because we live in a fallen world we are still subject to tumult and storms in our lives. We are still needy creatures. We need a rescuer, just like everyone else.

No matter what our condition, we all need the saving Lord. The exciting thing is that He is always waiting until we cry out to Him, waiting to bring the healing word and rescue us from our graves.

God wants us all to be able to sing the chorus, "I cried out to the Lord in my trouble, and He delivered me from my distress."

A Special Delivery

One morning I received a Scripture passage in the mail from a friend. No note, no explanation, no signature accompanied the delivery. But I knew who it was from, and I knew God was sending His personal word to me through my dear Christian friend. The passage read:

> "I am with you and will watch over you wherever you go, and I will bring you back to this land. I will not leave you until I have done what I have promised you."
>
> Genesis 28:15

We have a present God. We are people of His presence. These facts are incomprehensible; we can only experience them. The ancient song from Saint Patrick's breastplate, sung at nearly every ordination to the priesthood, says it all:

> Christ be with me, Christ within me,
> Christ behind me, Christ before me,
> Christ beside me, Christ to win me,
> Christ to comfort and restore me,
> Christ beneath me, Christ above me,
> Christ in quiet, Christ in danger,
> Christ in hearts of all that love me,
> Christ in mouth of friend and stranger.

To know His ever-encompassing presence is to know He is constantly working in me to bring me to that place, that land, where

He is, so He can perfect me. I have a peaceful sense of security in knowing that Another lives within me. This is the reality of the incarnation.

Whether, like Noah, you are tossed and driven with no help in sight, or like Job, you are overcome with disaster at every turn and see no respite or like me, you have problems just because we live in a sinful world: You can know for certain that He is with you.

The reality of that knowledge comes down to this:

- When I am in solitude, I am never alone; my best Friend is by my side.
- When I am sick, my Healer is always with me.
- When I am in trouble, my Counselor is always listening.
- When I am at a crossroads, my Guide is always leading me.

Practicing God's Presence

Jesus looked at them and said, "With man this is impossible, but with God all things are possible."

Matthew 19:26

1. What impossibilities are looming in front of you today? Try to dialogue with God about them specifically, using your prayer journal. You may want to use script form, as I demonstrated on page 74.
2. Consider sending a meaningful Scripture anonymously to a friend. Share the divine presence you are experiencing.

Region 2
Listening Prayer
to Hear the Healing Word

BASED ON THE EXPERIENCES OF ELIJAH, AS FOUND IN 1 KINGS 17–2 KINGS 2

Day 8

A Maelstrom of Miracles

My FRIEND AND I KNOCKED TIMIDLY AT THE IMPRESSIVE FRONT DOOR OF A stranger's home. Our pastor had asked us to call on a woman who had suffered for years from debilitating depression so severe it kept her housebound. He had seen little change in her condition under his ministry. Despairingly he asked us, two young women who were newly committed Christians wanting to "do something for Jesus" to pay a call and follow the Holy Spirit's leading. The assignment was a new one for both of us; we had zeal but no experience.

I had never witnessed depression like we saw that day. In a magnificent setting, a beautiful home, sat a lonely woman watching her plants die because she had no incentive to water them. My general impression of the situation could be summed up in one word—"brown." Everything about her life was dull, and her demeanor expressed it clearly.

Small talk and social amenities were impossible. As brand-new Christians all we knew to do was to pray, so we did. One after another the two of us invoked the Holy Spirit in a litany of praise and intercession, acknowledging Jesus' presence and asking God to heal our new friend.

The next day the lady called, wanting to know when a prayer group would be meeting. She wanted to get involved! God had healed her condition miraculously. We could tell by her voice that her enthusiasm for Him matched ours! Never did we meet another person who more earnestly and intensely continued to follow our Lord.

This story is not an isolated example. For the first several months immediately following my Christian commitment miracles happened every day. I watched a cut finger heal over as the wounded cells responded to prayer. My nine-year-old son's turned-in feet had required braces when he was younger; I saw them straighten from the ankles! I saw legs lengthened and teeth filled. I watched a large goiter disappear from a woman's neck as she received healing prayer. I saw a crippled woman throw down her crutches and run, shouting, "I've got new feet!"

I had laughed cynically about such occurrences before I knew the risen Lord. Now they made our new life of faith stimulating, thrilling and awesome.

But a life revolving around expecting miracles was also terrifyingly supercharged, exhausting and addictive. We began judging a successful prayer meeting by how many individuals were healed. If we saw no immediate miracles when we prayed we second-guessed ourselves and one another. The need to go to one more meeting, hear one more speaker, learn one more "technique" or have one more spiritual experience took precedence over quiet devotional time and intimacy with Jesus. Our children were with baby sitters more than with their parents; family meal time became rare. Phone calls during dinner and people dropping in for prayer became more the norm than the exception.

Plunging from a worldly comfort zone into this maelstrom of miracles was about to take its toll on the stability of our family life.

Walking the Christian path is not always one fireworks show after another, as we soon found out. Days and weeks eventually came when God's voice seemed quieter, even silent. Miracles were fewer and farther between and the humdrum routine of life crowded into the spectacular. I knew God had not changed or left us but I could not seem to reach Him; I could not seem to communicate with Him as well in the everyday sameness as I had in the initial rush of excitement. Peace was settling into my body, but a lonely hunger was creeping into my heart—a hunger to hear His words to me.

What I needed was to practice the presence of Jesus through times of listening prayer. As I traveled into this region of the journey to wholeness I learned to incorporate listening prayer into my life. And so did a fellow traveler from long ago, a prophet named Elijah.

A Prophet of Fire

Elijah was a fascinating man, a wild-looking free spirit who came out of the wilderness much as John the Baptist would many centuries later. Elijah wore coarse camel-hair garments and leather belts; long hair hung down his back. He lived and ate off the land, wandering, as God led him from one place to another to speak His words to whoever would listen.

Elijah was anointed by God to call attention to spiritual darkness in the kingdom of Israel, to call the Hebrews back to the one true God and to overthrow the evil kings who practiced Baal worship.

Elijah was a prophet of fire, a prophet of the spectacular. He became well-known not only because of his unusual appearance but because everywhere he went, miracles happened. He was either feared or respected by everyone he met, and sometimes the two reactions were mixed.

Called the "crisis prophet," a man of action, not words, Elijah predicted a complete drought that lasted for years (1 Kings 17:1). He called down fire from heaven on more than one occasion, and watched God's divine, destructive purging in action (1 Kings 18:16–45). At one point God sent ravens to Elijah with much-needed food (1 Kings 17:6). A single parent shared her last pieces of bread with him and then watched the little flour and oil she had left multiply miraculously to feed Elijah, herself and her son for as long as Elijah stayed in her home (1 Kings 17:7–16). When the woman's son died, Elijah prayed over him and watched God resurrect him from the dead—the first recorded incident of the dead coming back to life (1 Kings 17:17–24).

Yes, Elijah's life was full of action and protests and exhortation and fireworks. He saw the awesome majesty of God as few men and women have seen it. So when Elijah faced a great need in his life, he longed desperately to hear God's voice clearly above all the chaos in his world. Then he remembered Moses, and how Moses had heard God.

A Blast from the Past

Five hundred years before, Moses had been led by God to Mount Sinai (also known as Mount Horeb) in the desert south of the Promised Land of Israel. There, surrounded by thunder, lightning, a thick cloud and a trumpet blast, the Lord descended in fire. The mountain trembled violently and the noise of the trumpet grew louder and louder. And in the midst of this amazing spectacle God spoke clearly to Moses (see Exodus 19:16–19).

This was Elijah's style! He had lived his life among shouting, violence, fire and miracles. Now he was hungry to hear God speak to him, so he made the long journey to Mount Sinai to hear God as Moses had so long ago.

In preparation for his divinely appointed journey angels fed him twice a day. Then Elijah traveled for forty arduous days and nights, braving the elements and not pausing even for food, urged on by the assurance that he was going to hear from God. Earthquakes, wind, fire—he could not wait! Finally he reached the holy mountain and collapsed in a cave to spend the night exhausted, but expectant.

Sure enough, the Bible says, "the word of the LORD came to him: 'What are you doing here, Elijah?'" (1 Kings 19:9).

Elijah recited all he had done for God and how, after he had obediently accomplished all God had told him to do, he was seeing God's prophets killed! Why, he was the only one left, and now the evil ones were after him, too. He could see no positive results after all the spectacular things that had happened. He was disillusioned, ready to have his spiritual action batteries recharged.

"Go out and stand on the mountain in the presence of the LORD" [God told him,] "for the LORD is about to pass by" (1 Kings 19:11).

This was heady stuff, but not new for Elijah. He was not fainthearted. Had he not seen God bring fire down from heaven on Mount Carmel, fire that destroyed an army? Had he not seen the dead raised to new life?

So Elijah, geared up and ready for fireworks, went obediently to do as God had requested. "A great and powerful wind tore the mountains apart and shattered the rocks before the LORD" says 1 Kings 19:11.

Elijah listened. He waited. "But," verse 11 goes on, "the LORD was not in the wind."

Then an earthquake rattled the mountain. Expectantly Elijah recalled that Moses had heard God in the earthquake. He listened. He waited. "But the LORD was not in the earthquake" (verse 11).

After the earthquake came a fire. Ah yes, fire! Had not God spoken many times through His wild prophet with fire? Now surely he would hear God speak!

Elijah listened. He waited. "But the Lord was not in the fire" (verse 12).

How do you suppose Elijah felt? Abandoned? Powerless? Where was the spectacular? Had God turned His back, taken away the energy and thrills he craved?

Disillusioned, Elijah stood alone in the quiet aftermath of the fireworks. Then, quite suddenly, he heard a gentle whisper. Could he trust it? It was so calm. But yes, it was the Lord!

In the still, small voice of quiet came the intimacy Elijah longed for with the One who loved him, called him and cared for him. God was teaching him the same lesson about listening prayer that, centuries later, He would teach me.

One or the Other—or Both?

Elijah appears again in the Bible, hundreds of years after he listened to God on Mount Sinai. Jesus had taken His friends Peter, James and John up on another mountain for a day's retreat. While they were there Jesus entered into the holy presence of God for a few moments. As Peter, James and John watched Him with His Father they saw His face shine like the sun and His clothes become as white as light, all reflecting God's glory. And then their eyes were opened to see Moses and Elijah standing right there, talking to Jesus! (See Matthew 17:1–4.)

Moses, the mighty man of God, had been so shy and quiet he needed his brother to speak publicly for him. But Moses had also heard and responded to God in earthquake, wind and fire.

Elijah, the prophet of fire, thrived on the spectacular and shouted words of warning to kings. Yet Elijah also heard and responded to God's gentle whisper.

Now Moses and Elijah came together to authenticate the ministry of Jesus, the Lord of miracles, and Jesus, the Lord of the heart.

As we are indwelt by this same Jesus, we will experience both the spectacular and the still. We need both, you and I. In our world our motors are revved and our senses are overcharged most of the time. Like Elijah, we find the quiet heart harder to engage.

And, like Elijah, we have to purpose to stay with God and wait for His Word to come to us.

Listening to God

You will keep in perfect peace him whose mind is steadfast, because he trusts in you.

Isaiah 26:3

1. Look up the references in your Bible's concordance on "quiet" and/or "quietness." You will learn a great deal about how God works. Remember to make them personal in your prayer journal.
2. Choose one "quiet Scripture" as a reminder for yourself. Place it on a mirror, in your car, at your desk or on the front of your prayer journal. Mine is Isaiah 30:15: "In quietness and trust is your strength."
3. What area of your life is restless for a quiet word from God right now? With your journal in hand, sit quietly and wait upon the Lord for at least ten minutes. Invite Him to speak His peace into your heart. Write out in your prayer journal whatever you hear in your quiet time with Him.

Day 9

Divine Serendipity

ONE AFTERNOON AS I WAS PRAYING FOR SOMETHING ELSE ENTIRELY, A PIC-
ture of my paternal grandfather, Opp (short for Theophilus), quite
suddenly materialized in my mind and heart. I "saw" him lying
in a hospital bed. Although I knew Opp was in the hospital in a
city several miles away and that he was not expected to live, I
had not been praying for him at all.

I was not close to Opp; he was a difficult man for me to understand. He had probably spoken no more than a hundred words
to me in my lifetime, even though I had grown up in the town
where he and my grandmother lived. Our family had shared
Christmas and Thanksgiving dinners in Opp's home for years
when I was a child, and until I went away to college I had probably seen him once a week at the family business. He always seemed
to me like a bitter, distant man, and I was a little afraid of him.

So you can imagine my surprise when, while I was basking in
God's presence, not only did I see the vivid picture of Opp, but I
distinctly heard Jesus speak these words to my spirit as well:

"Go to see your grandfather. Pray for his healing—tonight."

I looked at the clock; it was 4:00 P.M. Conlee was not home from
work. The boys had not eaten, and I needed to supervise their
homework. Driving to the hospital would take an hour and a half.
It was just too late to go.

Besides, I was not sure Opp would welcome my prayers. To my
knowledge he had never attended a church, and I had no idea
what his beliefs were.

But inside *I knew that I knew that I knew* God had spoken. Suddenly everything in me tuned in to the frequency that said I must go pray with Opp—tonight!

Nothing about this assignment was easy. That very afternoon the daughter of some dear friends from another city had left her campus dorm in our college town and moved in temporarily with us. She was upset about the situation that provoked her move and needed a "mama's" love. Our own children had just come in from soccer practice, and I had not even begun to plan supper. I wavered; maybe the whole venture was just out of the question.

I hit Conlee with the word I had from God as soon as he opened the door. Tired, hungry and a bit perplexed, he looked lovingly at me and said, "If God said it, you'd better do it. I'll go with you."

I could have cried with relief. We ate a quick supper, called a baby sitter and left at 7:30.

We arrived at the hospital at 8:56, noting signs everywhere that visiting hours were strictly enforced and that they ended at 9:00 P.M. We got lost finding Opp's room. As we finally opened his door an announcement sounded on the intercom: "All visitors must leave."

We entered the room and closed the door.

By Faith Alone

Opp had been a thin, wiry man when he was well. Lying in bed, wasted away at ninety years of age, it seemed this surely was his time to die. Why should we pray for healing?

Opp stared at me and asked, "What are you doing here?"

It had always been hard for me to talk to him, so I prayed for boldness. I tried to tell him how I got there, but he just kept looking at a western playing on the wall-mounted television. Finally I turned off the TV and said, "Opp, we'd like to pray for you."

Conlee and I each took one of Opp's emaciated, wrinkled hands, closed our eyes and began to pray. I heard the door open and looked up to see a nurse enter the room, but as soon as she realized we were praying she backed out and closed the door. This gave me more courage to be obedient to God. We prayed for healing and for an awareness of God's presence to surround Opp.

Conlee and I both were aware of an incredible anointing as we prayed. It was a short prayer, but powerful.

We opened our eyes and I looked at Opp. His rheumy, pale blue eyes were staring up at the blank television screen, but a tear was sliding down his cheek.

He's been touched; he has sensed God, I thought.

But, not looking at either of us, all Opp said was, "We had a good crop of pecans this year."

God's Agenda, Not Mine

Can you imagine all the second-guessing I did on the hour and a half drive home? Whatever you can think of, I thought it, said it and then some. But I had to admit it felt good to have been obedient to God.

That strange, nocturnal mission yielded surprising results. For openers, Opp fully recovered, did not need surgery and lived eight more years. To my knowledge, however, his spiritual condition never changed.

But my obedience to God affected my father, Opp's oldest son, in an extraordinary way. Daddy was dismayed, to say the least, by my conversion to an active Christian faith and commitment. He developed a habit of having several drinks and then spending hours arguing with me. I watched his relationship with my mother deteriorating. I had not told him of our visit to see Opp.

When Opp recovered, however, he told Daddy that Conlee and I had been to see him in the hospital and had prayed for him. Although Opp laughed about it when he told Daddy, my father was deeply affected when the reality of what had transpired hit him. He related later that all at once he could see clearly that my Christianity was real, not for show, and that the power involved in this healing must be God! Within a few weeks' time this simple fact of my listening, hearing and being obedient to God became the catalyst that resulted in a complete change in my father's life. And, in contrast to my lack of prayers for Opp, I had been praying for Daddy every day for months!

Daddy lived six more years after the incident. He became an actively committed Christian who shared his newfound faith in every area of his life. I watched my parents' marriage restored. At Daddy's funeral dozens of friends and business acquaintances told me how my father's testimony and simple faith had saved their lives, marriages and businesses.

After Daddy's death, as she went through his papers, my mother found his testimony typed out, a legacy of God's profound wisdom and divine serendipity for his family to cherish.

Listening to God

> To obey is better than sacrifice. . . .
> 1 Samuel 15:22

1. Is there something God has been telling you to do for some time? Something you have been putting off for various reasons? Perhaps He wants you to write a letter to someone, or make a visit, take a gift, say a prayer or ask someone's forgiveness. Would you be willing to pray specifically for His directions, making plans with Him to take concrete action as soon as possible?
2. Have someone's unexpected, serendipitous actions toward you been a blessing in your life? Have you told him or her what it meant to you, and thanked God for prompting him or her to action? Write some thank-you notes to God in your prayer journal.

Day 10

Practice Makes Perfect

MY FRIEND MARIE IS A PROFESSIONAL ARTIST WHO HAS TAUGHT ME A LOT about self-discipline. She quotes an art teacher who once told her, "If you want to paint well on Monday, you have to paint on Sunday."

Her idea was that a slump in work can result from slothfulness in practice. I can relate to this concept in many areas of my life—tennis, writing, exercise, dieting, even relationships. Let's face it: When the creative juices are flowing, anything is fun. But when it comes down to discipline in the ditches, we do not like it, we do not want to do it and we will accept any excuse to do something—anything—else.

If you have had trouble maintaining a listening prayer time on a regular basis (and I know you have, because you are human), or if you are just starting to realize the value of setting aside a special period of time each day for you and God to meet together, I want to encourage you. I need encouragement so often in my walk with the Lord. We all do. The writer of the letter to the Hebrews in the New Testament knew that, because he tells us to

> encourage one another daily, as long as it is called Today, so that none of you may be hardened by sin's deceitfulness.
>
> Hebrews 3:13

I am often tempted to "float" after a particularly spiritual "high," resting on my spiritual "warm fuzzies" for a few days instead of continuing to spend regular time with God. What a big mistake, and definitely part of "sin's deceitfulness"! I have also been known to substitute conferences, tapes, books and spiritual conversations for real Bible meditation and listening prayer. Again, such rationalization is a tactic of the deceiver. All of those admittedly good things cannot accomplish the same purpose that listening prayer achieves, and we are cheating our intimate relationship with God to believe that they do.

What are you thinking right now? *Listening prayer is too hard; I cannot do it. I am just wasting time when I could be doing something meaningful.*

I know those thoughts. They used to be in my repertoire! Let me share a story with you that changed my attitude about listening prayer.

From the Mouths of Babes

When our youngest son, Ben, was just a baby we had a weekend house by a lake in the Ozarks, about an hour's drive from where we lived at the time. It was a wonderful, quiet place with no television and few distractions—other than the beauty of God's creation! Many prayers were prayed in that special spiritual retreat for our family and friends, and for several years we spent as much time there as we could.

One day when Ben was just starting to verbalize in sentences, he and I were back home after a restful family weekend at the lake. He was playing on the floor and I was ironing while I watched a movie on television. I did not think he was paying any attention to what the actors, one of them a girl named Angel, were saying.

But suddenly Ben cried out, "That's not an angel!"

"What are you talking about?" I asked.

He pointed decidedly to the girl on the screen and repeated, "That's not an angel!"

"Ben, what does an angel look like?" I asked, thinking he remembered pictures from one of his Bible books. "Describe an angel to me."

"Big!" he said, spreading his little arms as high as he could reach.

His emphatic gesturing intrigued me, so I turned off the television, unplugged the iron and sat down on the floor with my little one.

"Ben," I asked him seriously, "have you ever seen an angel?"

He looked right back at me and nodded. "I see them at the lake."

"Do you mean they're in our house at the lake?" I questioned.

"Yes, and Mommie, they talk to me."

My heart did a flip, and I asked a question that brought tears to my eyes. "What do the angels say, Ben?"

"They say Jesus loves me."

I was stunned. This was not Ben's imagination; this was real. Wanting to make sure he understood the gravity of what he had just told me, I took both his little hands in mine and, looking seriously into his big blue eyes I said, "Ben, I've never seen the angels or heard them speak."

He responded with the same degree of seriousness and childlike sincerity, straight from the heart: "Mommie, they talk to you all the time, but you don't listen."

There's No Place like Home

From this experience I began to believe that, like Adam and Eve, we are born with the ability to "hear" God and to "see" the holy. But somewhere along the way we either decide or we are taught that the gift of intimacy with our Holy God is less valuable than other things in our lives. And once we quit listening, we quickly forget that we once heard.

It did not take long for Ben to forget those amazing experiences with God's messengers. He has heard me tell this story many times and he believes me. He can even recall other events that happened at about the same time in his life, like the time his dog, Charlie, kept him out of the water at the lake. But he has no recollection at all of the angels.

It is as if by living in a fallen world we go through a spiritual lobotomy at a very young age. To go back to the Garden of Eden relationship we all hunger for, we have to *choose, make the effort* and *practice diligently* our part in the dance with God.

My dear friend Claire Cloninger, who is a gifted songwriter, wrote the lyrics to a Christian ballad that Paul Smith set to music for Word, Inc. An all-time favorite of Conlee's and mine, it is called "Homesick for Eden":

The garden was green, the water was clean
The animals came without names,
And love was a girl who walked through a world
Where passion was pure as a flame.
In the back of our minds is a time before time
And a sad irreversible fact:
We can't seem to think why we left there,
And we can't seem to find our way back.

For all of us are homesick for Eden,
We yearn to return to a place we've never known.
Deep is the need to go back to the Garden,
A yearning so strong for a place we belong,
The place that we know is home.

Friends, this home is the place we find when, in listening prayer, we begin to "hear" again and "see" again and "know" again the things God created us to experience. The low-grade homesickness we have never been able to articulate is healed. The restlessness that has motivated our bad decisions and wrong choices is eased.

No, we are not back in the Garden, not yet, but we have found our *home within,* our *hamewith.* This wonderful Scottish word so beautifully describes our intimacy with our Lord that Conlee and I have named our new home "Hamewith Cottage." More than wood, stone and mortar, Hamewith is the place where we know we belong, where God wants us. It is the center of our being, where He resides.

Hamewith is where we hear the still, small voice. After we have rocked through our earthquakes, hung on for dear life through our windstorms and raced through the flames in our lives we, like Elijah, can come to a place where we say, "Lord, I am ready to be still, to sit and be at peace, to bask in the quiet and to listen to what You have to say to me."

Listening to God

Jesus replied, "If anyone loves me, he will obey my teaching. My Father will love him, and we will come to him and make our home with him."

John 14:23

1. A quiet place—is this where you are now? Or where you want to be? I want to encourage you in every way I can. If staying in that quiet place of listening prayer is a struggle, remember: It is worth it! If you are afraid of what God might say to you when you hear His voice, read the story of the forgiving father in Luke 15:11–32. Use your sanctified imagination to put yourself in the story.

2. We tend to hurry things in this frantic day and age, racing through even the best that life has to offer. Give yourself permission to enjoy the luxury of moving slowly through your prayer journal, pausing to see the beauty of what you have already written, receiving healing and love from Jesus, all over again, through your reading. Be thankful, aloud, for even the smallest thing that has blessed you.

Day 11

Time after Time

I JUST CAN'T GET EVERYTHING DONE. THERE AREN'T ENOUGH HOURS IN THE day. Oh, for just a little more time!"

Unfortunately neither you nor I can do one thing about adding more hours to a day. All of us have the same 24 hours with which to work. Knowing how I squeeze things into every second of every day, I wonder how government leaders like the President of the United States stand the pressure of having the same limited 24 hours a day that I have.

People struggling to keep discipline in their God-time each day usually say their biggest problem is "not enough time." We often say we are creatures of time, but that is not true. Time is a creature, too. Time, like men and women, was created by God. And, as He did with the rest of creation, God gave men and women dominion over time.

So why do we feel so trapped by time? Why do we feel it controls us, instead of the other way around? Why do so many seasoned Christian believers seem unable to maintain regular time with God?

Time for a Change

Once when time was creating a major crisis in my life, when fatigue, panic, irritability and pressure were suffocating me, God told me something about time that revolutionized my life and let me see a whole new dimension of His character.

Conlee and I had decided to spend a week at Lake Martin Marriage Retreat, near Tallassee, Alabama, a marriage enrichment experience led by the Rev. Forrest and Nancy Mobley. Scheduled into this wonderful week is an opportunity for each couple in attendance to have two lengthy, private counseling sessions with Forrest and Nancy. Husbands and wives can talk and pray about anything they want, about any obstacles looming in their relationship.

At that point in our lives our biggest problem was time! Conlee was working as a full-time minister, with administrative, spiritual, counseling and preaching responsibilities. Ben, our only unmarried child, was in high school, active in sports and school activities. I was working full-time for a caterer, managing a kitchen staff, a gourmet take-out shop and full-service catered events.

This was the first full-time job I had ever held. When our children were small and Conlee was active in the construction business, we had been able financially to provide our children with a stay-at-home mom. That job really used my gifts of homemaking, decorating, entertaining and hospitality. I loved staying at home and found it fulfilling.

When Conlee went into the ministry, however, we had two children in college, another at home and a much reduced income. I had to join the vast ranks of "working moms." The natural place for me to use my gifts was in catering, and God provided both a wonderful opportunity and delightful people to work with.

But the job was not a nine-to-five proposition. People do not hold extravagant galas during normal business hours. They want Friday, Saturday and Sunday night events, lasting until the early morning hours. They schedule Saturday and Sunday morning brunches. They love to entertain during the holidays. So I worked long days on my feet, dealing with other peoples' stress over their entertainment problems, and nearly every weekend evening as well. People pay well for that kind of service, but for someone with a family, catering can be a killer job.

What happened to family time? Chats after school? Milk and homemade cookies? Soccer games? Family devotions? Private devotions? Lazy Saturday mornings? Family dinners after church? Midweek prayer and praise? Dates with Conlee? Parties with friends?

"Sorry, Signa's working!"

Going Under for the Third Time

I saw no way out. I felt trapped. God had so obviously provided the job; how could I be ungrateful? We needed the income, but how could I continue at this killer pace? I was tired all the time; if I sat down at home I went to sleep. I was gaining weight because I did not eat regularly, did not get the right kind of exercise and my metabolism was shutting down. I could not remember when Conlee and I had last had fun together.

This was the problem I took to our counseling session with Forrest and Nancy Mobley.

Forrest and Nancy listened patiently and lovingly to our "unique" situation and then said, "We hear this story all the time. It is the biggest problem active married couples have; it is an epidemic. We have no answers for you."

I felt deflated. Nothing could be done. Our predicament was a part of the human condition, and I was going to have to live with it.

Then Forrest threw me a lifeline.

"My only advice is that you spend some time this week listening to God about time. After all, He created it." Forrest and Nancy prayed that we would be able to hear the Lord clearly as we purposed to listen.

That listening time saved our lives.

Time Out

To begin our time of listening for God's word about time in our lives, Conlee and I checked all the references in our Bibles on "time" and "days of life" to see what God had to say. The answer? A lot!

Do these words match up with your life? They did with mine:

Our days on earth are like a shadow. . . .
                1 Chronicles 29:15

My days are swifter than a weaver's shuttle. . . .
                        Job 7:6

My days are swifter than a runner; they fly away. . . .
                        Job 9:25

The most meaningful reference we found in this study of time was in the book of poems written mainly by King David. Two specific psalms literally shouted their relevance to our situation:

> Therefore let everyone who is godly pray to you while you may be found; surely when the mighty waters rise, they will not reach him. You are my hiding place; you will protect me from trouble and surround me with songs of deliverance.
>
> Psalm 32:6–7

And,

> Rescue me from the mire, do not let me sink; deliver me . . . from the deep waters. Do not let the floodwaters engulf me or the depths swallow me up. . . .
>
> Psalm 69:14–15

Is There Really a Bridge over Troubled Waters?

The Psalms' strong imagery of dangerous water spoke to both of us, describing to a "T" how we had been feeling—like drowning victims. I thought about the fearful emotions that overtake us when we think we are in dangerous, deep water. First we think we can stay afloat and bravely tread water, even in the midst of turbulence. Then fear creeps in and we begin to thrash about, looking for something, anything, to cling to. When finally we think we have found a possible lifesaver, we clutch it so desperately that we tend to pull it down with us. After we wear ourselves out with the struggle we finally give in, allowing the water to have its way with us, even if that means death.

The "sea" in which I was "drowning" was not wet, but that was the only discrepancy between David's scenario and the one I was living. As I read those verses with godly insight I burst into tears. Someone finally understood!

And the promises were there, along with the understanding. God would be my hiding place, my protection. He would surround me with deliverance. I now knew there was a way out. I did not yet know what it was, but I had hope because of God's revealed word to me.

99

Following our scriptural research, Conlee and I prayed quietly and listened. And in the listening solitude came a plan of deliverance so quickly organized, so intricately detailed, so completely unexpected I had no doubt it came from God's heart to mine.

His word to me? "You have allowed yourself to be bound by time to the extent that you have become its prisoner. Instead, I will empower you to harness the strength of time and use it for your benefit.

"Begin your day at sunset rather than at sunrise," He continued, "as was the custom of My people for generations. At the 'beginning' of your day, read My Word that I have given you, speak to Me from your heart and then listen. Allow Me to prepare you for the rest you need to begin the next morning with Me."

God-Time

A true deliverance from my predicament came out of this creative word about restructuring what I had thought was cast in stone. On weekdays Conlee and I began our day at sunset, as God had directed. We prayed, read Scripture, shared, listened and prayed for one another and for our children. We went to bed early. What we discovered was that we were actually beginning our day together in the evening by coming together spiritually and physically, loving and resting, rather than beginning our day with morning schedule stress and several hours' separation.

On this new schedule I was wide awake, showered and dressed by 5:00 A.M. and ready to continue the remainder of my day. I drove through dark streets to arrive at the catering office at 6:00. This became an intimate time with Jesus as I sang along with praise tapes all the way to work.

Because I was alone in the office until 8:00, with no ringing phones or other distractions, my efficiency level increased one hundred fold. I was even able to watch the sun rise over the lovely Celtic cross on the steeple of the church across the parking lot. I, who had never considered myself a morning person, thrived on this new perspective. And by 2:00 P.M. my work was organized and delegated when appropriate, and I was home to meet Ben after school. On afternoons when I had evening parties I was even able to get naps. It was so simple, yet so revolutionary!

I realize that as you read this it may appear I was playing a mind-game with myself, but when God speaks to our hearts about something, He anoints it with His presence. That made all the difference. Because He had said it, He was in it. His solution became a living word to our family and brought life to us.

For eight months this deliverance from the "flood waters" saved my sanity and my health. At the end of that time God had other plans for me and I quit working in the catering business. He has faithfully provided in every instance where there seemed to be no way.

This is not a recommendation to reorganize your day as I did, unless God tells you to do so. It is intended to convey to you that the God who created time is still the Creator. He knows what kind of deliverance you need and He has the plan and the means to bring it into your life. It may be as totally untraditional as my deliverance or it may be quite "normal."

Either way, God's desire for your wholeness is that you "pray to Him while He may be found," so His Word might be your "song of deliverance."

Listening to God

From the LORD comes deliverance. May your blessing be on your people.

Psalm 3:8

1. Write in your prayer journal about your "impossible" situation, schedule or quiet-time conflict.
2. As you place your hand over the words you have just written, pray with me,

Lord, here are all my reasons for not being able to have quality time with You. I give them to You because I am drowning in them and see no way out. Please speak to me a word of deliverance. I believe it is Your will for us to have quality intimate time together every day and I desire to share that with You. I trust that You have the lifeline I need and I listen in Your presence for Your solution. Please empower me by Your Spirit to obey You as You show me what to do. Thank You, Jesus. Amen.

Day 12

The Window of My Heart

MOST OF US HAVE GROWN UP WITH TWO MAJOR MISCONCEPTIONS ABOUT how we should "examine ourselves" in order to "do better" with our lives. First, most of us have learned to *look to other human beings* for verbal or nonverbal feedback. Some of us choose to look to people we trust and respect, and others choose people we want to imitate or hope to impress, whether or not they are worthy of such imitation.

The second way in which many of us examine ourselves is by *looking inward* (which is called introspection or, more popularly, "navel-gazing"). This can be a debilitating habit and, like looking to other human beings, can produce a highly distorted picture.

The best way to see accurately what is in our hearts is not by looking within or without, but by looking straight up to Jesus. He knows our hearts. He can tell us what is there, what we need to know about ourselves at this particular time in our lives. He alone can open the window to your heart, and to mine.

Learning to listen to Jesus, asking *Him* to search our hearts and show us what we need to know about ourselves and where we need to take action, is a liberating experience. It frees us from dealing with the *symptoms* of dis-ease in our spirits and allows us to deal with *root causes*. No longer do we need to be paralyzed with guilt, either true or false, as we let our Healer show us the core of our problem, confess our complicity in any sin attached and receive His forgiveness. No one knows your heart or mine like the One who created us and calls us His own. No one—including you or me.

Here is how it works. As I spend time loving, worshiping and listening to Jesus, I can give Him permission to show me any diseased attitudes clinging to my heart. It is important not to strive or dig frantically for what He is not willing to show me at that moment. He alone knows what I am able to deal with at any given time. I find that when I come honestly into His presence, the thing that disturbs Him most at that moment surfaces immediately.

If an attitude displeasing to Jesus surfaces, I write it in my prayer journal, neither condemning nor making excuses for myself. Then I give it to Him, confessing it as sin. Next I picture Him taking it from my hands, taking it into Himself and offering me His forgiveness. I accept His gift wholeheartedly, wrapping it around me like a cloak.

Clothed in Jesus' forgiveness, I now wait in His presence, listening for the healing words He will offer in exchange for the negative attitude of my heart. His healing words will begin to define my heart in its redeemed state. I will see myself in a new way through His eyes.

Let me demonstrate this life-changing exchange more concretely by telling you Jennifer's story.

A Holy Transaction

I prayed with Jennifer at the altar of a church where we were holding a healing conference. This young woman could hardly lift her head from the floor, where she was huddled in all-consuming grief.

I finally persuaded her to tell me what was tormenting her. Out came stories of emotional, physical and sexual abuse from nearly every person she had ever cared about. Her identity had deteriorated to the point that she thought of herself as something to be disposed of, as refuse. The foremost thought in her mind that evening was of suicide.

Jennifer and I invoked the presence of God's Holy Spirit to speak a healing word to her heart. To our surprise His immediate response was to show her her own sin, sin she had justified because of the abuse heaped upon her by others.

To my natural mind this seemed like a harsh, unloving thing for God to do. *Maybe it isn't God,* I rationalized. *Maybe Jennifer's own victimized, poor self-image is expressing itself. How can we be so cruel as to focus on the sin of an individual suffering so deeply from depression, shame and rejection?* My natural inclination was to affirm her, take her mind off her pain and speak loving words to her, not heap more shame and degradation on someone already so hurt.

But His voice was strong in my spirit: *Until she deals with her own sin, the sins of others will continue to torment her.*

Acting according to His divine character and wisdom, God went right to the source of Jennifer's pain. As I assured Jennifer that His presence surrounded her and that she was in a safe place, she received His power to see, acknowledge and confess her own sin: that she had hated and despised those who had hurt her; that she had wished them dead; that she had hated herself for being their victim; and that she wished herself dead as well. In His presence Jennifer recognized immediately the sin that had been part of her life for years, and she asked God to have mercy on her and to forgive her, as she would forgive others.

As Jennifer looked up from her prayer I assured her that indeed, because of her confession, God was pouring His forgiveness into her (1 John 1:9). Now that her sin was released she could receive His healing word for her.

"Listen, Jennifer," I said, "listen to His healing word to you. God wants to begin replacing the negative thought patterns you have carried for so many years."

We listened together and immediately she received one word very clearly: *Forgiven.* This was the first word of many that established Jennifer's new identity in her forgiven relationship with Christ.

At that point I gave Jennifer an assignment: She was to get a new notebook to begin a prayer journal, and she was to start the first page with the title "Who I Am in Christ." I suggested that she put *forgiven* at the top of the list. She and God had completed a holy transaction, and I suggested that each day she ask God for one more word to describe her as He saw her, continuing until the pages were filled.

The next morning when I saw Jennifer I could not believe my eyes. Her face was shining! She told me that before she even got out of bed that day God told her she was "loved." Joyfully she added this new adjective describing her identity in Christ to her prayer journal.

Jennifer continued to listen for and write down God's healing words for her every day of that conference. On the last day, at the Sunday morning service, the pastor asked if anyone would like to share what God had done in his or her life that week. Jennifer raced to the front of the church to declare that she now knew who she was because God had spoken to her and she had listened. She was not who people had told her she was; she was not even who she had thought she was herself. God had revealed her true identity, the one He had seen in her since she was conceived. Joyfully she shared some of the words He had given her that week: *forgiven, loved, accepted, strong in Him* and *victorious.*

God's healing words had saved her life.

Listening to God

I will write on him the name of my God and the name of the city of my God, the new Jerusalem, which is coming down out of heaven from my God; and I will also write on him my new name.

Revelation 3:12

1. You have been keeping a prayer journal diligently for at least ten days now. Are you beginning to see a pattern of what is in your heart? Are you beginning to know more of God's heart?
2. Are you willing to take the steps Jennifer took to hear God speak words of truth to you about who you are in Him? In order to listen to Him effectively you may need to picture yourself symbolically, as Jennifer found herself literally, on your face before the altar of the Holy One.
3. The New English Bible's translation of Psalm 95:7 reads, "You shall know his power today if you will listen to his voice." Think about this promise of blessing for a few minutes. What kind of power do you need today? The power to forgive? To come out of depression? To be victorious over sin? Write out your deep heart needs as God reveals them to you.

Day 13

The Desire of Your Heart

"**W**HAT IS THE DESIRE OF YOUR HEART?"

At each healing conference in which we take part we ask the attendees this question. For years my own response, even if I was simply asking it of others, was an image that exploded out of my heart into my conscious mind and consisted of one word— "home." I could see it written out as if on a banner, flying high over an actual house on the water where each wave sparkled in the sun. Other details were fuzzy, but a peace I knew came from God surrounded the image.

Yes, the desire of my heart was definitely "home."

"Home" has always been important to our family. We have guarded who and what was allowed in, not forsaking hospitality, but preserving holiness. To us "home" always meant more than a lovely house: It meant a sense of belonging, of having roots and a refuge from whatever chaos was going on out in our world.

"Home" took on a different dimension for us after we left our family roots to go to seminary. Our children were scattered in different states, attending college and then marrying, with one even living in Europe. Four moves within a few years taught us which roots were most important. We had given ourselves to God's call on our lives with no qualifications, so the concept of "home" was no longer a specific house, decorated in a certain way. Instead it was a place set apart by God for us to be part of and be responsible for. It was a place from which we could reap the benefits of the peace He would provide.

Consequently I carried down deep in my heart this desire for a true "home," the image of a place for us to go back to after ministering to others, a place full of God's presence and restoration for all of us. And always that image was associated with water.

A Special Place

I remember vividly our first family vacation to the Gulf Coast in the summer of 1973, when we fell in love with the white beaches and the blue-green water and the sea air's salty smell. I seemed to feel closer to God in that place, and could hear His voice more clearly than I could at home in the mountains. (Friends have told me they feel closer to God in the mountains; obviously this is an individual matter, but the point is the same.)

After we packed the car at the end of that first week at the Gulf for the two-day drive back to our hometown, I raced to the beach for one more taste of our beautiful view.

"Oh God," I whispered, *"please let us come back here. This is where I feel complete, where I belong. How I would love to live on the water all the time, to wake up each morning and see the wondrous changes that have occurred, the new colors, the energy, the calm, the life of the sea. At least let us come again to visit, Lord, please."*

For the next two decades we spent every family holiday somewhere on the water. Rick, our oldest son, now a married man, a chemical engineer and an environmental toxicologist with his Ph.D., always took his aquarium and pump, nets and snorkel, fins and mask. As soon as he had helped us unpack the car he was in the water, or rather, under the water, collecting "rare specimens" for the salt-water aquarium he set up in the living room of our rented beach house. Several times a day he came in with a new trophy and we watched it in the glass tank as we read about it in our field guides. At the end of our holiday the collection went ceremoniously back into the sea, leaving memories of pipe fish and eels and sea horses and starfish. (I always thought the sea "critters" took special memories of us back with them, too.)

Matt, married and the father of two, has served as an officer in the Navy and is now a civil engineer working in construction. As a child he spent hours building forts and castles and tunnels in the sand. He also had dreams of being "Cap'n Matt" on a fishing boat or a lifeguard like Earl, his hero on the beach. Each day he brought sand dollars in to bleach and carefully pack in paper towels for decorating our tree at Christmas.

Ben, who is a college student studying environmental engineering, took his first steps on the beach, squealing at the sand and waves between his toes. He was so covered in sand at the end of each day that we nicknamed him our little "sugar cookie."

Our routine every morning was to erect a large canvas dining shelter on the beach where we set up sand chairs, a cooler of cold drinks and Ben's playpen. Rick and Matt to this day still groan when they recall putting up that tent each morning and getting all sandy before they were fully awake. Conlee and I always had good books we had saved for "beach reading" and, under cover of the dining shelter, would stretch out to tackle tomes we had not had time to read at home. One summer I industriously read all the works of Alexsandr Solzhenitsyn!

A Jewel from Jesus

These wonderful beach experiences and memories made it natural for me to desire a home on the water, but the timing seemed all wrong. We were in full-time ministry; our priorities had changed and our bank account had decreased dramatically. Whenever Conlee and I talked about a waterfront home it was always associated with his retirement in the far-off "someday."

Then a few years ago at a particularly moving Holy Week service at our church, I heard again the story of the Last Supper. I heard how Jesus lovingly washed Judas' feet along with those of the other disciples, how He lovingly offered Judas the morsel of bread as He did the other disciples and how He freely offered Judas His life, just as He offered it to the others.

Lord, I found myself praying, *I am not plotting against You as Judas did. I am not willingly betraying You, as Judas did. I am opening my heart to You as fully as I know how. How much more should I be able to receive this love You are offering so freely! I want to let You wash my feet and feed me Your bread of life.*

I went to the altar expectantly to receive His life in the bread and the wine. Immediately I was bathed in His love, aware of new depths of it in my life. As I returned to kneel in my pew I felt the long-time desire of my heart surface—that desire for a home on the water.

At first I felt guilty. After all, this was a holy moment. I had just given myself to Jesus as fully as I knew how, and I had sensed His presence with me in a much deeper way than ever before. I was supposed to have my mind on holy things, holy desires, not the desires of my own heart.

Oh Lord, I cried, *take this selfish thought from me. I have dwelt too long on this dream of a home on the water. Even now it is coming between us in a holy moment. Once again I give it to You. It is all right with me if that dream never comes true. I want only to look on You. I want only You in my life.*

Then His word came to me clearly:

I love you more than you know. Do not turn away from the love I am offering you. I am going to plant you firmly in a home with roots that run deep. [I had an impression of a large sturdy tree with roots deep to the water.] *It will be the perfect little jewel for you on the water.*

Many times I had put the image of "home" on His altar and said, *"Lord, if this is not of You I want no part of it. It is Yours."* And each time I sensed God lovingly giving back to me that desire, rooting it, in fact, in my heart. As He spoke to me that day after communion I knew without a doubt that the desire that had been in my heart for so long was one the Lord Himself had placed there as an act of love. It was planted there to draw me closer to Him, not to the material value of the dream. As long as my identity was found in Him, not the home, it was His good pleasure to give me the gift.

One week later I was with a friend from Houston whom I had not seen in several years. She prayed for me in almost the exact words Jesus had spoken, that God's love would penetrate our lives so we would have roots deep to the water. Her prayer confirmed my belief that the desire of my heart was also the desire of God's heart, and that He was allowing the two desires to become one. What I was afraid might be selfish and materialistic, God was intending for the continued wholeness of our family.

I shared my experience with Conlee, and we decided to relax in the knowledge that the "little jewel" God had promised would appear in His time, and not before.

One year almost to the day after God spoke to me about the "little jewel on the water" we were given the desire of our hearts. It happened so suddenly there was no doubt it was a divine act. For only a very few days a particular home and property, tied up in an estate with no heirs, was on the market. Because it was in such a state of disrepair even those few who looked at it turned away, dismayed by the amount of work it would take to make the place livable.

But as soon as we stepped onto the property we *knew.* It was the only house we really looked at, and we did so only because a friend took us to see it. Because the executor of the estate lived out of state and wanted a quick sale, it was also the only waterfront property within our reach financially.

Most importantly, we saw the property as God saw it, through God's eyes. He saw, and we saw, its beauty and worth and the deep peace present beneath the outward appearance of neglect. A sense of prayer seemed to pervade the grounds, and as we began to renovate we found numerous evidences that praying Christians had lived in the house—crosses, Scripture passages, drawings and prayer lists.

As I write this we have lived in our "Hamewith Cottage," our "home within," the "little jewel," for barely a year. Renovating it has taken lots of hard work, but it has been a mission that has borne much fruit, blessing us beyond belief. Sitting here this morning, looking out on the still waters, watching a large heron fishing at the water's edge, I think how much like Judas I could have been. As Jesus lovingly offered me this morsel of "home" I could have rejected it, not believing it could happen. Or I could have attempted to grab it for myself. Had I not chosen to *listen* to His words for me, to *wait* and to *believe,* I never would have known the intimacy of His love or received love's gift.

Listening to God

> I waited patiently for the LORD; he turned to me and heard my cry.
> Psalm 40:1

1. What is the desire of your heart? Write it out. Let God speak to you about it as you listen.
2. Look up Psalm 37:4. Write it in your prayer journal and personalize it before the Lord. Why would your "delighting in the Lord" be a prerequisite for Him to grant your heart's desire?

Region 3

Overcoming Temptation So I May Know My God-Given True Self

BASED ON THE EXPERIENCES OF JESUS, AS FOUND IN MATTHEW 3:13–4:11; MARK 1:9–13; AND LUKE 3:21–22; 4:1–13

Day 14

In over My Head

TODAY WE ENTER REGION 3, WHERE OUR DAILY LEAVES OF HEALING WILL help us consider how overcoming temptation, as Jesus overcame it, can help us discover our God-given true selves. To get us started I want to tell you a bit more about my own spiritual journey toward wholeness, and specifically what I learned about temptation and God's calling to wholeness and mission as they related to my baptism, my confirmation and my experience of the baptism of the Holy Spirit.

My Baptism

First, can you recall your own baptism? Do you remember the exact date? Where did it take place? Do you have pictures of this important event? Is it indelibly imprinted on your heart as an annual day of celebration and remembrance, just like your birthday?

Perhaps you have never been baptized. Maybe you never felt quite comfortable with the idea, equating it with local church membership or a social rite of passage. Certainly it can be reduced to either of these when approached without the Spirit's leading.

When I was twelve years old, the church I attended promoted a seventh-grade rite of adolescence to become a full-fledged member of the church—and called it baptism. About fifty of us were herded forward one Sunday morning while our parents watched proudly. As we knelt at the large, semicircular altar, the minister took one white carnation after another, dipped it in water and touched each head (hair stiff with Spray Net) three times, baptizing us in the name of the Father, Son and Holy Spirit.

I am ashamed to admit it, but my only recollection of the event is that I giggled, embarrassed, hoping my new dress looked good from the back. I was totally unprepared, yet "something" was supposed to have happened.

My Confirmation

About three years after we married, Conlee and I joined our present denomination. We were required to study church history and tradition for six weeks. We were told that if we had previously been baptized, or if godparents had made statements on our behalf when we were infants, we could now affirm what had been done and enter into a new relationship with God.

Both Conlee and I anticipated our confirmation eagerly. We did not know what we expected, but we were serious; we wanted to know God! I hoped at least to gain whatever it was I felt I had missed at my baptism.

The little church in South Miami, Florida, near to where Conlee was stationed as a lieutenant in the Army, was quite informal in many ways. But when it came to confirmation, we might as well have been in Rome. I was to wear a white dress and a white veil. Because we were married, Conlee and I were to walk down the aisle together, kneel before the seated bishop (whom we had never seen before) and receive the laying-on-of-hands, an ancient rite in the Church whereby the Holy Spirit is imparted.

We were keyed up for our confirmation. We invited a nonchurch-attending couple to witness the event and join us for lunch afterwards to celebrate with our infant son, Rick. I think our friends were a bit uncomfortable with the whole idea but they were good sports, so they accepted.

Conlee and I held hands and carried prayer books as we walked slowly down the center aisle behind a dozen or so children. We were the only adults to be confirmed and many eyes were on us—Conlee with his military-style haircut and dark suit, I in my white pique pleated dress, white gloves and short white veil.

The bishop sat in a high-backed red velvet chair in the center of the aisle. We approached him and knelt on a cushion placed at his feet. Someone on his left held a book while the bishop placed his hand on my head and read, "Defend, O Lord, this Thy child with Thy heavenly grace; that she may continue Thine for ever, and daily increase in Thy Holy Spirit more and more, until she come into Thy everlasting kingdom. Amen."

As he read *increase in Thy Holy Spirit,* the bishop, as was his custom, gave each confirmand a little slap on the cheek as a tangible reminder that he or she was, indeed, receiving the Holy Spirit. I was ready. I wanted to be different. I wanted God.

But I felt nothing—nothing more than a slight sting on my cheek. I wanted to cry.

It was February 21, 1965.

My Baptism of the Holy Spirit

Seven years later, on February 27, 1972, Conlee and I each had a living encounter with the same Holy Spirit we thought had eluded us. I am not saying nothing happened at my baptism and confirmation. I am saying that until I was totally surrendered to Jesus Christ, I never experienced the reality of what I had vowed. When I surrendered, I began to learn who God had created me to be and how I could be that person.

I firmly believe, in fact, that even without my conceptual understanding and with no tangible evidence, something very real did happen to me when I was baptized and confirmed. In some way these unemotional acts of my will set me apart for God, giving Him permission to get involved in the course of my life.

Although I believe strongly that one baptism is sufficient for the symbolism of my death with Jesus, I wanted more than anything to experience immersion, or going under the water, as my Lord did in the Jordan River. In 1973, after much prayer, I felt His permission to be baptized in that manner. For the first time I had the "sense" of dying with my Lord, and out of my immersion came the beginnings of the true mission for my life.

This act of being baptized a second time may not line up with the doctrines espoused in some denominations (including my own), but to this day I believe it is one to which God called me, one that demonstrated my sincere longing to nail my unredeemed desires to the cross where they belong.

The Mission

If you have your Bible handy, please read aloud, one right after the other, the following four passages about Jesus' baptism and His temptations: Matthew 3:13–4:11; Mark 1:9–13; Luke 3:21–22; and Luke 4:1–13.

Notice that immediately after Jesus' baptism the Holy Spirit led Him into the desert where He would be tested by the devil. Why at that particular time? What happened at His baptism that made Him appear to be "ripe" for the devil's temptings?

We know that from His baptism on Jesus had the power to do miracles as His Father directed. And it was clear that Jesus had a mission—a clear-cut goal given by God: He was to redeem the world from sin and He would do it by changing human hearts, one at a time.

Dying to Self

Perhaps as Jesus submitted to the great symbol of His own mortal death in baptism, as He lay "in death" below the baptismal waters, God imparted the full knowledge of His mission. Whatever personal desires for family, education or career He may have had were apparently put to death in the Jordan River that day as He demonstrated His willingness to do only the will of the Father. We know He pleased the Father because as soon as He came up to breathe again He received the touch of the Holy Spirit and heard God's words from heaven: "This is my Son, whom I love; with him I am well pleased" (Matthew 3:17).

Enlightened and empowered by this act of God following His own obedience, Jesus had to get away from the crowds to absorb the profound commission He had received. His Guide, the Holy Spirit, knew just what He needed and led Him into a desert place where no one would bother Him—no one except the devil.

Why was Jesus ripe for the devil's temptations at this particular point in His life? Being willing to die to certain important issues in our lives enables us to receive the life of the Spirit and the power to do what He calls us to do. It seems to be a fact, however, that we receive our most powerful temptations from Satan after triumphs and spiritual "highs" with our Lord. And until we undergo those temptations and conquer them, we will not be fully effective in our divine calling. The temptations are real. We can expect them. But they seldom come in easily recognizable forms, and we are often taken unawares.

Satan, of course, wanted to thwart the vital mission for which Jesus had volunteered, but whoever would have thought he would do it by appearing to make the mission easier for Jesus?

Many Christians have speculated that Satan offered Jesus personal fame and power to follow him. Knowing the character of Jesus as he must have known it, it seems unlikely even Satan would expect Jesus to succumb to that carrot.

No, Satan knew Jesus was totally committed to His divine mission—that of bringing redemption from sin to the world by changing one heart at a time. How could he best thwart this? *By short-circuiting, by eliminating, the only means by which God said it would be accomplished—the pain of the cross.*

Satan tried to convince Jesus that what God wanted could be accomplished without pain. Instead, Satan offered a spectacular, pain-free instant fix to accomplish Jesus' mission, one that would not require Jesus to go through the agonizing death of crucifixion. What if there were a way to comfort and satiate everyone with no pain involved? Jesus would get fame; people would follow Him. He would accomplish His goals, and would have untold resources to establish His Kingdom. And Satan would provide it all in a much more "humane" way than God proposed.

We can almost hear the voice of Satan echoing from the Garden of Eden: "Did God really say that? Surely that's not what He meant." Satan lifted himself up as a more appealing being to worship, much more humanitarian.

But Jesus had heard God's voice clearly. God had said that His death in our place would purify, would purge out sin as nothing else could. It was vital for Jesus to go through the pain, to die the death, in order to accomplish the mission. No matter how much the humanity of Jesus dreaded the physical torture and death of the cross, the obedient divinity of Jesus was committed to carrying out God's plan to the letter. *There would be no compromise.*

Remember: Jesus used God's Word to combat Satan, and it proved a sturdy, effective shield to deflect the darts of Satan's "what ifs." Jesus was victorious.

No Compromise

What pain are you experiencing right now that tempts you to compromise? What spectacular bursts of power have you longed for in order to avoid the healing pain of the cross?

Perhaps you, too, have been baptized into Jesus' death and resurrection. You have confirmed those vows time and again both publicly and in private. You have been open to the work of the Holy Spirit in your life. And you are beginning to sense the mission to which God is calling you, even if at this point it is simply to walk into the wholeness He has for you.

Remember, setting your will to walk with, listen to and obey God makes you a prime target for the enemy's insidious suggestions. But we, like Jesus, cannot complete the mission of finding our true selves by overriding God's plan through tempting short-cuts. The cross is the only place for the sin, victimization, neglect, deprivation and hurt of our past to go.

Unlike Jesus, however, we do not have to enter into the pain of the cross by ourselves. He is waiting there for us, with hands outstretched to receive all the baggage that hinders our journey to wholeness, that keeps us from having our hearts changed to beat in harmony with His.

Finding Your God-Given True Self

I want to know Christ and the power of his resurrection and the fellowship of sharing in his sufferings, becoming like him in his death, and so, somehow, to attain to the resurrection from the dead.
Philippians 3:10–11

1. If you have never been baptized, ask Jesus to show you how, where and under whose instruction you might receive this sacrament and participate in this act of obedience to Him, symbolizing your willingness to die along with Him.

118

If you have been baptized, consider asking someone to pray with you to reaffirm your baptismal vows.

2. As you submit to the death of Jesus through baptism or reaffirmation of your baptism, ask Him to show you the true resurrection identity toward which He wants you to walk. That state of *being,* aside from *doing,* is your true mission.

3. You will need a baptism of His Holy Spirit to accomplish your mission and to resist temptations that would lead you aside. Purpose to pray daily for more and more of His Holy Spirit.

4. In what ways have you attempted, or been tempted, to short-circuit your healing? How have you focused on quick fixes or instant deliverances? Write them out as a confession to Jesus. See how you have left Him on the cross alone, waiting for you to join Him so you might triumph with Him.

5. There is a place for your pain to go! No longer does it have to be recycled over and over in your memories, your relationships and your actions. As you sit alone in your desert with Jesus, willingly give to Him the sin and pain of your life, past and present, that it may be nailed with Him on the cross, the only acceptable receptacle God has provided.

Day 15

The Mission of the Heart

WHAT DO YOU WANT TO BE WHEN YOU GROW UP? WHOM DO YOU WANT to be?

These are not rhetorical questions. Whether you are twenty or eighty, you probably do not feel truly grown up yet, even though you are legally an adult, and maybe even a great-grandparent! If you are like me, you hope someday to completely become the person you are meant to be, to find your God-given true self.

When I was a child I wanted to be a ballerina . . . or maybe a nurse, or a teacher . . . or a mommie. Later I wanted to be an obstetrician, and still later, a rock star. (What does this say about my development?)

I became a teacher and a mommie, but even then realized I was not necessarily grown up. Lots of places inside of me did not mature automatically. I could disseminate information I had learned, and I could reproduce biologically, but how in the world could I love unselfishly, not questioning my own motives or seeking constant reciprocal affirmation?

I made many mistakes as a young mother, needing affirmation for myself so desperately that I was often unable to love my babies with abandon. I was afraid of spoiling them, or letting them see my weakness or even more foolishly, of letting them see my unabashed love for them. This sounds crazy to me now, world-class, spontaneous hugger that I am, but I remember well the compulsive ways in which I used to analyze my every word and action.

Today I look with awe at my precious sons and daughters-in-law. I watch in astonishment the fine parenting skills evidenced by Matt and Margo, the father and mother of my two grand-daughters, Alex and Macy. I am amazed to see their maturity and the unselfconscious ways in which they love, affirm, encourage and exhort each other and their children.

While Conlee and I were in their home for a few days not long ago, I observed with amazement a natural—yet holy—thing that Matt and Margo did with their babies. Matt, under pressure with a new position in an engineering firm, had had a long, stressful day. Margo had cleaned, cooked, laundered, taken care of the children and dealt with numerous unexpected mini-crises. By late afternoon Margo understandably was relieved when we took the family out to a favorite Mexican restaurant. She had an appointment after our early dinner with a prospective client in her part-time business. She had worked hard on the presentation and was "up" for the interview, hoping to make a sizable sale.

But when we returned home from dinner a message on the answering machine announced that the client had canceled. The sale was thwarted. I could sense Margo's disappointment. The adrenaline that had kept her going evaporated. Her fatigue intensified. Alex began crying. Nothing was going as planned.

I knew that as a young mother in this situation I would have exploded in tears, anger, frustration, or all three. Instead, these godly parents picked up their crying baby, showered her with kisses and reaffirmed their love for her and for each other in words and actions. As quickly as it came, tension was dispelled and love, laughter and peace took charge. Jesus was there! Matt and Margo had allowed Him to sit in the place of honor in their home and in His presence they found it easy to be the lovers of each other and of their little ones that God had called them to be.

I cannot begin to tell you how grateful I am to see all my children in godly relationships. They are still seeking career goals and the fulfillment of their desires, but are content in knowing who they really are and what priorities are important. It took their mother a long time to learn the same lessons.

For most of my life, until I came into a serious relationship with the Lord in my thirties, I was adept at analyzing and adapting myself to the dictates of any situation. I was witty, urbane and flirtatious at cocktail parties; pious, respectful and caring at church; gossipy, irreverent and a shopping fiend with friends; submissive, child-like and charming with my parents; and a temperamental, overachieving martyr at home. I constantly stepped outside myself and watched how I interacted with other people, judging what they expected, noticing their reactions to me, trying to adjust my behavior to be more acceptable to them.

Not only did I not know who I was, I had no idea who I was supposed to be. Everyone seemed to expect something different from me. I wished I had a single source to model. Sometimes I felt pulled in so many directions it seemed I would snap.

I often asked Conlee to tell me who I was, and who he wanted me to be. Because I loved him I wanted to please him. But Conlee, too, was struggling to find himself; he could not empower me to be the ideal wife and I had no power to do it on my own. It was a frustrating time in our marriage, and ultimately I blamed my husband for wanting me to be someone I was unable to be and yet not helping me become that someone.

Today, years later, life is still trying to weigh me down with expectations. Take the "pastor's wife" image, for example. I certainly do not fit that stereotype, whatever it is. And being involved in healing ministry gives many people the impression that I am available for every need and never have problems of my own. Pardon me while I laugh—and then cry!

But while the expectations are still present, today the pressure is gone. After struggling through much painful healing with my Lord, I am me. I have learned to set healthy boundaries in my relationships. At long last I feel the freedom to say "no." I can be honest. I have begun to learn who God wants me to be, the "me" I know is a perfect fit. Even though I am not successful all the time, God's design for me is a definite focal point that helps cut off peripheral temptations and voices. Since I have started to get familiar with the real "me" I have had incredible peace in my life.

The Painful Process

When I began to let Jesus clearly show me who I *am* (a sobering reality) and who I *can be* (an awesome possibility), the temptations began in earnest to short-circuit the route from reality to possibility. The route to my full potential, my true self, involved getting in touch with real pain, and I do not like pain. Surely God was not going to make me experience anything uncomfortable.

I wanted a miracle of deliverance, not a trail of tears. Sometimes finding my true self hurt so badly I wanted to settle for compromise. I learned, however, that for individuals, prayer groups or churches to go back or even to stop mid-stream in the growth process is not simply to settle for less, it is to die.

I can only compare the process of growing up to my true self to childbirth. After I became pregnant there was no going back to being "un-pregnant" unless a part of me died. During the delivery of a child comes a time called "transition" in which the mother's body moves from the completed phase of dilation to another phase—expulsion. Those of us who have gone through the process unmedicated remember well the feeling of panic when we either said or thought, "Let's just stop this; I don't want to have a baby today. Let's call it off and do something else!"

But our bodies had taken the momentum: For life to come forth we had to surrender to the satisfying, if painful and difficult, work of pushing a new life out into the world. Our only option was to put to death the child within, struggling to be born.

You may feel like you have been "pregnant" forever. A vision of who God wants you to be is a part of you; it seems rooted inside, yet you cannot quite reach it. What inhibits the "delivery"?

Jesus' Identity

To answer that question we need to look at our role model, Jesus. What expectations were placed on His life?

1. *The expectations for a son.* Jesus was a Son. Certainly He was a unique Son, conceived in a miraculous way, known from conception by His parents to be the Messiah, God's Anointed One. How do you think Mary and Joseph attempted to form their boy's personality and leadership qualities according to their perceptions of "messiahship"? Mary and Joseph certainly remembered vividly the royal kings who had presented gifts to Jesus as a child. Surely their son was destined to be as powerful on earth as those who had bowed before Him. How might they have tried to overprotect Him or inadvertently misdirect Him, possibly preventing Him from walking in His true identity according to God's timing?

Being good Jews, Jesus' parents no doubt wanted Him to marry the right woman and give them many grandchildren. Recognizing His great mind, they also must have wanted Him to study with the best teachers available, to achieve many degrees and be a distinguished member of the Sanhedrin. We know that even at twelve years old He had mature interests, wanting above all to be in His Father's house (Luke 2:42–52).

Yes, the human expectations for sonship must have been strong in Jesus' life. But He looked through them and listened to the voice of His Father to find His true self.

2. *The expectations for a healer.* After Jesus' empowerment for ministry at His baptism, after He had affirmed to God and to Satan in the desert that nothing—not even pain—would deter Him from being the Person He was called to be, He began to disciple His friends, preach to large crowds and heal the sick. His reputation as a healer spread quickly, and both people with acute illnesses and those who had suffered for a long time flocked to Him.

Jesus' "patients" resented the time He spent alone or with His closest friends. They wanted to monopolize His every waking moment with their great needs and clamored for His attention. Many wanted only an instant healing, not a heart-relationship with Him.

Jesus knew the multitudes had more needs in one day than He could heal in a lifetime. He had to look through people's expectations for Him as a healer and listen carefully to one voice only: the voice of His heavenly Father.

3. *The expectations for a teacher and leader.* Jesus was both a teacher and a leader to the multitudes. He spoke more often to the hearts of ordinary people than to the logical minds of the trained professionals, although leaders in the synagogues continually tried to pull Jesus aside from His mission to debate minute points of theology. They liked to pit their brilliant minds against His. They recognized the captivating ways in which He could win any argument by a twist or subtle nuance of a train of thought.

Many Jews thought Jesus would turn out to be a great revolutionary, a zealot. His ability to sway a crowd was uncanny.

His enemies saw that His charismatic personality could easily lead the people to overthrow the oppressive Roman government.

Even some who called themselves Jesus' friends tried to lead Him away from His God-given mission into the political arena, where they were convinced He could influence many more people through displays of force and manipulation. The very temptations of power and influence that Satan had placed before Him in the desert after His baptism were in evidence every day of His ministry.

Jesus had to look through what people expected of Him as a teacher and leader, and listen constantly to the voice of the Father to give Him direction.

4. *The expectations for a friend.* Jesus did have several close friends, and when He began to explain to them in more detail how the mission of His heart (to bring redemption to all people) would be accomplished (through His death on the cross), they were horrified. They could not believe He must die young. In their eyes His mission was not accomplished yet; there must be another way.

One of Jesus' friends, Peter, took Him aside to try to talk Him out of His "foolish" mission. When Jesus heard Peter He instantly remembered hearing the same arguments from the mouth of Satan during the forty days he spent in the desert. Just as in the wilderness Jesus did not entertain the thought of deterring from His mission for even a moment, so it was now. He spoke directly to the author of Peter's thoughts: "Get behind me, Satan! You are a stumbling block to me; you do not have in mind the things of God, but the things of men" (Matthew 16:23).

Jesus had to look through the expectations of His friends and believe implicitly in the Word of God.

5. *The expectations for race and nationality.* Being a Jew in Jesus' day meant being hated and despised by the Romans, the ruling political authorities. The Roman leaders treated the Jews much like slaves, burdening them with oppressive taxation and regulations. Those Jews who worked for the Romans (tax collectors, for example) were despised by their fellow countrymen. As a gifted leader, Jesus was expected

to hate the Romans and either participate in or lead a revolution to overcome their tyranny. Instead, He forgave them and gave His life for them.

Although they were despised and persecuted themselves, the Jews of Jesus' day were also bigoted and prejudiced against other cultures. They considered the neighboring Samaritans no better than dogs. They did not believe that God's salvation should extend to anyone outside their race. They hesitated even to travel through the neighborhoods of certain nearby residents lest they be contaminated.

Instead of adopting the prejudices of His race and culture, Jesus chose to listen to the voice of His heavenly Father and believe that every person, Jew or Gentile, was created in the image of God, destined to become more than they—or anyone else—thought they could be.

6. *Human expectations for a painless existence.* Jesus certainly did not want to go through the horrible death of crucifixion. No doubt He had seen crucifixions, or heard about their agonies.

But nowhere do we get the impression that Jesus was afraid to die. He knew, rather, that as He died on the cross He would be taking all the sins of the world, past, present and future, upon Himself. What a destiny for a Man who in His divine image had never experienced sin. What an end for a Man who in His human identity desired a comfortable, painless, long and productive life.

But Jesus looked through the expectations of His humanity and trusted the Father to bring resurrection life and power into His pain and dying.

Your Identity

Could the obstacles preventing the birth of the mission of your heart—to find your true identity in God—be as old as the obstacles with which Satan and others attempted to deter Jesus?

- Have parental and family expectations helped or hindered your search for your true identity?
- Have you spent more time searching for miracles and quick fixes than you have spent working on an intimate relationship with Jesus?

- Have you allowed logical argument and severe introspection to deter you from a godly course?
- Has the influence of well-meaning friends kept you from seeking God's will for your mission?
- Have the customs or traditions of your race or nationality been more important to your spiritual development than the Word of God?
- Has the fear of pain paralyzed you from facing the hurts of your past, present and future and taking them to the cross?

The mission of your heart is the same as Jesus' mission was and still is. Just as He needed to listen to and obey the Father in order to be the Person God asked Him to be, so you need to listen and obey God in order to find your true identity in Him.

Remember: The mission is not to *do* for Him, it is to be formed in His image, and to allow His character to be formed in you. Out of that "being" great deeds may be accomplished, but whatever mission to others God has for you will never be effective unless first you are at peace inside, at home with the real you God intended you to be in Him.

Finding Your God-Given True Self

Therefore, since we have been justified through faith, we have peace with God through our Lord Jesus Christ, through whom we have gained access by faith into this grace in which we now stand. And we rejoice in the hope of the glory of God. Not only so, but we also rejoice in our sufferings, because we know that suffering produces perseverance; perseverance, character; and character, hope. And hope does not disappoint us, because God has poured out his love into our hearts by the Holy Spirit, whom he has given us.

Romans 5:1–5

1. Spend time in conversation with Jesus via your prayer journal, seeking His undistorted answers to each of the above questions about your personal identity.
2. Continue to pray daily for a greater infilling of His Holy Spirit.

Day 16

I Will Change Your Name

I SAW A PICTURE IN TODAY'S PAPER OF A 64-YEAR-OLD WOMAN POSING seductively in a slinky, glittering gown against a backdrop of satins and furs. She looked rather artificial with long, fake eyelashes and a bouffant wig, but she did look youthful for 64.

The newspaper article told in detail of multiple face lifts, tummy tucks, skin peels and weekly injections she received to restore her youthful appearance. What got my attention, however, was the reference to her history of depression, suicidal tendencies and drug abuse. She may have looked young and glamorous, but she was an extremely unhappy woman.

You and I might not have the money for cosmetic surgery, but we get different hairstyles, new clothes, better jobs or a membership at a weight-reduction center to improve our self-images. Still, inside is where I must feel right about myself, no matter what I do to fix up the exterior.

Spending lots of time and energy on physical fitness and improving our minds is good for self-preservation and self-esteem, but ultimately we must realize that no matter how healthy, how tanned, how fit our bodies, how many honors we receive, how intelligent we may be or what we own, if we fail to understand our identity in Jesus we will have no peace within.

An Identity Crisis

Jesus, with His heart-changing mission, has a unique way of coming right into the midst of a person's carefully planned personal campaign for self-improvement and turning everything upside-down. Conlee and I found that out first hand.

From the time we met in college until we were in our tenth year of marriage, Conlee and I consistently set goals for self-improvement and personal success. Conlee had always wanted to own his own business, and we experienced several lean years as we sacrificed to make that dream a reality. Accomplishing that goal offered an incredible boost to his self-worth, his status in the community and his ability as a businessman. Like many men he felt the need to prove to himself that he could compete successfully in those arenas.

I had always wanted to have a lovely home to decorate and entertain in. I wanted it to reflect my creative talents, provide enjoyment for our family and hospitality to our friends.

Successful self-employment and owning a beautiful home are not bad goals. To many they represent the American dream. The danger, however, is that the dream can become our *identity*. There was a time when the thought of losing my home implied losing everything I was. My "things" gave me my identity. In my mind people could categorize me by seeing what surrounded me, and somehow I felt that certain accouterments gave me an advantage I lacked within. But when things or accomplishments are our standards for self-acceptance and self-worth, abundance is never enough.

In a loving and dramatic way, Jesus stepped through the careful boundaries of accomplishment and accumulation I had erected in my life to protect who I thought I was. Looking back I know now that He could see I was on a collision course. It was only a matter of time before my "want-tos" would exceed our family income. In the midst of my apparent prosperity Jesus took a look at my empty heart and made a Scripture from Revelation 3:17 come alive to me:

> You say "I am rich; I have acquired wealth and do not need a thing." But you do not realize that you are wretched, pitiful, poor, blind and naked.

God's Word exposed my worst fear. Without "things" that money could buy surrounding me I felt I was nothing, that I had no identity at all. But Jesus offered me His identity. At the time I could not have articulated it, but that is exactly what He did. He offered me godly identity that was as real as putting on a coat. It was a perfect fit. It covered all the places that had been naked and pitiful. It gave me a firm, godly center on which every desire, choice and decision could be grounded.

No one coerced me to accept God. No one argued endlessly about the merits of materialism versus the merits of godliness. I was never encouraged to sign a pledge or make a vow. No outward requirements were presented and I was not asked to give up anything. I do not know for sure, but if these things had been required I suspect a natural rebellion would have taken over and prevented me from seeing the truth.

Instead, in the midst of a simple prayer one night in my den, a prayer for a guest who was hurting, God revealed His presence to me. One minute I was a reluctant observer. Suddenly I was so caught up in the supernatural reality of a living God that I was willing to change forever, to be whatever He wanted me to be. The working out of the process begun that night will take a lifetime, but much healthy change has already occurred.

The Identity Exchange

A pastor from Arkansas named H. D. McCarty wrote a newspaper article years ago that I have never forgotten. He told about a dog who constantly carried around an old dry bone. He would bury it, dig it up, gnaw on it and protect it with bared teeth and growls. There was no way that dog would give up that old dry bone—unless someone offered him a piece of juicy steak. Then he would drop his familiar possession in an instant to devour something of substance.

Same story, different actors: In Warren Bennis' book *On Becoming Leaders* (Addison-Wesley, 1989), John Scully, former CEO at Apple Computer, comments on the success of constructing and offering to the public the best prototype of a computer his company could produce:

> Often people don't know what they want and can't describe it until they see it. If we've done market research on the Macintosh prior to production and asked people to describe what they want in a personal computer they come up with something entirely different, but when we show people the Macintosh and say, "Is this what you want?" they say, "Yep."

We always think we know what we want, what is best for us. But until the best is placed before us we will seldom lay aside the inferior choices we have already made.

I was shown and offered the very best—the heart of God. I had never thought, dreamed or imagined it could be so wonderful to know Him. I experienced a wave of peace that satisfied a hunger I had had all my life, the excitement of adventure with Him combined with a calm restfulness in the midst of all my activity. Quite literally He filled me up, filled long-empty spaces so full there were times I thought I would burst. Without a moment's hesitation I laid down the old dry bone to which I had been so attached and embraced the full-course meal. Upon first sight of the "perfect prototype" I knew this was what I had always wanted, and I embraced it gladly. I was changed, saved, converted, born again, redeemed, sanctified, baptized in the Holy Spirit and renewed. All that—and more, much more.

The Gift of God's Identity

The gift of God's identity is impossible to understand until we accept it. Jesus accepted it fully at His baptism; He affirmed it in the desert. There He saw how cleverly the devil could attempt to steal it away from Him, and He determined to offer Himself as God's prototype of who each of us can be as we, too, allow God's identity to be fused into our own.

No longer do I have to dwell on my past, my hurts, my deprivations—or even my healings. They are no longer my identity; they no longer have the power to shape me. Even the "spiritual" distinction of being "one who is healed" is not my primary identity: I must put that aside and press forward to enter more and more into Jesus' identity. As Saint Paul said, "Not that I have already obtained all this, or have already been made perfect, but I press on to take hold of that for which Christ Jesus took hold of me" (Philippians 3:12).

No one needs to be labeled "homosexual," "alcoholic," "overachiever," "failure," "abused" or "promiscuous." When we accept the gift of God's identity we become simply "children of God" with all the benefits accompanying that honor. Being a child of God overcomes all that has happened in our lives. "Jeff-the-former-homosexual-whom-God-has-healed" discards his crippled past to put on his absolutely accurate new identity, "Jeff, child of God." "Sue-the-overachiever" stops her anguished striving to relax in a new security as "Sue, child of God."

As "Jeff" and "Sue" and all the rest of us begin to realize all our new names and identities include, we begin rightfully to take on God's family characteristics of joyfulness, freedom, confidence and peace. The spiritual welding we experience with our Father is far stronger than the genetic linkage to our earthly parents. It quite literally changes our names—and our inmost beings—so we become what He has wanted us to be forever.

Every time we sing the song "I Will Change Your Name" at one of our seminars, at least one person, and often several, has a fantastic revelation about the enormous change God wants to make in his life. He literally sees labels worn all his life, labels like "wounded," "stupid" or "clumsy," labels that have shaped his whole being, fall away like worn-out clothes. Through tears he has the joy of hearing his heavenly Father call him by a new name that will now shape him and give him his true identity in Jesus.

Watching each new birth is a thrill!

Finding Your God-Given True Self

Every good and perfect gift is from above, coming down from the Father of the heavenly lights, who does not change like shifting shadows.

James 1:17

1. What labels have others put on you? You may have to go back to childhood to remember nicknames or taunts. What labels have you put on yourself? Write them out in your prayer journal.
2. You will need to exercise your will to forgive the people who gave you these labels if you sincerely want to be rid of them. Unforgiveness will bind you to sin in your life, even if you are the victim.
3. Allow your heavenly Father to sing you a love song, naming you as His child. Receive from Him a picture of the person He has always seen you to be.

Day 17

The Christian's New Clothes

Y ESTERDAY I MENTIONED SOMEONE WHO RECEIVED HIS NEW IDENTITY FROM God. It was as if his old, wounded identity fell off him like worn-out clothes. During a time of great concern about our youngest son's involvement with drugs and alcohol in high school, I was surprised when God spoke clearly to me three times in the period of one week using the same metaphor—that of clothing. Each time the truth was presented to me differently, but because I wrote it all down in my prayer journal, I could look back and make the connection between all three entries.

God was obviously imparting a basic principle—one it was time for me to learn. And He was making it real in many ways, ways that would touch my heart, mind and emotions.

Take Off Your Clothes

The first day I heard God's message on this subject I was with a group of women praying before a Bible study. We were praying for a woman in the group who had been in a car accident and was continuing to have severe back pain.

As I prayed for her healing I listened for God's voice. Can you imagine how amazed I was to see (with the eyes of my heart) Jesus standing in our midst, asking each of us to discard all our clothes and be vulnerable before Him? It was such a strong impression that I looked up, startled, at the other women. But they were all still in an attitude of prayer for our friend.

I felt Jesus' voice inside me again saying, "Take off your clothes." His voice seemed so loud I was sure they all heard it, but the message was for my ears only. I knew it was a symbolic message, not literal. Inside, though, part of me was amused to imagine how the women would react if I told them what Jesus was asking us to do.

Jesus was using a powerful symbol, for there was no way any group of women I had ever known would take their clothes off in front of one another, leaving them naked and vulnerable. I gained a deep sense of how much we all wear camouflage clothing, needing our adornments to define us to the world.

What could I remove literally, I wondered. *A skirt, belt, blouse, jewelry, undergarments, shoes?* But that was not His intent. Jesus then began to show me garments I wore every day without realizing it. I had become so used to them I never thought about putting them on or taking them off. They had become permanently attached to me.

Jesus did not name them for me—not yet—but something left me. Now I felt naked in a way I had never experienced before. I felt exposed to the elements, in danger of death.

Then Jesus began to hand me new clothes. In fact, I saw Him give all of us new garments; a blouse to one, a robe to another, a dress to another, until we were all clothed appropriately. Each garment was a perfect fit, especially made for each of us by a master tailor.

Finally I saw labels inside each garment, labels that read "Truth," another that read "His Way" and another "Compassion." The garments were His presence! We were wearing Christ!

I shared some of this revelation with the women before we went in to our Bible study, but I did not adequately convey the power of the image because there were several blank looks and giggles. Apparently this was to be like one of the gems Mary received when Jesus was a baby, gems she had the wisdom to keep in her heart and allow God to make real on His timetable. So I wrote the experience in my prayer journal and asked God to imprint upon me the truth He wanted to teach me.

Untie the Cords

That night I had a dream, so vivid I knew it was another message. Although in this dream some real people in my life were present, I knew they were not to be taken literally. The dream was highly symbolic. Each person was used by God to represent a truth about myself in a way I could recognize. It is important not to assign value or fact to another person because of a dream. Ask God to show you what that person symbolizes to you. A dream speaks to your heart in its own language, that of symbol.

Here is what I wrote about the dream, with names disguised:

> I am in a hallway and a very young, very feminine Anne (a cousin who has been deceased for many years) comes to me. She hands me clothes, her own lovely clothes that she wants me to have.
>
> I go into a room where Myra, another relative, is frantic, wanting to know where I have been. She is worried because she was expecting me hours ago even though I had not told her when I was coming. She is on the phone with Robert, a friend who, being practical, has sent out the sheriff and search parties to look for me.

I awoke frustrated and confused and angry. After writing the dream in my journal I sat down with God, asking Him to interpret the confusing mixture of emotions with which it left me. He showed me three strands of a cord that had become so imbedded within me that I was unaware they were present. Closely entwined, they were strangling me slowly until one day the true person I was supposed to be would be unable to breathe.

The three strands were represented in the dream by:

1. Myra—accusing, seeing every possible thing that could go wrong and jumping to conclusions;
2. Robert—taking inappropriate actions, constantly digging, leaving no stone unturned, overly practical, analytical and efficient;
3. Anne—the true feminine, offering me the clothing of my God-given true self to put on so I could respond to God by living creatively, nurturingly, intuitively and obediently.

In my spirit I handed the strands of cord to Jesus and watched Him untwist them, separate them one from another and, taking the one named "Anne," tie it around me as a ribbon.

135

Look in the Mirror

The next day I asked Jesus for enlightenment concerning the truths He had shown me. I sensed it was time to name all the "clothing" I had long been wearing that was restricting me. I sat down with my journal to let Jesus help me give form to what had been elusive. He told me to begin with things related to my children and my perceptions of motherhood.

Here are those reflections, just as I wrote them:

Jesus, I ask You to show me those things I have been wearing that have restricted me from being the woman You created me to be, especially where my child is concerned. I pray You would help me name each one. I choose to take off and cast aside the following garments I have been wearing unconsciously:

Fear
Pride of motherhood
Loss of control
Anxiety
Sense of failure
Sense of futility
Gloom-and-doom attitude (painting the worst scenario)
Comparing my child to others
Pride of Christianity
Grasping for solutions
Looking for the quick fix
Making my own agenda
Establishing unreal expectations
Involving all resources unselectively
Letting others decide my course of action
Getting too many people involved in personal problems
Relying on statistics
Forging ahead without prayer
Tearing down my child's boundaries by prying
Blaming his friends

I never knew I had clothed myself in such ugly, inappropriate garments. As I wrote them out, I sensed layer upon layer of restrictive coverings that prevented my being all I could be. Many I had put on for a specific occasion and never taken off. When I finished writing I saw them for what they were: multi-layered filthy rags covering my true self as Jesus created me.

"Lord," I wrote, "I am handing You all this clothing You have shown me that I have been able to name. I stand before You naked, empty, vulnerable, at the bottom of my storehouse. Unless You clothe me, I will stay here naked."

I was impressed to go back to my list and check two items: pride of motherhood and pride of Christianity.

Here, God showed me, were two items of "designer clothing" I had been wearing to win approval from others. I showed off with them, and took pleasure in flaunting them. These two were the most disgusting to Him and until they were discarded the others could not be removed easily.

In response I said to Him, "I take off the pride of motherhood and the pride of Christianity. I give them to You."

"Now you are truly naked," Jesus told me. "Go and look in the mirror."

Still with the eyes of my heart, I saw myself walking, with great reluctance, to a full-length mirror. I stood in front of it, my eyes downcast. I did not want to see what I knew was there.

"Look at yourself through your own eyes," He said.

Slowly I looked up. Just as I feared: the vulnerable, naked body of a middle-aged woman who had borne three children. I saw stretch marks, a flabby stomach and sagging breasts, the telltale signs of motherhood, the parts of us we always camouflage.

"Look at Me," Jesus said.

I looked up at Him. He looked lovingly at me, deep into my eyes, and said, "I think you are beautiful."

I dissolved. Never before had I allowed anyone, not even Jesus, to see me so exposed. I looked back at the mirror and then saw what He had seen—a beautiful woman, wanting to love and be loved. He was not looking at a physical body, but at hurts of the past, scars, wounds and bruises. Some were self-inflicted, but most were not.

With love and compassion He said again, "I think you are beautiful."

A Mother's Wardrobe

I wrote the words He then gave me in my journal:

> For you to be a godly mother, I must first clothe you in *truth*— the truth of "the way it is" and "the way it will be." You can only receive this from Me.

Next I clothe you in *heart vision.* Man looks on the outward appearance but with Me you will look on the heart.

I give you an *alligator hide.* This protective covering will keep you from internalizing stinging words, rejections and rebuffs.

I give you *God-sense.* No longer will your center be your emotions or head knowledge. It will be My presence.

I give you *longanimity.* [I had to look this word up. *Webster's* defines it as "patient endurance of injuries; forbearance."] Your effectiveness will not be measured in days, months or years, but in increments of spiritual growth. Do you remember wanting your son to take his first steps? Do you remember working with him, seeing him almost succeed, and then fall? But you were certain he would walk one day and you waited. Nothing you could do would hurry the time. Your growth and your child's growth will be like this. It will happen in My time.

I crown your wardrobe with *love.* Even when your child is the most difficult, the most unreceptive to your love, the most cynical about needing it, it will be the one stabilizing stronghold in his life. Do not withhold it; lavish it. The more you give it away the more it will be increased in you.

As I attempted to put on each of these garments of motherhood, I felt at first as if I were wearing someone else's clothing. But I chose to keep them on, because they were gifts from God, made for me by the Master Craftsman. I chose to put on Christ!

Finding Your God-Given True Self

I put on righteousness as my clothing. . . .
                                        Job 29:14

1. Ask the Lord to show you what you are "wearing" that is inappropriate in His eyes, especially regarding any difficult relationship in your life. Write out each article of "clothing" as you and Jesus name it together.
2. Are you willing to give Jesus your "protective adornments" even if it means you will feel naked? If so, make the transaction with Him now in a verbal or written prayer.
3. Ask God to clothe you in garments appropriate for attending the wedding feast as His bride. Read Isaiah 52:1, seeing your own name in place of "Zion" and "Jerusalem."

Day 18

Victim or Victor?

THIS WEEK DURING A "JOURNEY TO WHOLENESS IN CHRIST" SEMINAR WE
heard a powerful testimony from one of God's children who
had been severely wounded emotionally and sexually by both
family and spiritual authorities in her childhood. The pain she
described made us weep and stirred up righteous anger at the
evil in the world today. Some of her pain was still evident as
she told her story, but wholeness shone forth, a wholeness
birthed as she chose to forgive those who had wounded her.
(The importance of forgiveness will be covered in more detail
in Region 6.)

As I listened I wondered, *How does this pattern get established?
What sets up a person for repeated abuse?*

Then I remembered another healing conference at which I had
heard another young woman, whom I will call Lisa, tell her story.
It was all too similar to this one, a painful account of frequently
repeated molestation and sexual harassment throughout her life
by various people in various situations, times and places. I remembered wondering then as well: *What causes this to happen to a person over and over?*

I am well enough acquainted with both of these women to
know there was no seduction involved on either of their parts
(an excuse many undiscerning people will latch onto in an
attempt to find answers). No, these women were certified repeat
victims. But why?

Giving Life to the Lie

I seldom have impressions as graphic as the one I had concerning Lisa. When the vision came she and I were seated next to each other on the front pew just after she gave her powerful and courageous testimony. She had moved many in the congregation to tears, and about five hundred people had just given her a standing ovation. Lisa had overcome incredible obstacles, had been victorious and was now involved in a worldwide healing ministry. Hers was a remarkable story of Jesus' healing love, available to all of us.

After she took a seat next to me I was suddenly and vividly aware of her presence, but not as she had appeared on the platform only moments before—attractive, neat, poised and invitational. I was not looking at her, but I sensed her to be emitting a disgusting odor, so filthy and repulsive that it literally made my stomach heave. I unconsciously moved away from her, feeling contaminated.

I closed my eyes and again I could see her, this time even more graphically. She was sitting on top of and covered with piles of steaming manure. Flies buzzed all over her body, so thickly that I could barely see her face. The stench was unbelievable. I was so nauseated by this time that I got up and left the church by a side door. I went to a ladies' room and washed my face and hands, trying to scrub away the images. *Oh Lord,* I prayed, *where did this come from? Is it demonic? What am I seeing?*

As soon as possible I told Conlee what I had experienced and asked him to pray with me. He felt strongly that I should share this vision with Lisa. I could not imagine telling her what I had seen. The vision's impact was still so vivid that I found it hard to be objective enough to share it with Conlee, let alone with Lisa.

I prayed, lifting up to God as best I could my reactions. Amazingly, I sensed in my spirit that Conlee was right: I should tell Lisa what I had seen and felt.

It is important that we do not wound our Christian brothers and sisters by impulsive words and actions that have not been submitted thoroughly to God. But God was clearly initiating this encounter with Lisa. He was going to minister to both of us.

It seemed best to invite another person on the healing team to meet with Lisa and me. I was impressed to select a man whom I knew to be a trusted, godly friend to both of us, one who knew Lisa far better than I did. The three of us gathered in a private corner of the team's meeting room and I reluctantly told Lisa of the horrible images I had seen and the revulsion I had felt. I wanted to be Lisa's friend and I was certain that after she heard my story she would reject me or, at the least, feel embarrassed and uncomfortable around me from that time forward.

To my astonishment she was neither surprised nor upset. In fact, she sensed God's love coming through the vision as I related it.

"This is exactly how I saw myself after I was first abused sexually," she explained. "I carried this image of myself around in my heart, giving it more and more permission to define me. I believed I was refuse, the worst kind imaginable. I was convinced that nothing but creatures who fed on refuse could be attracted to me, and after a while I was not even surprised when further abuse came into my life. I expected it. I thought I deserved it."

The Image of God

Lisa related that out of much pain had come much healing. She had learned to resymbolize "woman" in God's image, a holy image. She had begun to love herself in a biblical way (Matthew 22:37–39), to respect herself, to see her identity as God sees it and to put to death the false identity she had adopted.

Our male friend then prayed for Lisa to receive more of the gentle, trusting, receptive, nurturing characteristics that are more natural for me, and for me to receive more of the strength of purpose, the strong will to make godly choices and the ability to see objectively that are more natural for Lisa. All of these are godly characteristics of a woman made in God's image.

Lisa and I could not have more dissimilar physical appearances. We could not have come from more different families, cultures and geographies. Yet we are so much alike. We are both made in the image of God, and we are on the same journey. Both of us are seeking Christ's wholeness in areas of our lives that have been abused, neglected or wrongly defined by ourselves or others.

Although Lisa and I see each other infrequently, I keep her picture in my journal and pray often for her. When we are together we always experience a strong bond of love and kinship. We are becoming the women God has called us to be.

A Symbolic Vision

When God gives a powerful vision or dream like the one I have just described, it takes an act of our will to choose to look through the "picture" to find the symbols He intends us to see. Dreams or visions do not assign fact or value to people; they point toward truths, usually about ourselves. Even though I was emotionally affected by this vision, if I had assigned fact or value to it concerning Lisa I would never have gone near her again.

Dreams and visions most often come when we are seeking truth. Remember, I had been seeking answers to the question *What sets up a person to receive repeated abuse and injury?* God showed me in a graphic way.

Lisa had taken on the "clothing" or identity of a victim and eventually believed she deserved everything that had happened to her. Through forgiveness and healing prayer she had chosen to take off those false garments and to begin to walk in wholeness, clothed in the righteousness of Jesus. She could now tell her story and help others.

God used the vision to show me some areas where my true identity was hidden, too. How I needed that power to see with God's vision—not just with my own subjectivity, but with His divine objectivity! How I needed to overcome the fear of rejection ("I can't tell Lisa!") that kept me from responding in godly love! How I needed to lay aside cultural niceties clinging to my personality that kept me from speaking the truth in love and calling forth wholeness!

This experience brought heart-healing that has affected my ministry profoundly. I began to see that I, too, had accepted a false identity, one of passivity. It literally attracted confusion and indecisiveness to me like flies to a refuse pile. I had adopted what I had been taught "nice little girls" should be like. Nice little girls did not question authority. They did not argue. They were not controversial. They were never forceful. And if they could not say something nice they did not say anything at all!

To be a "nice little girl" I had assumed a false sense of the feminine and nearly suffocated the godly, womanly virtues of strength, truth and divine objectivity. It was no wonder I had been confused about who I was and who I was supposed to be. I had been getting too many mixed messages.

God Polishes the Tarnished Image

By the time I sat on that church pew beside Lisa and saw the vision, God had already done much healing in my life. I had grown considerably as a Christian and was walking much more in my God-given identity. But there is always more! The power of that vividly graphic message strengthened me further.

How important it is to ask for heart vision. We each need to see the image of our God-given true self and steer toward it. Your God-given true self is so lovingly entwined with God, and such a perfect fit, that it defines and surrounds you with the wholeness of Jesus Christ.

Finding Your God-Given True Self

"When a prophet of the LORD is among you, I reveal myself to him in visions, I speak to him in dreams."

Numbers 12:6

1. Have you preserved certain images of yourself from childhood? Write them in your prayer journal.
2. Did God or someone else plant these images in your heart?
3. Ask God for heart vision to see yourself as He sees you. Purpose to pray for the strength to choose to walk toward that image of wholeness, even if it seems impossible at this moment. Write your intentions in your prayer journal.

Day 19

Life out of Death

WHILE SERVING ON THE LEADERSHIP TEAM AT A LARGE, WEEKLONG PASTORAL Care Ministries seminar on the West Coast, I was approached early in the week by a woman I will call Margaret. She seemed quiet, reserved, and was perhaps thirty or forty years of age.

"Will you have some time to pray with me during this conference?" she asked.

"Yes, of course I will," I replied. "But let's wait until later on in the week. God will certainly do a lot of healing in you in the meetings, and it is much more important that *He* speak to you than that *I* speak to you. Check back with me in a few days."

She nodded and left. The needs were great at this particular conference and I spent many hours praying with other men and women who needed to hear a healing word from God.

Midweek Margaret approached me again, during a break. She was quiet but agitated.

"I have seen you praying with several people all week," she said through tight lips. "It's not fair, because I came to you first."

I reached out and took her hand. "Margaret, are you feeling that God wants to touch everyone here but you?"

"Of course," came her quick reply. Her response spoke volumes about how she saw herself in relationship to God.

"Let's talk about that," I said, and invited her to a secluded part of the large auditorium. "How long have you felt so rejected by God?"

"Always," she said grimly, still clenching her teeth.

144

I observed her closely. Her posture was rigid, her hands balled into fists. Her face, too, resembled a clenched fist, its tight muscles and pinched expression accentuating deep lines. Her wall of defenses firmly and protectively in place, she had come to complain and argue her case.

From Margaret's point of view, she had taken a back seat to everyone in her family all her life. They expected her to have no feelings. Everyone she cared about had rejected her. Her parents criticized her constantly. Prospective friends quickly lost interest. Her lifelong dream of a loving husband was unfulfilled. God was disappointed in her.

"Margaret," I asked, "how do you feel about yourself?"

"I should be dead," she replied evenly, her self-control an obvious effort. "I have no right to live."

Deadness was already apparent in her expressionless face and it seemed to me that a numbness much like *rigor mortis* was invading her soul.

By this time music was beginning to draw the conference participants back to their seats for the next session. Margaret reached out, gripped my hands with surprising strength and said, "Don't you leave me! I can't go back home like I came. If I don't get some help here I am going to die."

The meeting was beginning so I led her to a quiet place.

"Margaret," I told her, "there is a reason you feel so rejected, a reason you feel you deserve to be ignored, a reason you believe even God has turned His back on you. No prayer I can pray over you will make these feelings go away. Only God Himself, the One against whom you are defending yourself, can help you. But you are expecting Him to reject you, too, so you have closed yourself off from hearing His healing word to you. Is your worst fear that if you do listen He will refuse to speak to you?"

My question pierced her facade, and she collapsed into deep sobbing. The tough exterior barriers she had erected fell away and she literally began to gasp for breath, for life. She trembled all over, fearful of complete destruction without her hard, cynical protective coating. I let her cry for a while, watching her get in touch with her long-suppressed pain.

"Margaret, now that you are vulnerable toward God, let's listen to Him together, expecting Him to speak to your heart."

We held hands and I prayed a simple prayer, inviting Jesus to hold her in safety as she lifted her heart to her heavenly Father. "Father, speak Your healing word to Your child, Margaret, and show her what is in her heart."

After a brief time of silence Margaret began to cry. But her cries were no longer those of an angry woman. She sounded like a frightened, grieving infant. She clung to me and I simply let her cry, rocking her in my arms, knowing God was doing a healing work in her heart. When the crying and grieving ceased and she could speak, she shared God's tender revelation and ministry.

A Spiritual Diagnosis

God had brought to Margaret's conscious memory the fact that she was a surviving twin born several months after the miscarriage of her brother. Ever since her months in the womb she had carried the grief of this tremendous loss and, since she had not been in touch with it consciously, had never been able to release it to God. As He allowed the memory to surface vividly, she realized her pain and was finally able to give it to Him from the bottom of her heart.

The sense of loss for an intimate relationship with a twin she could not even remember had had a marked effect on Margaret's personality all her life. Discerning her parents' grief and their disappointment that the son they had wanted so desperately had died instead of the daughter, she had always felt unwanted and of little worth. She felt God had made a mistake in letting her live and her brother die.

As Margaret matured she developed little or no self-esteem, until she decided that she should never have been born. This conviction eventually led to thoughts of and plans for suicide. She assumed the identity of a nonperson, feeling that she deserved no love, no attention, no affirmation, no acceptance, from her parents, her friends or from God. Finally she could relate to others only through self-pity or anger, and these emotions became her identity.

In the brief time I held Margaret as she sobbed, God had shown her the root of her lifelong identity, but more importantly, the root of His deep, deep love. Before now she had been afraid to seek it. With a hungry heart she now asked God to forgive her for what she had mistakenly harbored against Him. Afterward she found it easy to forgive her parents and others whom she had always believed to be resentful of her very existence. Simply, without dramatics, we rebuked the spirit of death that had lingered about her, whispering in her ear, all her life. I held her and prayed that God would give her a deep-centered sense of being. She was set free in a most remarkable way.

Margaret's whole demeanor changed. Every line in her face softened. She was expressive, relaxed and quite lovely. She looked about 25 years old, and at peace with herself for the first time in her life.

At the end of the week, as Conlee and I headed for the airport, I saw Margaret waiting by the curb for her ride. She was twirling around in the breeze, childlike in her joy of life. I asked our driver to stop while I ran across the street to embrace this newly joyful creature. She said it was beyond her wildest dreams to experience life; she had thought it only an illusion before. Words failed, but her face, her body, her laughter and her embrace told the story. I will never forget that picture.

Not everyone will be instantly released from the false identity he or she has assumed as Margaret was, but it does happen frequently. Some deep healings take longer, but they always happen in God's time. Either way, what remarkable transformations occur as the prisoner allows God to unlock the door that has kept him or her bound! Almost always the key that opens the door is forgiveness. It may seem like the hardest thing a person could ever be asked to do, but it leads to a freedom he or she never thought possible.

God set Margaret free to be the woman He always intended her to be. She would struggle when she returned home to live into that freedom in the midst of family and friends who still related to her in the old ways. She would be tested and tried to see if indeed the change was real. She would have to establish a new kind of relationship with God—one of intimacy.

I never expected to see Margaret again, but I continued to pray for her. Almost two years later she came up to me during a conference in another country and said, "Remember me?" I almost did not recognize her; the transformation was complete and remarkable. Serenity, peace and life permeated her whole body and demeanor in a way that could only have come from God.

I have seen many other "Margarets" since then—men and women alike who have come into abundant life in beautiful ways. The freedom to be our true selves in Jesus is a great gift, one too many of His creatures abuse, neglect or throw away. It is a "pearl of great price." It is of such value that anything a person must relinquish to seek it and obtain it is worthwhile (see Matthew 13:45–46).

When you begin to wear your God-given true self with freedom and joy you will have traveled a tremendous distance on the journey to wholeness.

Finding Your God-Given True Self

If you accept my words and store up my commands within you, turning your ear to wisdom and applying your heart to understanding, and if you call out for insight and cry aloud for understanding, and if you look for it as for silver and search for it as for hidden treasure, then you will understand the fear of the LORD and find the knowledge of God.

Proverbs 2:1–5

1. In what ways can you identify with Margaret? Write them out in your prayer journal.
2. Have you felt a child of the opposite sex was wanted more than you? Have you felt that God made a mistake at your birth? Write Him a letter about the ways in which you feel disappointed by what He has or has not done in your life. Read it aloud to Him. He is big enough to handle your honesty.
3. Give yourself permission to allow your true feelings about yourself to surface. Can you give them to your heavenly Father? Choose to forgive all those who have wounded you so the sin of unforgiveness does not stand between you and God. Then you will see Him and yourself in a godly perspective. Just saying the words "I forgive" aloud will help. The *feelings* of forgiveness will follow eventually.

Day 20

Garden of the Heart

AS WE GET SERIOUS ABOUT FINDING THE GOD-DESIGNED TRUE SELF WITHIN us, the great temptation is to begin severe introspection and self-analysis. This is one of the most seductive and dangerous traps into which a Christian can fall. The excessive practice of intro-spection has, in fact, been called a "dreaded disease" and rightly so; in many cases it is terminal.

How then can you and I discover our God-given true selves? How can we learn what qualities we need to get rid of and what qualities we need to develop? Surely, we reason, as responsible Christians we need to examine ourselves. But how?

The Language of the Heart

The only way we can ever know what is truly in our hearts is to look up to Jesus. Only Jesus can give us the information we need at the appropriate time to begin healing our hearts and making us whole.

The heart speaks a language all its own, a language that can easily communicate with God once we learn to understand it. The heart receives and speaks to us in symbol. Symbol brings thought and feeling (the head and the heart) together. Some have said that bringing the head and heart together may be a bigger feat than defying the laws of gravity. At times it seems that difficult.

149

Those who have engaged in severe introspection find themselves cut off entirely from their hearts because they are so "heady." They may want to get in touch with feelings, emotions and subjective ways of relating to God and to others, but they literally do not know how. Beginning to express themselves in this "foreign" way can be painful and exhausting.

In the early years of our marriage I repeatedly demanded of Conlee, "Don't tell me what you think! Tell me what you feel!"

Invariably his reply was, "I don't know what I feel! I only know what I think!"

Conlee's inability to express his feelings to me was extremely frustrating. I was certain he was suppressing emotions he thought would make him appear vulnerable. Accusations would follow; my irrational responses and his logical, irrefutable statements only widened the breach in our communication.

It seemed to me that Conlee was demonstrating clearly his belief that his ability to be consistently rational, logical and analytical was far superior to my ability to be intuitive, sensing and feeling. Only genuine love for each other protected us from drawing battle lines and letting this difference become too important in our relationship. But it continued to be a real problem for many years, with occasional fireworks.

One of my friends relates that when she and her husband had a similar discussion she pleaded with him, "Just tell me what you feel!"

His reply, in all sincerity? "I feel you should clean out the refrigerator."

Being Formed in His Image

The point is not that men need to "feel" more and women need to be more logical. The point is that all of us need to become aware of the ways in which we are made in the image of God.

God is the embodiment of that which properly initiates, organizes, brings order in the midst of chaos, presses through in difficult situations, analyzes, edits, pursues truth, sets healthy boundaries, defines and constructs. These characteristics are grouped together as "the true masculine," having nothing to do with male sexual gender.

150

God is equally the embodiment of that which properly responds, receives, perceives, nurtures, senses and intuits. These characteristics are grouped together as "the true feminine," having nothing to do with female sexual gender.

Men and women, both made in His image, can, with His help, develop the true masculine and the true feminine characteristics of God. If we find ourselves lacking in one area, we must be willing to pray for all of God (both masculine and feminine) to be present in us as we grow into more complete persons.

As I began to seek wholeness in my life I had to pray regularly for God to form in me a strong masculine will. I needed to receive from Him the ability to organize, to edit, to set healthy boundaries in my life and to have godly definition in my heart. These were my weakest areas, ones in which I had trouble finding worth because they were so foreign to my nature.

Because the true masculine was so strong in Conlee, on a very carnal level I felt myself to be at odds with him much of the time. He could always win an argument, he always controlled our money and he handled time better than I did. I, on the other hand, discerned problems easily and sensed others' feelings accurately. I also had the ability to express globs of meaning, but with very little structure. As a result no one paid much attention even when I shared items and thoughts that were immensely important to me. If I had not been able to ask for and receive more of God's "true masculine," I never would have been able to teach the seminars we do, minister with God's authority or write this book.

Conlee has prayed equally hard for God-given freedom to respond to His leadings, to receive from Him correctly, to sense the things of the Spirit and to nurture his family and the church flock God has given him to shepherd. Had he not been willing to receive the "true feminine" of God he would be far less effective as a minister, a nurturing father or a loving husband.

When we strike out in foreign territory, such as allowing God to develop uncharted areas of our hearts, fears normally arise. If they are ingrained in us deeply enough, they will inhibit our ability to grow into the image of Christ. We may, in fact, be consciously unaware of them. But our frustration and longing to be all God is calling us to be may motivate us to expose our fears to the healing presence of Jesus.

Cleansing the Imagination

In all our seminars we use a simple and profoundly effective little exercise called "The Garden of the Heart Prayer" to allow Jesus to show us the fears within our hearts. Conlee and I learned it from Leanne Payne and Pastoral Care Ministries, and it has helped both of us considerably in our own journeys. We have seen remarkable healings take place as we have incorporated it into helping others learn and speak the language of the heart.

To do this little exercise, however, we must allow God to use our imaginations for the purposes for which they were intended—holy purposes.

Perhaps you have watched New Agers misuse the godly gift of imaging the holy, and you have been afraid even to entertain the idea of exploring your imagination with God. Perhaps you have been taught that your imagination is evil and dangerous to use.

Your imaginative faculties (along with all the other fearfully and wonderfully made parts of your being) are a gift from God. Certainly the imagination can be misused for evil purposes, as can anything God intends for our good. But it can also be used to honor and glorify Him.

Your imagination is much like a movie screen—blank and neutral. It is neither good nor evil, merely a receptacle on which images from your heart can be projected. If there is evil in your heart, your imagination will bring up evil images. If goodness and beauty find lodging in your heart, your imagination will allow you to see them, too.

Because of the age in which we live, and the negative visual images and harsh words with which we are bombarded, all of us have a lot of garbage stored in our hearts and minds. This garbage is projected from time to time onto our imaginations. They may show us stored images from something in which we participated, something we witnessed, pictures from magazines, scenes from television or movies. There may be images of pornography or violence or demonic activity. We need to get rid of whatever does not belong in God's holy presence.

Over and over men and women have told us of unholy images intruding into their most holy moments in God's presence (such as in church, in prayer or in loving, holy relationships). These images may have plagued them for years, haunting their dreams and thoughts and perverting reality. Shame and embarrassment often lead these Christians to shove the images back down into the garbage cans their imaginations have become; they want to forget they ever had such thoughts.

How relieved they are when we tell them that when we seek the holy presence of God, God Himself brings up these images from the depths of our imaginations! He does so in order that we will hand them over to Him so He can cleanse our imaginations, readying them to receive pictures of His reality—

> Whatever is true, whatever is noble, whatever is right, whatever is pure, whatever is lovely, whatever is admirable— . . . anything . . . excellent or praiseworthy. . . .
>
> Philippians 4:8

—not the illusory decption of the enemy. To allow this cleansing I ask God to bring up every pornographic, violent, unclean image out of my imagination. As they come into my conscious mind, I place a hand on my forehead and pull the images "up and out" of myself and hand them to Jesus.

Some men and women see so many perverted images on the screens of their imaginations that it is as though they have to pull them out like long movie reels from their minds to Jesus' hands. This may take some time.

Then it is important to see what Jesus does with what I give Him. The imagery of how He disposes of my garbage makes a lasting impression on my heart of the completeness of His cleansing power.

When the release comes, I ask the Holy Spirit to fill, wash and renew my imaginative faculties as I stand cleansed before God.

After you have asked God to cleanse your imagination as I have described, it is appropriate to ask Him to speak to your heart in its own language, employing your cleansed imaginative faculties.

Weeds of Fear

How can I learn the language of the heart to see if there are any fears within *my* heart? One way is to simply ask God to show me my heart as a garden. The garden imagery is, of course, highly biblical.

Prayerfully and quietly, not striving, allow Jesus to show you whatever is in your garden. Allow time to look around, noticing everything that is there. Then ask Him to show you if any weeds of fear are growing in the garden, anything that does not belong. If you find any, pluck them up and name each one. Then hand them to Jesus and watch carefully to see what He does with them.

Some weeds may be as large as trees, with deep roots. You will need Jesus' assistance in pulling these out of the ground. Some weeds may be disguised and you will need His assistance to see them. It is important to give Him permission to show you anything He knows you are ready to discover. As you watch what Jesus does with your surrendered fears, you may see Him transform them into something useful or beautiful. Some fears must be destroyed. All this imagery is symbolic of something important happening in your spiritual growth.

Remember that in this exercise Jesus is your Guide, leading you into truth, not illusion. Using your holy imagination in this way differs significantly from New Age "guided imagery" exercises in which you are told what to see and how to respond to it. We do not tell you what is in your garden. Jesus does. We do not explain to you what Jesus does with your fears. Jesus shows you.

The pictures shared from this exercise are astounding. Some who have struggled for years in their search for hidden barriers to their freedom of the Spirit discover reams of truth. Seeing their true hearts for the first time, they feel freedom they have never known and experience remarkable heart-healing. Others may simply begin to believe God can really speak to their hearts, when once they had doubted their ability to receive.

To help you understand more fully the power of the garden exercise, let me share what both Conlee and I heard from the Lord on one of the many times we have looked at the gardens of our hearts.

Conlee's Garden

I saw a neat, orderly garden with a manicured lawn and hedges in front of a precisely built brick wall. I had laid a brick sidewalk that was bordered by symmetrical plants. I saw nothing out of order.

I was satisfied with the symmetry and lack of clutter, but as instructed, I asked Jesus to show me any weeds of fear. He took me to the neatly trimmed hedge and showed me, deep within the greenery, a vine so entangled with the hedge that it looked as though it belonged. But it did not: It was a weed.

154

I began to uproot the vine but I realized it went under my sidewalk; to pull up the roots would destroy my handiwork. Jesus took my hand and helped me pull up the vine, roots and all, totally demolishing the sidewalk.

When the root came up I saw its name: "Fear of the Unknown." I gave it to Jesus. He took it in His hand and took off running, crashing through my perfect hedge and my perfectly constructed brick wall, leaving a gaping hole and bricks scattered everywhere. All of the carefully constructed order in my garden was gone.

Jesus paused outside the wall in what looked like a wild olive grove and turned to me, smiling, beckoning me to go with Him. Taking a deep breath I ran in His direction.

Conlee received a healing of his heart and an empowerment for ministry as he was able to name his fear of the unknown and release it to Jesus. Can you see how Jesus was encouraging him to become freer in the true feminine attributes of God? He was encouraged and strengthened to respond to God in new ways, without arduous analysis of each detail. His heart could continue to contain order and symmetry, along with the new freedom and joyful expression of his desire to follow Christ. Because of this freedom he continues to be able to respond to God's call into uncharted areas of ministry.

Signa's Garden

I went into my garden where I saw a huge, live oak tree in the center. Its limbs nearly touched the ground. Weeds of grass were growing up around its base. Apparently I had trimmed the weeds regularly with a weedeater and the garden usually looked neat, but below the surface fears were obviously alive and growing.

I took a shovel and began to dig a nice, neat circular bed around the base of the tree. Jesus put His foot on the shovel with me to help, so the digging was quite easy. I lined the bed with bricks.

As we removed each weed, Jesus shook the dirt off its roots and we put it into a large, black garbage bag. I waited for Him to take them away but He didn't. Then I knew I must name every weed in that whole bag. I took a white marker and wrote on the sack, "Weeds of fear that the timing and circumstances won't work out right and we will end up where God does not want us to be."

Jesus took the sack and crushed it in His hand until it was small, condensed. He put it through His clothing where it was absorbed into His body.

Those fears are gone!

Jesus gave me this garden image during a long search process period in which Conlee was being interviewed by several churches for the position of pastor. I had never articulated this fear until I saw it in the garden. Can you see the masculine ordering of emotions that resulted?

Finding Your God-Given True Self

So God created man in his own image, in the image of God he created him; male and female he created them.

Genesis 1:27

1. Write in your prayer journal the listing of God's characteristics that I have categorized as masculine and feminine (see pages 150–51). Find biblical examples of God expressing each one. Example: "defining" in Genesis 1:4.
2. In which of the groupings of God's characteristics are you deficient? Begin to pray for a more complete integration of your head and your heart, your thoughts and feelings.
3. Go through the cleansing of the imagination exercise as described on pages 152–53. Ask God to bring up out of the reservoir of your imaginative storehouse any images that do not belong there. As they come up, lift each one out of your mind into God's hand. Receive His breath upon you as a cleansing wind.
4. Ask God to show you your heart as a garden. Following the examples given today, ask Him to show you anything that does not belong in your garden—weeds of fear, anxiety or other hindrances that paralyze the development of your true self. Be sure to name them and give them to Jesus. Notice carefully what He does with them. Write all He shows you in your prayer journal.

Region 4
Believing I Have Worth to Receive All God Has Promised Me

BASED ON THE EXPERIENCES OF THE LEADERS OF ISRAEL, AS FOUND IN NUMBERS 13–14

Day 21

Continuing the Journey

YOU ARE NOW AT A CRUCIAL STAGE IN YOUR JOURNEY. PERHAPS YOU ARE excited about every turn in the road and cannot wait to get to your destination. Or maybe the journey seems tedious to you, fraught with delays and distraction. Maybe the journey has proven so painful that you are seriously tempted to quit, to dig in right where you are or even to turn back.

Historically Speaking . . .

Let's look at some scriptural examples that illustrate the importance of the decision you will make today about continuing your journey. Look carefully at chapters 13 and 14 of Numbers. You may need to read them aloud to get the gist of the story. (Deuteronomy 1 also offers a good synopsis of the same events.)

The Hebrews, led by God's own man, Moses, had been delivered miraculously from their captivity in Egypt. There they had not been free to exercise their God-given identities, to be the people God called them to be. Now they were assured that God had prepared a place for them, a place He had always wanted them to be. Through Moses He was going to lead them to this place of wholeness, but first He had to teach them how to relate to Him and to each other in intimacy, trust and obedience.

The Hebrews were eager and excited. They could not wait to take the next steps. Before long, however, they realized that some of the old habits formed in Egypt were not going to be easy to give up. Old, familiar ways of relating to one another were no longer acceptable to God.

Getting in touch with their own sin, deprivation and neediness brought pain the Hebrews would rather have avoided. Being led into wholeness was not as easy as they had thought it would be. Overcoming their enemies was hard work. Some folks wanted to go back to Egypt—and slavery! Some wanted to dig in and accept whatever seemed to be the norm right where they were, even if it was not a godly place. Only a handful wanted all God had for them so desperately that they were willing to move on as God led, even if it took time and hard work.

Eventually God told Moses to choose a leader from each of the twelve tribes to check out the land He had been promising them from the beginning of the journey. All along God had described this land in picturesque language, telling His people it was "flowing with milk and honey" (Exodus 3:8). It had always seemed real, but real in the "sweet-bye-and-bye."

Now, however, in God's perfect timing, the Promised Land was actually in sight—it was a certainty. They could see it with their own eyes across the river and they could walk into it. God allowed a representative group of Hebrews to walk in and look at it and feel it for themselves and to bring back a report about how wonderful it was. He gave them forty days to discover the possibilities in this new place.

A Modern Application

I want you to see the original Promised Land as a prototype of your own wholeness in Christ, the "land" to which you are traveling. *This is your promise from God.*

Nineteen hundred years ago a believer named Paul prayed the following prayer for the people of Ephesus—and for us:

> I pray that out of his glorious riches he may strengthen you with power through his Spirit in your inner being, so that Christ may dwell in your hearts through faith. And I pray that you, being rooted and established in love, may have power, together with all the saints, to grasp how wide and long and high and deep is the

love of Christ, and to know this love that surpasses knowledge—
that you may be filled to the measure of all the fullness of God.

Ephesians 3:16–19

I believe this prayer is being prayed from heaven today for each of us! When it becomes a reality in our lives, we will be living in the land of wholeness in Christ.

Entering into that land of wholeness is no longer just a "pie-in-the-sky" Christian promise, a "place of milk and honey," a vague hope for the "sweet-bye-and-bye." You are already experiencing more wholeness in your life right now than you thought possible a year ago. You actually know or know about people who can testify that it is indeed true—there is a place where one can be healed, be real and live in peace. And it is worth every effort to get there!

Back to the Bible

Twelve men were sent out to investigate the land, to see if what God had said was true. To a person, they all agreed the Promised Land was everything God had said it would be, and more. It was beautiful, it was fertile and it was a perfect place to raise their families. Every one of them wanted to live there.

But of the twelve, ten said it would be impossible to conquer the land. They could see only the hard work ahead—clearing the land of its enemy inhabitants, tilling the soil, building new foundations. Fear of the unknown, of hard work and of enemies, seen but not yet faced, paralyzed them. They refused to move on. God promised to go before them and fight their battles, but they did not believe He knew the strength and size of the foes they would encounter.

And so, because of their unbelief and unwillingness to endure pain to win the great prize, not one of those ten men ever lived in the Promised Land. Each died prematurely because of his fears, leaving his family to wander in circles, searching for an elusive goal.

Today's Stumbling Block

What is your biggest stumbling block? What keeps you from pressing on, facing the enemies of your soul and conquering them? Do obstacles from your past loom so large that you hesitate to face them head-on? Are you, like the leaders of Israel, continually circling around major issues in your life, unwilling to engage them in God's power? Are you still remembering words said to you years ago such as, "You don't deserve anything more than what you already have; you're not worth the trouble it would take for God to bring you to wholeness"?

Arriving at the belief that you have worth in God's eyes is a major milestone on your journey to wholeness. Hearing God speak your name, accepting His personal invitation to come on the journey, experiencing His presence standing with you in the face of the enemies that surround you and receiving His power to overcome them all strengthen your belief in the incredible value you have in God's eyes.

If you have been consistently devalued by those close to you, you may have difficulty realizing your priceless worth to God. He longs to prove how much you mean to Him, but He cannot unless you provide the opportunities for Him to do so.

During this week you will go out on a limb for God. If you are serious about continuing the journey to wholeness, allow yourself the next few days to establish trust with Him. This may involve asking Him to examine your childhood impression of Him so He can correct any misperceptions. It may mean facing old enemies of fear and, though they loom very large on your horizon, choosing to see that God is larger yet. It may mean choosing to keep moving toward wholeness, one step at a time, even though you are tired and discouraged by your seeming lack of progress.

Wholeness is the state in which God prepared for you to live before you were ever conceived. You may rationalize your present existence, but wholeness is where you have always longed to be.

Believing You Have Worth

> Consider it pure joy, my brothers, whenever you face trials of many kinds, because you know that the testing of your faith develops perseverance. Perseverance must finish its work so that you may be mature and complete, not lacking anything.
>
> James 1:2–4

1. Write out Ephesians 3:16–19 in your prayer journal, making it personal (i.e., "Lord Jesus, I pray that from all Your

glorious riches You will strengthen me with power through Your Spirit in my inner being . . ."). Then, from your heart, read the prayer aloud to your Lord.

2. Are there areas of your life about which you feel God does not really care, does not have time for you or has given up on you? If so, I invite you to write them out in your prayer journal. Ask Him to speak to you personally about each area. Write His answer in your journal.

Day 22

Dealing with Darkness

During the last 25 years I have been in more prayer groups than I can count. I have tried all flavors: traditional and charismatic, in churches and in homes, women-only and mixed groups, liturgical and informal. In some groups I felt such a sense of "belonging" that I remained integrally involved for several years. Others just did not seem right for me and I only visited occasionally.

It is exciting to know that groups of people gather regularly in every city, town and village of the world to praise and pray and give testimonies to the goodness of our God. To walk into such a prayer group, even in a strange place, is to feel instantly at home, kin with others who love Him also.

But I have encountered one practice in prayer groups in which I cannot willingly take part. I call it "practicing darkness" rather than "practicing light." Perhaps you, too, have found yourself in a group of Christians who spent a great deal of time speaking to Satan, rather than praising God, worshiping, rejoicing in God's goodness or interceding for others.

How often have you heard or prayed:

I bind you, Satan, in the name of Jesus. You have no place here. I tell you now to be gone. Satan, we speak words of defeat to you; you are consigned to outer darkness. We tell you to get your hands off God's children. Satan, we tell you to leave this place, to leave this city.

"What's wrong with that?" you ask. "We need to protect ourselves so we can pray more effectively. This is spiritual warfare."

Let me ask: Whose presence are you invoking? With whom are you dialoging? Are you focusing on the light or on the darkness?

If we focus on darkness, invariably a heaviness will descend on the group and the power of the Holy Spirit will be less perceptible in our midst. Often the efficacy of our prayers is diminished and confusion and dissension reign.

Giants in the Land

In the book of Numbers, ten leaders of Israel focused on the darkness in the Promised Land and led a whole nation down the same dead-end path. You will recall that God had allowed twelve leaders forty wonderful, revealing days in the Promised Land. They saw amazing richness and beauty, a place with Garden-of-Eden-like potential where they could live with the Lord as their God. He told them repeatedly that yes, there would be enemies in the land, but they were *not to focus on those enemies*. God would drive the enemies out if His people were obedient. He offered a laboratory in which trust could grow. But fear overcame ten of the leaders, fear that God would not be able to do what He said He would do.

Once they accepted and coddled that fear rather than asking God to put it to death, every problem and obstacle in the Promised Land seemed insurmountable. Every difficulty obscured their vision of God.

The same is true for us. Like the leaders of Israel, we are asked to take God at His word. We are asked to trust that He will do what He has said He would do, even though we are given no tangible guarantees. We are asked to act in faith, choosing to walk into uncharted areas of our lives praising our Lord, not giving undue attention to our enemies. Praise is our ultimate weapon in the warfare against darkness. Praise invokes God's presence, strengthens our spirits and gives us freedom to operate in all His gifts.

Is there ever a time to rebuke Satan? Of course. When we are operating in the power of the Spirit, the gift of discerning other spirits will let us know if we are indeed dealing with Satan. Then, in God's power, we can send Satan packing quickly and effectively, without undue conversation.

What about Matthew 16:19, in which Jesus tells us, "Whatever you bind on earth will be bound in heaven, and whatever you loose on earth will be loosed in heaven"? This Scripture (repeated in Matthew 18:18) must be taken in context to see that Jesus clearly is speaking of binding and loosing sin in our lives through the binding of unforgiveness and the loosing of forgiveness. The power of unforgiveness is mighty and will keep us bound for a lifetime if we do not choose to loose it through confession, forgiveness and repentance.

Many Christians have trouble believing that God will go before them and fight their battles because they do not believe they are valuable to God. Some of these dear brothers and sisters have been led to feel that they are expendable in God's eyes, and that the fight toward any degree of wholeness will have to be made in their own energy or not at all. Perhaps this is why they feel compelled to fight Satan with a constant war of words, rather than in the power of Christ.

Our own unbelief is an enemy far more subtle than Satan. Doubt that God will bring us to wholeness is a deadly antidote to the saving work of Christ.

Other travelers on the journey to wholeness have shared with me negative thoughts that kept them from entering in. Here is a sampling:

- Satan has as much authority in this situation as God does unless I pray the right prayers.
- I have suffered at the hands of too many people and my scars are too great for God to heal me.
- Admitting aloud how unworthy I feel constitutes a negative confession, and God will not heal me. I must, therefore, deny my feelings.
- I have committed too many sins for Jesus to want to rescue and redeem me.
- I have already decided that I am not worth the trouble it would take Jesus (even if He were able) to clean up all my messes and bring me to a safe place.
- God has too many important things to do to listen to my problems.
- I must deny the problems in my life and my family's life so the world can see an effective "Christian witness."

Each of these statements is a lie!

166

I recently received a letter from a church leader who had been under the illusion that true spiritual warfare was conducted only on the level of dialoging with darkness. At a seminar I led for her Bible study group I was alerted to this practice by her initial prayers for me. After invoking the presence of the Holy Spirit she immediately launched into a long list of warnings to the evil one, telling him all the things he must do and must not do. A sense of darkness came immediately over our prayers and I received a holy warning from God that I must pray light into our meeting.

Later in the seminar I was led by God to exhort my hearers to put aside "practicing darkness" and choose to fight their battles in the light of Christ. Because this leader loves the Lord with all her heart she saw the truth and repented. She wrote to me:

> A sense of pride had begun to get at me, especially when I heard (our leadership team) referred to as "fearsome" after word began to spread of prophetic prayer and some deliverance. And all too soon, as forces arose and dark shapes loomed up out of the shadow, I had fallen into studying the darkness, as if by understanding its dynamics I would somehow be better able to disable it. Deadly. It was "the cross plus" mentality. Jesus caught me before I stumbled.
>
> Even this morning the Lord reminded me that if I look in the face of the darkness, my faith and courage run out of me, leaving me weak as water. My face must always be turned up to look at Him, to listen to Him. And it is His power, it is He who disables the darkness, not my understanding of it.

Breaking Up with the Enemy

My youngest son, Ben, a college junior, has given me many godly gems of wisdom. Since his complete transformation from three years of living on Satan's playground of drugs, sex and alcohol, he has attempted with all his might to live for Jesus Christ in every way possible.

One of the first things Ben did was to give back all the "tokens of affection" Satan had given him—at least a hundred CDs, posters of rock musicians, T-shirts with suggestive slogans, mementos of drug scenes and his long pony tail. Ben did this ruthlessly, likening it to a breakup with a long-time steady girlfriend, then returning to her all the pictures, gifts and remembrances of their former relationship.

Ben also closed the door on his unholy lifestyle by ending lengthy telephone conversations with people who were bad influences, people who might have tempted him away from Jesus. He chose to "hang out with light" and "hang up on dark."

I marveled as Ben went through this process. The change in his heart was foremost, but it was not long before the outward appearance of his person and his lifestyle followed. His determination to cut himself off completely from darkness and fill his life with light has enabled him to mature very quickly in his Christian walk.

It will be the same with all of us: If we persist in conversing with Satan in our prayers, maintaining even a negative dialogue with someone we "broke up with" a long time ago, we will not mature as Christians. Nor will we travel as rapidly as we long to on the journey to wholeness.

We can choose with our wills to seek the light, to walk in the light, to choose light over darkness, to dialogue with light, to be bathed by light.

We are children of the light! Let us choose to live with our heritage!

Believing You Have Worth

This is the message we have heard from him and declare to you: God is light; in him there is no darkness at all. If we claim to have fellowship with him yet walk in the darkness, we lie and do not live by the truth. But if we walk in the light, as he is in the light, we have fellowship with one another, and the blood of Jesus, his Son, purifies us from all sin.

1 John 1:5–7

1. Examine, through God's eyes, the weapons you have been using in spiritual warfare. Have they been effective in the battle?
2. Can you identify with any of the negative statements listed on page 166? They are lies. If you have been passive in the midst of your enemies or have focused on their darkness rather than on God's goodness, ask God to forgive you. Now assume a posture of turning toward the light. Look up the

references in your Bible on "light." Write in your prayer journal some that speak to your heart.

3. Put on the full armor of God's own presence as your protection. Personalize Ephesians 6:10–18 as you pray it aloud each day. Write it out as your own prayer in your prayer journal.

Day 23

Accepting Myself

IN HER BOOK *RESTORING THE CHRISTIAN SOUL: OVERCOMING BARRIERS TO COMpletion in Christ through Healing Prayer* (Baker, 1991), Leanne Payne cites three great barriers to wholeness: the failure to accept oneself, the failure to forgive others and the failure to receive forgiveness.

"The failure to forgive others," she says, "and/or to receive forgiveness for ourselves—have to do with more or less specific memories and rejections. In contrast, the failure to accept oneself is an attitudinal block. It has to do with how we perceive and feel about ourselves and others."

The reasons for "how we perceive and feel about ourselves and others" are legion. In my own life there have been so many reasons why I could not accept myself completely that I was able to sort through them only by focusing deliberately on the presence of Jesus. I could not focus on my obvious stumbling blocks. In His light I found an orderly way to deal with each problem, one at a time. Eventually I could love myself aright and accept the woman God was calling me to be.

Many of us realize that we experienced some painful deprivation of childhood affirmation. We may have had wonderful, loving Christian parents who did the best they could to raise us. But guilt or fear of disloyalty may make us reluctant to admit that we simply did not receive from them what we needed to feel complete. The freedom to express that need honestly to God without judging our parents is an essential step to accepting ourselves.

170

There is a delicate line between molding character, disciplining behavior and guiding a child into the image of God, and the unhealthy counterfeits of those parenting tasks: breaking a child's spirit, molding the child into what society demands, forcing rebellion and guiding the child into the parents' image. The godliest of parents is still human. It should come as no surprise (but often does, to those who see it for the first time) that children from godly Christian homes often feel inadequate, unable to accept themselves or believe they have any worth at all in the Kingdom of God. Such children inevitably have the most difficulty identifying the lack of worth that has plagued them all their lives. They cannot force themselves to appear disloyal to such "perfect" parents, so the enormity of their guilt in speaking the truth about their childhoods keeps their struggle with unworthiness crammed inside. Eventually they project their own self-hatred not only onto themselves, but onto those closest to them.

Some mothers and fathers simply are not able to love each child in the way he or she needs to be loved in order to become all God intended. Premature death, illness, poverty, job demands, family responsibilities, ignorance or their own emotional deprivations are just a few of the reasons why even "good" parents fall short in this area. I have had to forgive my parents for some deprivations in my childhood. I have also had to ask my children to forgive me.

We Come as Children

Many dedicated ministers' children have come as adults for healing prayer because of the terrible sense of inadequacy they have felt, especially in the presence of God. Why? Because their parents (especially the ones who were clergy) seemed to have time for each person in the congregation—except their own children. While we may look at these clergy families from afar and marvel at the pastors' unselfishness and dedication to God, the lack of personal attention and affirmation was imprinted on the minds of the wounded children to the extent that they felt unimportant to their parents and, ultimately, not all that important to God.

I recall the successful pastor of a large, well-known church who cried as he related an incident from a long-ago Saturday afternoon when his father (also a successful pastor) promised to play ball with him in the backyard. This was his "time with Dad" and he felt very special as they began to throw the ball back and forth to each other.

Then two lay leaders from his father's congregation appeared at the gate to the back yard asking his father if they could visit with him about some church business. Instead of telling them he had promised this time to his son and would be happy to meet with them later, the father said, "Oh, I'm not doing anything important, just playing ball with Johnny. Come on in the house."

Even though he was in his forties when he told this story, "Johnny" had never forgotten those words. They continued to ring in his ears, not just from his father's mouth, but also from his Father's mouth.

Overcoming the Obvious

For others the reasons for a lack of self-acceptance are more blatant. Some have experienced real evil in their families through physical and emotional abuse, abandonment, humiliation, violence and/or neglect. These sufferers may find it much easier to determine the cause of their sense of unworthiness, but much harder to forgive those who have so cruelly sinned against them. Still, forgive them they must! Forgiving our enemies is always the key to our own wholeness.

Over the years I have heard many confessions about cruel things parents have done and said to their children, actions and words that affected those children for the rest of their lives. All too often I have heard the cries of adult daughters who remember their fathers ridiculing their womanhood at the onset of their monthly periods. These women recall their fathers' words vividly, as if they were spoken yesterday. Shaming their daughters and calling them "dirty," these fathers frequently prophesied in an unholy way what their daughters would become.

In each instance I have known where shame, hatred and ridicule were heaped upon a young woman's perceptions of her own femaleness, serious adult gynecological problems developed, problems requiring healing prayer. Where once the self-hatred of her own sex had cursed and shamed those parts of her body that proclaimed her "woman," we now asked the power and presence of God within to proclaim blessings upon the intrinsically female parts of her body. We have encouraged many such women to go into the privacy of their own bedrooms or bathrooms to bless their breasts, uteruses, in fact, their whole unclothed bodies. While they may cause initial embarrassment, these private times of blessing bring acceptance and release from shame. And they sometimes bring healing of disease.

Even the woman who has fulfilled the unholy prophecies spoken over her, prophecies of wantonness and promiscuity, can now begin to see herself as Christ sees her. I remember praying with a woman who had been a long-time prostitute on the streets of New York City. Cleansed by confession, forgiveness and repentance, she had a vision of herself as a renewed virgin, ready to await God's direction for her life. This is the work of our God, who makes us worthy!

A Prayer for Parents

When we as parents begin to understand what we have done, are convicted of our sin and/or ignorance in raising our children and perhaps see the disastrous results of our mistakes in our children's lives, we can easily fall into heavy sorrow and self-condemnation. What we need, instead, is true conviction unto repentance.

God has shown me many mistakes I made in raising my own children. I was a very young mother and ignorant about young children. I was an only child and had never held an infant in my life until my first son was presented to me in the hospital a full 24 hours after delivery. I had no idea what to do with him, and was terrified I would do something wrong. I was too quick to follow the poor advice of the medical professionals, whose main goal appeared to be making their own jobs easier. Little good literature on child-raising was available at that time and I was unaware of any support groups. I made numerous errors in judgment as a young mother and some are evident in my children to this day.

I have had to forgive doctors, medical staff, relatives, friends and myself for the mistakes I made. In some cases I have asked my children to forgive me for my ignorance and passive love.

The following prayer from my journal has helped me:

Lord, give me divine insight into my parenting experience. Help me to see the situation in truth, not exaggerated or diminished, but the situation with my child as it really was.

Where sin or ignorance led to the neglect of my child, reveal it to me in truth.

Show me, Lord, the physical, emotional and spiritual voids in my child due to my negligence.

Lord, I confess my failures to You. I ask You to forgive me and cleanse me. Wash my sorrow from me and release my child from my sin and the sins of society. Lord, You make up the deficit as only You can.

Prepare my child to receive my confession in an appropriate time and way, and to extend forgiveness to me.

Fill the empty places in my child's heart and heal any division between us.

Thank You, Lord. Amen.

Seen by the Holy

We will never know our own children as God knows them. We will never even know ourselves as God knows us. The most important thing any of us will ever do to find our true selves is to sit in His presence, to listen to His words, to trust His voice. To get to the core of the worth He sees in us we may have to uncover much pain, confess much sin and repent of many bad habits. But the worth of the individual creature has already been paid, the highest price God could offer—the life and death of His only Son.

Your intrinsic value to God is so important that He staked Jesus' life on it! Jesus' resurrection from the hell of sin and death is proof that you, too, can rise from the hell of self you may be in at this moment.

Believing You Have Worth

It should be that of your inner self, the unfading beauty of a gentle and quiet spirit, which is of great worth in God's sight.

1 Peter 3:4

1. What degrading images or words from your past come to your conscious memory at this time? Write them in your prayer journal. Give each one to Jesus and ask Him to redeem it and resymbolize for you the images of "father" and "mother."
2. Make a list of people you know you need to forgive for things done and things left undone in your life. Submit their names to Jesus.
3. In words, aloud, begin to bless any parts of yourself that have been clothed with shame, embarrassment or self-hatred. Choose to see them through your Creator's eyes.
4. Thank Jesus specifically for dying so you might live. Write your thanks to Him in your prayer journal.

Day 24

Ordering My World

WE CAN BECOME UNBELIEVABLY SELF-CENTERED WHEN WE ARE HURTING. When we are preoccupied with our own pain the world stands still; we put every other person or agenda on the back burner. Individuals who are struggling desperately through grief or divorce or depression actually may resent the rest of the world for operating as though nothing is out of order.

When my father died I felt as though the whole world had stopped—or ought to. I remember driving my mother home from the hospital that night and wondering why traffic was progressing as usual, why people were going out to dinner and movies and visiting with one another as if nothing had happened. My family was in the midst of cataclysmic change. Our world would never be the same. It was inconceivable to me that no one else seemed to feel the powerful changes overtaking us at that moment.

In his book *Ordering Your Private World* (Oliver Nelson, 1985), author Gordon MacDonald relates an incident from his years as a pastor that my husband could have reproduced verbatim from his own experience:

> One Saturday afternoon the phone rang in our home, and when I answered the woman's voice at the other end of the line sounded quite upset. "I've got to see you right away," she said. When I learned her name, I quickly realized that I had never met this person before and that she had rarely ever visited our church.

176

"What is the reason that we have to visit right now?" I asked. It was an important question, one of several I've learned through experience to ask. Had this been many years ago when I was young, I would have responded immediately to her sense of emergency and arranged to meet her in ten minutes in my office, even if I had previously hoped to be with the family or involved with study.

"My marriage is breaking up," she responded.

I then asked, "When did you become aware that it was going to break up?"

She answered, "Last Tuesday."

I asked another question. "How long do you think the process of breaking up has been going on?" Her next comment was unforgettable.

"Oh, it's been coming on for five years."

I managed to muffle my real reaction and said, "Since you've seen this coming for almost five years, and since you knew it was going to happen since last Tuesday, why is it important to visit with me right at this moment? I need to know that."

She answered, "Oh, I had some free time this afternoon and just thought it might be a good time to get together with you."

I Need You Now!

We have all had times when our emotions have peaked and, like the woman who called Pastor MacDonald, we think we need immediate attention. Often it takes all the courage we have to ask for help, and when our request is put off it is as if God Himself is putting us off. Once again we feel we lack sufficient worth in His eyes to command His attention.

But listen to how Pastor MacDonald handled this delicate situation so as to safeguard the woman's sense of worth and be true to himself as well:

> "I can understand why you think you have a serious problem. Now I'm going to be very candid with you. I have to preach three times tomorrow morning, and frankly my mind is preoccupied with that responsibility. Since you've been living with this situation for several years now, and since you've had several days to think about your situation, I'm going to propose that you call me on Monday morning when we can arrange a time where my mind is in much better shape. I want to be able to give you my utmost in concentration. But that probably is not possible this afternoon. How does that sound?"

The woman responded positively. Pastor MacDonald had set healthy boundaries around his time and his family's time.

God often responds to us in a similar manner. Have you noticed that when you ask God for something you are particularly anxious about, He seldom treats your need as an emergency? Often, at the very moment when we think we are at our wit's end and cannot survive another minute on our own, God begins to show us strength within ourselves that comes from His presence—strength that can get us through! If He, or someone He sent, came too quickly to our rescue we would never discover this incredible fact of incarnational reality—the presence of the living God within!

How wonderful it is when our dependency on others becomes refocused in dependency on Him.

Jesus the Provider

Let's look once more at our character model, Jesus Himself, to see how He handled the anxieties of those around Him.

> When Jesus landed and saw a large crowd, he had compassion on them and healed their sick. As evening approached, the disciples came to him and said, "This is a remote place, and it's already getting late. Send the crowds away, so they can go to the villages and buy themselves some food."
>
> Jesus replied, "They do not need to go away. *You* give them something to eat."
>
> Matthew 14:14–16, italics mine

Can you feel the anxiety building in the disciples? They see a potential problem in the making. Several thousand people have followed Jesus out to a remote place where He had gone with the intention of being alone with His disciples for the day as they grieved the murder of John the Baptizer. No doubt they all needed time alone to pray, to share their feelings and to hear what Jesus would teach them.

But Jesus had compassion on the crowds who persisted in joining them. Many who knew Him as the healer had come to receive His touch, and He did not disappoint them.

178

Now it was getting late in the day and still they thronged around Jesus. Probably frustrated, tired and hungry themselves, and certainly carrying unresolved grief, the disciples go to Jesus, imploring Him to send the crowds away to the closest villages to get themselves some supper. It is almost dark; He has to put an end to this marathon healing meeting. If He does not do something quickly it will be dark and then what will they do? Hurry, Jesus, hurry!

But Jesus, who always brings order into a confusing situation, shows the disciples how to slow down, listen to Him and collaborate with Him to bring a totally unexpected resolution to their problem. He tells them they are going to be involved in ministering to the people. It looks impossible because they only have five loaves of bread and two fish. That is scarcely enough for the disciples, let alone five thousand men and even more women and children!

Yet the disciples obediently do what Jesus tells them to do, and the miracle of the feeding of the five thousand from a simple, meager picnic lunch becomes history.

When Jesus comes to feed us, heal us and start us on our path to wholeness, He invariably creates situations down the road where we need to help other hurting souls. Once I learn to stop, listen to Jesus and collaborate with Him in the miraculous healing process He works in my life, I can look away from my immediate needs and begin to focus on getting my greater needs met by Him. I learn to absorb everything I can of Jesus; to sit quietly, listening to Him to take Him into myself; to practice His presence; and to concentrate on knowing and loving Him.

And as I do so, not only are my needs met, but my eyes are also opened wide to see others who are just like I have been, frantic and frightened that they will be ignored. Jesus lifts my self-centered blinders, and my outward vision improves one hundred percent from the narrowly focused introspection and self-pity of the unhealed soul.

Then, and only then, will I cry out, as the disciples did, "Jesus, heal them, too! They are starving for what You have to give them. I know You can do it. You did it for me."

To my surprise He begins to disciple me in earnest: "I AM in you. I AM the healing they need. *You* give them something to eat."

And when I dare to offer to a fellow sufferer the invisible food Jesus has given me, He once again miraculously multiplies the healing, feeds the hungry and satisfies His children.

In giving out what He has given me, as He directs me, I take more of His presence into myself.

Believing You Have Worth

For everything God created is good, and nothing is to be rejected if it is received with thanksgiving, because it is consecrated by the word of God and prayer. If you point these things out to the brothers, you will be a good minister of Christ Jesus, brought up in the truths of the faith and of the good teaching that you have followed.

1 Timothy 4:4–6

1. Have you felt rebuffed by God or by one of His ministers when you have cried out for help? Can you look to Him now and see that this could have been His way of having you look directly to Him for the help you seek? Can you forgive the one you thought put you off?
2. In what ways have you been reluctant to give out what Jesus has given to you? Have you felt yourself too unworthy to minister to one of His hurting children? Pray right now for those who have needed you.
3. Ask God for the wisdom to know when He is setting holy boundaries in your life and when He is calling you to reach out to minister healing to one of His hurting children. In order for Him to answer this request you will need to know how to be quiet in His presence and how to hear His voice.

Day 25

A Priceless Gift

Scene One

Imagine this scenario: You are sitting at your kitchen table one morning having coffee and reading the newspaper when the doorbell rings. You look out the window and there, parked in your driveway, is the Publishers' Clearinghouse van. The Prize Patrol is on your front porch! Scarcely daring to believe your eyes, you open the door. Sure enough, a smiling television personality hands you a huge bouquet of red roses and a check with your name on it for ten million dollars.

What is your reaction?

"Oh, I can't accept this; there must be some mistake. Even if you drew my name there are others much more deserving than I. You don't know that much about me, and I'm sure if you knew me you wouldn't want me to have this. Please give it to someone else."

Am I crazy? You would snatch that check so fast! You would laugh and cry and praise God and Ed McMahon and call everybody you know!

Scene Two

Now imagine this: You are sitting at your kitchen table one morning having coffee and reading your Bible when you focus on these words of Jesus in John 10:10: "I have come that they may have life, and have it to the full."

What is your reaction?

"Oh, I am so grateful, Lord. This is what I've been praying for for years. I am going to do so much good with this priceless gift You are giving me by coming into my life. This full, abundant life in You will affect every relationship I have. Thank You for loving me enough to give me the desire of my heart."

I hope you would respond like that, rather than rejecting such an invaluable offer! Unfortunately we often have a hard time believing we deserve the blessings God wants to bring to us. Over and over I hear sincere men and women saying, "I just can't make myself believe that God would really forgive (or speak to, or protect, or love) me."

A Strong Tower

Remember several leaders of Israel who said, in essence, "I just can't make myself believe that God would really protect us from the enemies in the land He has for us. I'm not sure I can take the risk. What if we moved all our families and belongings there and then had everything destroyed? What if we, ourselves, were destroyed? The place we're living right now may not be all we hoped for, but at least we're safe and secure."

I hope you see that believing in "safety" and "security" apart from God's will for us is a lie—and not just a lie, but a dangerous lie. Saint Paul wrote about this danger in a letter to some of his friends:

> While people are saying, "Peace and safety," destruction will come on them suddenly, as labor pains on a pregnant woman, and they will not escape.
>
> 1 Thessalonians 5:3

Paul was speaking about the dangers of clinging to a false security during the end times, but the godly principle holds true in the area of traveling toward personal wholeness as well.

A good gem of God's wisdom to write in your prayer journal comes from Proverbs 18:10: "The name of the LORD is a strong tower; the righteous run to it and are safe." Let His Word, His name, His presence be a strong tower for you today. May He be a place where you can know you will find safety and protection. If you are feeling especially vulnerable in moving into a trusting relationship with God, use your holy imagination to "see" Him as a tower, impenetrable by the enemy, yet warmly welcoming you to come inside where He can care for you. Yes, it takes faith to "see" this, to believe it, but a tiny, seed-like bit of faith will carry you a long way.

Jesus offers you a gift beyond price today: It is the gift of wholeness. Receiving it does not mean you can sit back and do nothing on your own behalf! Your active participation is required! Neither does moving into the gift mean you will never feel pain again. You will hurt deeply, but will see the beauty in releasing the pain so it does not resurface later in an inappropriate way or place.

For the first time you can know with joy in the midst of pain that there is a safe place for the pain of your past to go. When we look to the "tower of our safety," Jesus, who died on the cross for us, we can release our pain and grief into His waiting heart. He submitted to the agonizing death on the cross so He *could* receive your pain and fear and sin.

If we felt we had no place to put our pain when it wells up inside, we would naturally be reluctant to let it surface. What freedom to understand that, at last, we know where the pain was always meant to go.

Believing You Have Worth

When you were dead in your sins and in the uncircumcision of your sinful nature, God made you alive with Christ. He forgave us all our sins, having canceled the written code, with its regulations, that was against us and that stood opposed to us; he took it away, nailing it to the cross.

Colossians 2:13–14

1. If you have a crucifix or a picture of Christ dying on the cross, take it in your hands and picture Him there, dying for your pain, sin, fear and paralyzing vulnerability. If you do not have an actual crucifix, close your eyes and picture the image of what actually happened at Calvary two thousand years ago for you.
2. If you have never believed the truth, the reality of the wholeness your heavenly Father offers you right now, offer that disbelief to Him and ask Him to forgive you. He will still offer you the way to wholeness. Can you accept it in spite of your apprehension? Give faith a chance.

Day 26

Waiting to Have Worth

LAWRENCE (NOT HIS REAL NAME) GREW UP IN A FAMILY OF WELL-EDUCATED professionals. Education and good grades were the standard for acceptance in his home. His parents frowned upon a "B" as a sign that Lawrence had not applied himself to reach his full potential. An "A" was rewarded with the admonition, "Don't quit trying; there's always room for improvement."

Lawrence excelled in drama and art, but his parents belittled these pursuits, regarding them as a waste of time. Lawrence soon found he virtually led two lives. He seldom brought home friends who appreciated the arts, knowing they would be criticized. He continued to maintain a superficial interest in his parents' social activities, wanting desperately to win their approval. In truth, he felt out of place in either world.

As Lawrence grew older and received accolades from his peers in the arenas of theater and painting, he could neither believe nor accept their praise. Inside he never felt he measured up because of his unfulfilled, basic need to hear his parents say, "We love you, we're proud of you."

When Lawrence became an adult he finally expressed to his well-meaning parents that they had always denied him the one thing he had longed for—their acceptance and approval. They were dumbfounded. In their minds they always had intended to convey acceptance and approval, but had equaled those qualities with the constant pressure to do more and perform more excellently. They were appalled that Lawrence would insinuate they

184

did not care for him. They simply thought they had protected him from thinking more of himself than was "healthy."

Lawrence's healing came as he was able to forgive his parents for their lack of meaningful affirmation in his life. But his next step was to hear and receive true affirmation from his heavenly parent. As Lawrence began to spend quality time with Jesus, he was able to picture Him looking at the "B+" on his grade school report card and giving him a big hug. He sensed Jesus saying, "I'm pleased with you; let's go celebrate!" He was able to picture Jesus opening the front door to his friends, inviting them in, providing a place for them to be together.

But most of all, in listening prayer, Lawrence heard Jesus say to him, "Lawrence, I love you just as you are. I am going to encourage you all I can to grow into the man I know you can be, but know that My love is unconditional. I will never remove My love from your life, no matter what you do or do not accomplish. I will always be here for you. We are one!"

At some time in our lives each of us needs to hear God say those same words to our hearts, whether or not our earthly parents were ever able to say them. We will truly believe we have worth only when we hear our heavenly Father pronounce those affirming words. Just as Jesus was empowered within by hearing from His Father, "This is My beloved Child in whom I am well-pleased," so we, too, are empowered by hearing the same words.

Facing the Facts

Our parents are human, even as we are. They have suffered deprivations and a lack of meaningful affirmation in their lives, just as we have. We need to see them objectively to know that in most cases our parents were not evil, nor were we so unlovable that they were unable to nurture us in ways that would have ensured our wholeness.

In some cases with which I am familiar, there have indeed been instances of evil on the part of one or both parents that emotionally and spiritually handicapped their children. When this is true it is extremely important for the adult child to confront head-on the incarnate evil in his or her family. That adult child must also make a complete separation from the evil—spiritually, emotionally and physically—if he or she wishes to realize wholeness.

While we must never compromise with evil by rationalizing its existence or attempting to live side by side with it, we must forgive those who have perpetrated the evil against us. The act of forgiveness in no way denies the severity of the offenses. It does, however, release us from being violated over and over as we recall the offensive acts in our memories, thus continuing to experience their effects.

Far more common than living in the midst of true evil, however, is a scenario mentioned previously—that many of us lived with well-meaning parents or parent surrogates who, either because of ignorance or inability, were unable to affirm us adequately in healthy ways. We may find it easy to understand that no deliberate harm was intended, that we were not cruelly neglected and that, when the chips were down, our parents unquestionably would have been on our side. But something was still missing in our familial relationship, something we may have longed for all our lives.

Maybe you have always wished you had a mother who would enfold you in her arms and hold you, rocking you until the peace and warmth of her love penetrated your aching heart. Maybe you have always felt the need for a father who would put aside his evening paper, turn off the television and give you his full attention, if only for a few minutes.

Neither the father nor mother who could not or would not do these things intended to deprive you. Perhaps she was not comfortable with touching. Perhaps he had pressures and stresses you knew nothing about. But the impact is still the same. It hurts inside and a part of you is still crying for the kind of affirmation that gives you self-worth.

Father, Forgive Them

Again, the key to freeing yourself to receive healthy affirmation is to forgive your parents. How? Look right up to your heavenly Father and "see" your mother or your father in His presence. Now, looking into God's presence, "tell it like it is" from your perspective. Do not rationalize or make excuses; just give the facts, as you see them.

Your story might sound like this:

"I always wanted my daddy to take me up on his lap and hug me. I wanted him to say he loved me but he never did; he always seemed too busy. It made me feel unimportant, as if he didn't really love me."

After expressing the facts you will probably still experience some intense feelings. Their presence does not mean you are unable to forgive your parents! Forgiveness is an act of your will, not a reflection of your feelings. It will be necessary to say aloud the words, "Father, in Jesus' name I choose to forgive my father. I choose to forgive my mother. I release them to You and ask You to heal their brokenness even as You heal mine."

You may need to complete this process several times. Often the first or second or even third times we choose to forgive are more like rehearsals than realities. Even being willing to be willing to forgive is a big step. Do not let Satan, or anyone else, accuse you of failing to pray in faith the first time if you need to pray the forgiveness prayer again and again. Although incredible miracles of forgiveness bring remarkable instant physical healings and psychological freedom, the act of forgiveness often occurs in layers.

Once you have chosen to forgive, listen to your heavenly Father's words of affirmation to you. Receive from Him the truths your soul has craved. He has been longing to say them to you, but unforgiveness is always a barrier to your receptivity.

Believing You Have Worth

If we claim to be without sin, we deceive ourselves and the truth is not in us. If we confess our sins, he is faithful and just and will forgive us our sins and purify us from all unrighteousness.

1 John 1:8–9

1. In your prayer journal, list some of the major regrets you have had in your life in your relationship with your mother and father. Do this even if one or both of them is deceased.
2. Read and copy in your prayer journal Matthew 6:14–15. Then make the Scripture personal, inserting the appropriate names. (See the example below.)

Write the personalized Scriptures in your journal and say them aloud, prayerfully, concerning each person who comes to mind as needing your forgiveness. Remember, praying the prayer of forgiveness releases you from the effects of the sins against you. It also releases the one who sinned against you to be convicted by God, healed and redeemed. Example:

If I forgive my mother when she sins against me, my heavenly Father will also forgive me. But if I do not forgive my mother her sins, my Father will not forgive my sins.

3. Spend some time listening to God's voice. His heart yearns to speak to yours. Ask for spiritual ears to hear His words. Write them in your journal.

Region 5

Looking My Pain in the Eye
As I Stand before the Cross

BASED ON THE EXPERIENCES OF JONAH, AS FOUND IN
JONAH 1–4

Day 27

His Purpose Is Higher

THIS WEEK WE ARE GOING TO CONSIDER A HIGHLY UNPOPULAR SUBJECT: pain. We will avoid pain at all costs, take arduous detours to stay out of its way and spend a fortune to get rid of it or mask it when we are under attack.

Although physical pain is bad enough, most people who have endured intense emotional and psychological pain will tell you that the latter is just as debilitating. I have heard the heart cries of so many who tell me that their every waking moment is wracked with the pain of past events or relationships. The world's popular remedies for alleviating emotional pain—"Put things behind you" or "Let time heal your wounds"—will always fall short of the completeness of Jesus' healing power.

Jeremiah recited the cry of many pain-devastated humans:

> Oh, my anguish, my anguish! I writhe in pain. Oh, the agony of my heart! My heart pounds within me, I cannot keep silent.
> Jeremiah 4:19

And,

> Why is my pain unending and my wound grievous and incurable?
> Jeremiah 15:18

Only when we see Jesus as the risen Lord, the One who has been crucified to receive all our sins and all our pain, can we finally be assured that there is indeed a place for our pain to go. No longer must we recycle it in our minds and hearts, constantly reopening old wounds of the past. Saint John recorded beautifully for us the revelation he received from the throne of God:

> And I heard a loud voice from the throne saying, "Now the dwelling of God is with men, and he will live with them. They will be his people, and God himself will be with them and be their God. He will wipe every tear from their eyes. There will be no more death or mourning or crying or pain, for the old order of things has passed away."
>
> Revelation 21:3–4

Let's explore some ways you and I can give our pain to Jesus, allow Him to dry our tears and allow Him to heal our broken hearts. Looking at a well-known friend from the Bible will help us.

Getting to Know the Character of Jonah

When you look back over your life as you have already lived it, is there one particular event for which you would like to be remembered? The event most memorable to you would not necessarily be the event historians would acclaim. Jonah's life was like that.

Almost any Sunday schooler can tell you about Jonah and the "big fish." In most cases they will talk about Jonah and the "whale," although whales have very small mouths and it would be nearly impossible for one to swallow a man. But other kinds of large fish could do so. At any rate, the "big fish" story definitely gets top billing in Jonah's life history. We all remember it, but it is only a small part of an important story about a reluctant prophet.

You probably think you know this story well, that you have heard it since you were a child. But I am going to ask you to reread the whole book aloud, all four chapters, before you continue this day's journey. And I want you to read it from a particular perspective—the perspective of the tribal storyteller.

The story was probably written down many years after it had already become a well-known part of Hebrew oral tradition. Each Hebrew tribe or family had at least one person who was gifted with the art of effective storytelling. Traveling storytellers visited villages, towns and cities telling fascinating tales that carried truths designed to pierce the hearts of the listeners and change their lives. Being a Hebrew storyteller was a big responsibility. The storyteller had to be accurate in his portrayal of the hero's or heroine's character and, above all, accurate in his portrayal of the character of God.

God loves to use stories to touch our hearts. Jesus was masterful in His art of storytelling and taught profound truths through parables taken from everyday life that still have the power to change us today.

The art of the story reaches us on different levels. We may identify first with the hero, then with an insignificant character, then with a circumstance, then with the godly response. Stories can touch our emotions, reach deep into our hearts and cause us to respond in ways we do not need to analyze or evaluate.

Jesus obviously loved the story of Jonah and gave it great importance. His response to it, in fact, is recorded three times in the New Testament. When the Pharisees asked Him for a sign to prove His authenticity, He told them that the only sign they would be given would be the "sign of Jonah," that the Son of man, like Jonah, would also spend three days and three nights in the heart of the earth (Matthew 12:39–41; 16:4). He also said that the Ninevites would stand up in judgment over the Pharisees and condemn them because they (the Ninevites) repented when Jonah preached to them, while the Pharisees refused to repent when one even greater than Jonah, namely Jesus, preached to them (Luke 11:29–30).

It is time for you to read the story for yourself. To do this, imagine that you are the tribal storyteller. Picture your listeners hanging on every word as you relate to them Jonah's fascinating tale. Read it with drama, pathos, adventure, comedy, sadness, frustration and tenderness.

Do it now.

If you got into the story at all you now want to know more about Jonah, a humorous, complex, petulant and often confusing character.

The story takes place about 785 B.C., during the reign of King Jeroboam II. Jonah was a Galilean, as was Jesus, and grew up influenced, as Jesus was, by Hebrew attitudes and culture. He learned as a small boy that God was merciful, just and loving, full of compassion and quick to forgive—toward the house of Israel. He also learned that the Hebrews expected this same God to annihilate the enemies of Israel. For the pagan (the Gentile), no salvation or mercy would be extended. Instead, every true Hebrew passionately desired that the enemies of Israel be utterly wiped off the face of the earth.

The familiar Hebrew psalms of Jonah's time, some of which are excerpted below, contained words that enforced this belief:

> Strike all my enemies on the jaw; break the teeth of the wicked.
>
> Psalm 3:7

> Let evil recoil on those who slander me; in your faithfulness destroy them.
>
> Psalm 54:5

> Like a slug melting away as it moves along, like a stillborn child, may they not see the sun. . . . The righteous will . . . bathe their feet in the blood of the wicked.
>
> Psalm 58:8,10

> Do not let them [our enemies] share in your salvation.
>
> Psalm 69:27

> May his [my enemy's] children be fatherless and his wife a widow. May his children be wandering beggars; may they be driven from their ruined homes. May a creditor seize all he has; may strangers plunder the fruits of his labor. May no one extend kindness to him or take pity on his fatherless children.
>
> Psalm 109:9–12

These represent a sampling of the prayers of well-meaning Hebrews who sincerely believed God would always protect the house of Israel by destroying her enemies. In some cases God did so in order to protect the enormous investment He had made in His people. Until the Hebrews were stronger in godly experience, faith and belief, God was unwilling to risk having the truth of His Word diluted by the lies and compromises of the pagans His people encountered.

This, then, was Jonah's mindset when God's word came to him: "Go to the great city of Nineveh and preach against it, because its wickedness has come up before me" (Jonah 1:2). Jonah must surely have thought this word did not accurately portray God's character as he had been taught about it. God would want to destroy Nineveh utterly; to eradicate every living soul in the city. Surely He would not give the Ninevites a chance to repent and be saved.

Jonah knew a lot about Nineveh. It was the largest city in the world at that time, the capital of the great Assyrian Empire, the wealthiest, cruelest and most powerful nation in the world. Over one million people lived there, enjoying priceless wealth, artifacts and libraries, mostly pillaged from cities the Assyrians had conquered.

Nineveh's interior walled city, about eight miles in circumference, housed the royal palaces, the hanging gardens, the king's residence, his libraries and the government buildings. The walls were one hundred feet high and their width could hold three chariots side by side. The outer city, made up of suburbs of row houses for hundreds of thousands of inhabitants, stretched for about sixty miles in circumference. Jonah would find it a three-day trip just to get from the outskirts of Nineveh through the walled city to the other side.

Running As Fast As You Can

Now can you begin to understand that when God called him to go to Nineveh, Jonah's first reaction was to say, "I am not going to do that"? He did not argue with God or plead with Him; he just ran in the opposite direction. Jonah was in Galilee; Nineveh was on the Tigris River, located where Mosul, Iraq, is today. When God said to go northeast, Jonah went southwest. When God said to go up, Jonah went down. He wanted to get as far away as possible, and the route he took was clearly intended to accomplish that purpose. To go to Tarshish (in Spain) was, in the eighth century B.C., to go literally as far as a ship would take a person.

Because the Phoenicians had trade routes established throughout the Mediterranean, the ship Jonah boarded in Joppa was probably staffed by Phoenician sailors, pagans every one. After they set sail the Lord caused a terrible storm. Each pagan sailor on board prayed to his own god; together, they wanted every base covered for their protection. In spite of their fervent prayers, however, the storm continued to rage. The crew decided to throw all the cargo overboard to lessen the ship's load. This would cost them dearly, but it might save their lives.

But still the storm raged. In the process of checking the ship, the captain came upon Jonah fast asleep in his quarters below deck. Apparently Jonah had no fear of the storm; he felt he would rather die than watch God forgive and save his worst enemies. Jonah was not a coward, for he was not afraid to tell the captain that it was because of him that the ship was about to be destroyed. And he also told the captain that there was no other choice but to throw him, the offender, overboard.

The pagans were terrified when they learned Jonah had so angered his God, and were reluctant to take into their own hands the responsibility of throwing him overboard. A God who could bring on such a ferocious storm to get the attention of just one man might destroy the whole lot of them if they usurped His right to bring punishment upon the guilty.

The sailors decided, instead, to try another tactic first. They would row in to the shore—a very dangerous thing to do because of the possibility of being tossed upon rocks and jetties. But this ploy did not work either, and they finally realized they would all be destroyed if they did not get rid of Jonah.

Interestingly, these pagans prayed to so many gods they did not hesitate, in their fear, to pray also to the Hebrew God. They asked to be forgiven for the action they had to take in throwing Jonah to his death. Jonah felt their compassion but knew they had no other choice than to get him off their ship. Once they threw Jonah overboard, the storm ceased. Greatly impressed, the sailors made a sacrifice and a vow to this new God whom they had seen at work.

The Harvest of Disobedience

Jonah's disobedience to God caused suffering for others besides himself. Disobedience to God always leads us into a downward spiral that affects everyone around us. In other words, disaster always follows disobedience. Disobedience is always a detour away from wholeness.

Are there areas in your life where you have knowingly disobeyed the Lord? Quiet yourself before Him. With an open heart ask Him to show you disobediences you may have rationalized or masked, deceiving yourself. He will make them apparent. As you are willing to grieve for your disobedience before Him and ask Him to forgive you, you will be able to spare many others from the effects of your sin on their lives, also.

Standing before the Cross

Whoever serves me must follow me; and where I am, my servant also will be. My Father will honor the one who serves me.

John 12:26

1. You may want to read the story of Jonah aloud to one or more persons and invite their responses. Could you be vulnerable enough to tell them how you see yourself in the story?
2. Has God ever impressed you to do something that seemed utterly impossible? Did He ever tell you that something totally outrageous was going to happen, and that you were going to be part of it? How did you respond? Write about this scenario in your prayer journal.
3. In what ways have you presumed upon God? Have there been areas in your life where you have assumed a certain thing to be the will of God without thoroughly searching His Word, listening to Him and asking for His enlightenment? Coming face to face with this fact can be painful. It can unearth stones that may have been lodged in your family's tradition for generations. Are you earnestly willing to let God speak to you on a personal level so you and others might not be destroyed? Write your insights in your prayer journal.

Day 28

Dying to Live

NOW WE HAVE COME TO THE PART OF THE STORY OF JONAH YOU KNOW SO well: Jonah's rescue by the big fish. This is a poignant illustration of the unexpected ways in which God can—and often does!—rescue us and get our attention. When disobedience leads us down to destruction with no way out in sight, how like God to put us in a position of utter helplessness where we are forced to look up and out of ourselves toward His loving, saving arms.

Many a person has looked back on the worst tragedy of his or her life and said, "If I hadn't been in the deepest pit, I would never have looked up for God and allowed Him to save me and be an intimate part of my life."

Sacrifice of Thanksgiving

Jonah was headed for certain death, tangled in seaweed, falling down, down, down to the bottom of the sea, when God provided a holding place for him. His life still hung in the balance, because the likelihood of escape from the interior of a fish seemed remote.

For the first time Jonah was tasting death. He realized that for all his previous bravado he was experiencing the true meaning of *Sheol,* "the depths of the grave," where one is for the first time completely out of God's presence (Jonah 2:2). It was a sobering, terrifying thing to contemplate and from his innermost being Jonah called out to God to be his Savior.

198

Still in the depths of his prison, Jonah sacrificed a song of thanksgiving to God. Still unrescued, Jonah sang the song of the redeemed. Still bound, Jonah cried the victor's cry. Was he foolish? Was he making believe? Was he denying his circumstances? No. Jonah was confirming the true character of God regardless of the circumstances—God is a God who saves! Jonah was practicing true worship, and when we truly worship, God responds.

God's response in this circumstance was to cause the big fish, that could neither destroy nor digest its meal, to vomit Jonah out of its belly onto dry land. Immediately Jonah heard the word of the Lord a second time: "Go to the great city of Nineveh and proclaim to it the message I give you."

This time Jonah chose to obey.

A Response from the Heart

God had done an extraordinary job of preparing the hearts of the Ninevites to receive His message through Jonah. We do not know how long or detailed a message God put in Jonah's heart, but what he said was very simple: "Forty more days and Nineveh will be overturned."

Forty days was a generous amount of time for the Ninevites to have in which to respond to Jonah's warning. Forty days would have given them time to hear it, to think about it, to discuss it with one another, to digest it, to weigh all the consequences and then to decide whether to accept or reject it.

Instead, following Jonah's simple statement, the Ninevites responded quickly with all their hearts. Before Jonah could even reach the interior city where the king resided, the ordinary people along the way were hearing and acting on the word from God that had penetrated deep into their souls. God placed in their hearts a longing for something better than what they had experienced. They saw a promise of peace and an enriched life that surpassed anything they had known. They saw an end to the misery, frustration and confusion of their lives. To a person, they wanted what they felt was now within their reach—peace with God.

The true word of God initially does one thing to all of us—it causes us to see ourselves as filth before His holiness. The Ninevites knew immediately that they needed to be cleansed from the inside out, so they declared a fast and put on the universal sign of their times for recognizing their sin—sackcloth. This harsh, hair garment would scratch, chafe, itch and torment the skin of the wearer as a constant reminder of the way their sin tormented God. To fast and cover one-self in sackcloth alerted every part of a person's body and mind that he or she was in desperate need of a total cleansing from God.

Only after his people had responded did the king hear the word from God in his own heart. He, too, responded by repenting. Believing and acting in obedience to God's decree, he took off his royal robes and put on sackcloth garments.

In the need to be cleansed, to face the seriousness of our sin and unrighteousness before God, there is no distinction between royalty and commoner, between Jew and Gentile, between male and female. All of us need to look our sin, pain and worthlessness in the eye as we seek wholeness from God. We must say to Him, "I deserve to die for this. I am guilty and I stand before You with no defense." Then, and only then, do we make ourselves available for the inner healing and sense of worth God has always intended us to possess.

Our Salvation

Like the Ninevites, we have One before us to proclaim God's spoken word that brings salvation. But our messenger, unlike Jonah, has the power in Himself to deliver us because He, Jesus, is fully God. He not only went into the bowels of the earth for three days and three nights at His death, but He took with Him to the depths the power sin had always had over the world. His death was far more than that of a good man dying for His friends. No, Jesus' death was much more meaningful, something no other human being who ever lived was able to do. He accepted into Himself all the sin of the world, past, present and future, took it with Him to Sheol (that place apart from the presence of God) and left it there, separated from God "as far as the east is from the west" (Psalm 103:12).

When you and I take the weight of our sin and pain, walk up to the cross and identify with Jesus having died there, we can enter into Him and let our sin, pain and woundedness become one with Him. God the Father has provided for us a place in which to deposit this destructive load. No longer must we repress the pain in our lives, adding to our dis-ease. No longer must its overwhelming weight force us to project it onto others. No longer must we recycle pain through event after event, relationship after relationship. There is a place for it to go, a place acceptable to God.

I cannot begin to count the number of times I have witnessed troubled men and women sigh in utter relief as they grasp the truth of this fact—that there really is a place for our pain to go. *Knowing* that there is a place for our pain to go enables us to face the possibility of letting our pain surface without being destroyed by it. *Believing* that there is a place for our pain to go provides us with a means outside our own failed efforts to be free for the first time. *Depositing the pain at Jesus' feet* puts us that much closer to our destination—wholeness in Christ!

Recently I joined a large group in praying a salvation prayer for several persons who wanted to receive Jesus as their Rescuer for the first time. In the midst of that prayer I had an inner vision of myself moving toward Jesus, who was nailed to the cross. My arms were outstretched wide, matching His, and I was giving myself permission to turn loose all my hindrances to wholeness. In that posture, unable to grasp anything into myself, I felt vulnerable as I approached Him. His eyes invited me to keep moving closer. I walked *into* Him, my form taking the shape of His form, until we were one. I felt all the heaviness I had carried with me flow right into His body, leaving me lighter, cleaner and newer. My sin moved from my body to His and He put it where it belonged. Then I felt us both lifted from the cross, joined together as one without the bulkiness of sin separating us.

Perhaps you have been unable or unwilling to face past or present acts, memories or events in your life because you are afraid that the pain of those memories will consume you, even destroy you. It is wise to ask a trusted prayer partner, pastor, therapist or counselor to assist you in getting this pain up and out and allowing it to go into Jesus. Many times the pain does indeed seem so terrible that we are sure, as Jonah was, that it is going to consume us. It is possible that the pain can be so intense that we may wish it would just devour us and get it over with. Many who have felt intense, consuming pain for years have finally found wholeness in their willingness to face into the pain and release it in a redemptive way.

God provides wonderful boundaries to protect our wounded spirits, souls and bodies until He knows we are ready to be healed. His timing is so perfect that we are wise not to force up memories ourselves or allow someone else to force up memories that

He knows we are not yet ready to deal with. If even now you feel overly fearful as painful memories begin to surface, fix your gaze firmly on your Lord, Jesus Christ, and say aloud to Him,

> Jesus, I ask for Your divine protection. You know the healing I seek and I trust You to place me in the secure safety of Your presence. I want my healing to come in the perfect time and place You have provided. Please bring strong men and women of prayer into my life to assist me on my journey to wholeness. Above all I ask You to place healthy, godly boundaries about me as I begin to let the pain of my past come to the surface. I want to place it in Your heart. I trust You, Lord Jesus, with my life.

Standing before the Cross

> Dear friends, do not be surprised at the painful trial you are suffering, as though something strange were happening to you. But rejoice that you participate in the sufferings of Christ, so that you may be overjoyed when his glory is revealed.
>
> 1 Peter 4:12–13

1. No matter where you are spiritually or emotionally right now, whether in pain, depression or anxiety, it will help you to write in your prayer journal a psalm to God, your very own "sacrifice of thanksgiving." Let it come from your heart of faith rather than from your mind of circumstances. Allow the character of God to be revealed in your prayer.
2. What promise from God continues to ring in your heart? Even though it may not seem to be a reality in your life yet, say it aloud as Jonah said the word from God in the city of Nineveh. Proclaim it. Write it in your prayer journal. Decide what you are going to do about this promise. Tell the Lord your intention and ask for His help to follow through.
3. Let your sins come up before you as you pray. Be honest about each one. Call each by its scriptural name, i.e., "committed adultery," not "had an affair"; "stolen," not "misappropriated funds"; "hated," not "responded in kind."

   Make a list of each sin the Lord shows you. Now give each sin to Jesus on the cross. Let yourself become one with Him. As you give up your sins, let His love and forgiveness flow into you, filling all your emptiness.

Day 29

Putting Anger in Its Place

A FRIEND WHOM I WILL CALL BARBARA HAD BEEN TO EVERY KIND OF SELF-help group and private therapist she could find. Some were admittedly "off-the-wall"; others had strong public reputations for respectability. Some claimed to be Christian, while others openly defied any acknowledgment of a being higher than the power of a person's own mind.

Barbara was searching desperately for an answer to the inner turmoil that had plagued her since the onset of abuse in her childhood. Therapist after therapist employed technique after technique to alleviate Barbara's suffering. She was asked to take pillows and punch them to get the anger out. In the depths of her fury she not only punched the pillows, she literally destroyed them, and was scarcely able to stop the attack. She rammed her fist into a wall, seriously injuring herself. She burned the backs of her hands and arms with lighted cigarettes. She screamed "primordial cries," chanting, burning incense and cursing aloud her assailants. She tried sex, alcohol and drugs. She drew pictures of sexual assault and demonic sexual images in an attempt to cleanse her mind of them.

After years of these techniques and thousands of dollars spent, Barbara came for healing prayer. She had developed such self-hatred, hatred of spiritual authority and a twisted perception of God that she was nearly unable to function as a normal human being.

At first Barbara was so angry at God she could not even say His name. In her mind He had allowed these things to happen. He was a masculine figure she could no longer trust.

But Barbara did allow me to pray for her and to tell her about the place her anger could go—to the cross. This was a surreal concept in her mind, but she was willing to hold a large crucifix I gave her as a visual symbol of what Jesus had done for her. She looked at it as I explained to her how Jesus' death on the cross provided the only place where we could leave our sin, pain, anger, shame and guilt. I explained to her that until she was willing to trust Him she would never find an outlet for all that was tormenting her without destroying herself.

Barbara had to think about this for a few days. She was making a major decision, and she had a lifetime of pain to get rid of. When she came again for healing prayer, she was willing to talk a little more and again I prayed for her to be set free in a miraculous way. It took several meetings before she had an overwhelming desire to forgive her enemies, accept the sacrifice Jesus was offering her and deposit all her pain in the one acceptable place, the cross of Christ.

Barbara is free today because she knows how and where to place the emotions that rise within. She is still being healed (now with the assistance of a good Christian therapist and a believing church), because God is gently revealing more and more of her childhood pain as she is ready and able to deal with it. A gifted artist, she now expresses her healing, not her pain, through her work.

Saved from the Pit

Barbara, like Jonah, tried to run away from the only One who could set her free. Only when both Barbara and Jonah were at the bottom of the pit were they willing to turn to His saving power. Barbara, like Jonah, also found she had to deal with "layers" of distrust toward God. What must have seemed to both Jonah and Barbara to be the most incredible rescues of all time from the very pits of their own hells turned out to be just the beginning of our Lord's unending love and patience for those who are willing to let Him restore their lives completely.

Barbara needed to hold up relationship after relationship to the light of the cross. She needed to confess, repent and receive forgiveness for many activities that had led her away from

God's presence. He did not require all of this at one sitting. He was incredibly patient. He lovingly and gently continues to reveal His character to her as He leads her on her journey to wholeness.

Jonah's rescue from the belly of the fish was but the first of many lessons he had to learn about the true character of God. It is God's nature to take us as far on the journey to wholeness as we are willing to travel. The journey is exciting and full of adventures and surprises. Just when we think we are in for a season of "cruise control," He reveals further areas of our lives in need of His refining, provides an experience that deepens our faith or allows us the opportunity to serve Him in some stunningly risky way for which we know we are totally inadequate, thus causing us to seek more of His power.

The Peace and Will of God

Once we have experienced salvation through Christ, and the resulting freedom from sin, most of us expect lives of relative peace. We love Isaiah 26:3: "Thou dost keep him in perfect peace, whose mind is stayed on thee" (RSV). But we soon find that peace is not necessarily the simple absence of conflict, as we might like to think. True peace is knowing we are in the will of God.

The peace only God can bestow can be found, surprisingly, in the most hectic of circumstances, when everything around us is going awry. God's peace can be present in the deepest sorrow or in the most difficult relationship. As Philippians 4:7 tells us, it "transcends all understanding."

Jesus said that the peace He was leaving to us was the same amazing peace He exhibited; it was not the peace of the world (John 14:27). Jesus' peace did not arise from a life without conflict, but from life totally yielded to the will of the Father.

You can know for a fact that you are in His will when you are allowing Him to refine you and draw you closer to the divine image. You can and will experience the peace of God while you are in the midst of being healed, even while He still has much to do to perfect His image in you.

Standing before the Cross

Continue to work out your salvation with fear and trembling, for it is God who works in you to will and to act according to his good purpose.

Philippians 2:12–13

1. With your prayer journal in hand, think about all the ways you have tried to mask, project or deny anger (or any other sin that is persistent in your life). Have you thought not talking about it or thinking about it would make it go away? When it gets too intense, do you project it onto those closest to you? If you stay extremely active, do you hope you will have no time to think about your pain? Have you tried to harm yourself in an effort to appease the pain? How have you opted for the peace "of the world" rather than the will of the Father and the peace of Christ?

   Any of these actions or reactions indicate that you have not taken your pain, anger or other sin to the one acceptable place Jesus has provided—the cross.

2. Read Ephesians 4:17–32, a section in which Saint Paul writes about living as children of light. Write in your prayer journal the parts you know apply to you, especially those having to do with anger.

3. Now that you know what to do with your anger, identify who or what you are really angry with and deposit your heavy burden at the cross. See Jesus take it from you and allow it to flow right into His body.

4. Sing the song of the redeemed as you straighten up from kneeling at the cross. Even if you do not see yourself as a songwriter, write your own special song of thanksgiving to Jesus in your journal, and give yourself permission to sing it to Him. It does not have to rhyme in your head; it has to resonate in your heart.

Day 30

Grumbling at God

JONAH COULD RECOGNIZE AND APPRECIATE THE MERCY AND KINDNESS OF individual Gentiles, such as the pagan sailors he met on the ship to Tarshish. They were genuinely concerned for him, and even though they eventually threw him overboard, they tried every means they knew to preserve his life. One on one he had no problem with believing that individual Gentiles could be worthy of God's grace.

But watching a whole city of Gentiles being saved was quite another story. When Jonah saw the Ninevites repent and receive God's grace and salvation, he was so angry with God!

> "O LORD, is this not what I said when I was still at home? That is why I was so quick to flee to Tarshish. I knew that you are a gracious and compassionate God, slow to anger and abounding in love, a God who relents from sending calamity. Now, O LORD, take away my life, for it is better for me to die than to live."
>
> Jonah 4:2–3

Jonah was so furious he wanted to die! His deep, deep anger did not spring up overnight. His whole life had been based on a certain perception of God, and now God was teaching him a lesson totally radical to his way of thinking: He was to forgive his enemies! It was inconceivable! God was supposed to be angry at the Gentiles, not have mercy on them.

A Radical Teaching

When Jesus sat on a mountainside one day and taught His disciples, one subject He discussed was this:

> You have heard that it was said, "Love your neighbor and hate your enemy." But I tell you: Love your enemies and pray for those who persecute you, that you may be sons of your Father in heaven.
>
> Matthew 5:43–44

This was revolutionary teaching for Jews, who had been raised with the same values as Jonah. But Jesus had a reputation for doing radical things and giving radical teachings. He offered healing and deliverance to one of the hated Canaanites (Matthew 15:22–28). He offered the living water of eternal life to a village woman in the detested area of Samaria (John 4:4–42). He taught that one day people would come from east, west, north and south (meaning Gentiles) to take their places at the celebration feast of salvation in the Kingdom of God (Luke 13:29). He described Himself not just as the light of Israel, but as the light of the whole world, and offered any person who would follow Him the light of life (John 8:12). All these statements inflamed the Jewish leaders.

When Jonah saw God's compassion on the repentant city of Nineveh and the way He spared their lives after threatening destruction, Jonah was incensed in the same way the Pharisees were incensed by Jesus. Both God the Father and Son were challenging the traditions of the Hebrew patriarchs. Both God the Father and Son were redefining the facts upon which the Hebrews had based their lives. And both God the Father and Son were digging up the very foundations of the Hebrews' belief systems.

God Woos the Grumbler

Yes, Jonah was furious with God. The Ninevites had turned their hearts to the Lord and His wrath had lifted. Gentiles were receiving the gift supposedly reserved only for Hebrews. He knew in his heart that Nineveh was not going to be destroyed, but as we read the story we watch the grumbling prophet walk outside the city and sit down in a place where he would have a view of the destruction—just in case. Because he planned to wait until God's original timetable had been fulfilled, he made himself a shelter from the hot sun.

God, still loving His grumbling prophet, caused a quick-growing vine to spring up, giving Jonah even more shade and showing him that the door to intimacy with Himself was still open if he cared to confess and enter it. Jonah loved the vine's shade, and in the heat of a desert afternoon it may have saved his body from heat stroke. He was happy with his "good fortune," but was so preoccupied with himself that he failed to recognize the vine as a gift from God.

Twenty-five hundred years later, we see in this small act of giving the vine that God's character always loves, woos us to Himself, forgives, reconciles and restores right relationship.

God, the persistent Lover of each heart, continued to woo Jonah back to Himself, this time by another tactic. At dawn the next day He caused a worm to eat the vine so that it withered and died. By the time the heat of the day was at its zenith, Jonah was feeling faint. Remembering the cool shade he had enjoyed just 24 hours before, his deep-seated anger rekindled. Why had "his" vine been taken away?

Dramatic as ever, Jonah grumbled away, wanting to die rather than to endure discomfort. Then God spoke to him, asking, "Do you have a right to be angry about the vine?"

Jonah's answer was quick and intense: "I do. I am angry enough to die" (Jonah 4:9).

At this response our loving God delivered the punch line:

> "You have been concerned about this vine, though you did not tend it or make it grow. It sprang up overnight and died overnight. But Nineveh has more than a hundred and twenty thousand people who cannot tell their right hand from their left [small children], and many cattle as well. Should I not be concerned about that great city?"
>
> Jonah 4:10–11

Defining the Problem

Once again imagine yourself as the storyteller. You come dramatically to the conclusion of Jonah's intriguing story and your listeners lean toward you in complete attention. What wisdom will God give Jonah?

There is no nice, neat resolution or "happily ever after" tacked onto the end of this story. God leaves us with a poignant question: "Should I not be concerned about that great city?" Hebrew listeners who identified with Jonah would probably have responded with a loud no! But they had a dilemma: To say no to God now would be embarrassing.

God's divine love went into the creation of each individual who resided in Nineveh, just as it went into each inhabitant of Israel. His heart cried as each one turned away from Him, and He longed to be reconciled. Yes, He had invested heavily in the establishment of a holy nation, one that would personify His own character. But He also had a larger plan to reconcile the whole world to Himself, the true God, so all other nations of the world would be drawn to the truth.

We are not told what happened to Jonah, but God's main concern is our response. He asks, "What does this mean to *you* with your hatreds, prejudices and fears?"

God wants us to take our anger, hatred, prejudice and fear to the cross, where He will set us free from the invasive, malignant discontent of our hearts.

Standing before the Cross

> You are all sons of God through faith in Christ Jesus, for all of you who were baptized into Christ have clothed yourselves with Christ. There is neither Jew nor Greek, slave nor free, male nor female, for you are all one in Christ Jesus.
>
> Galatians 3:26–28

1. Who is your "Nineveh"? Is it a particular denomination? A particular race? A certain type of sinner? Define where your anger and prejudice are directed. Can you show mercy toward individuals from a given group when you know their circumstances and problems, but feel intolerant toward the group as a whole?

2. Are the foundations of your life crumbling? Upon what foundation are your faith, strength and courage built? On tradition? On habit? On superstition? On total reliance on

Jesus Christ? Read Matthew 7:24–29 to receive Jesus' own words on this subject.

3. Do you think God should have been concerned about the great city of Nineveh? Do you think God should be concerned about you? Do you think God should be concerned about your worst enemy?

4. Before we took off on this journey to wholeness I told you that one intercessory prayer section in my prayer journal is labeled "Beloved Enemies." Would you consider beginning that kind of prayer discipline? In your prayer journal write a prayer for the person(s) who continually comes to your mind when you think of an "enemy."

Day 31

Covered with Love

W‍HEN YOU AND I ARE IN PAIN WE ARE ALMOST GUARANTEED A FREE RIDE on an emotional roller coaster. Our feelings and judgments careen wildly out of control and we lose our ability to see things around us objectively; it does not take much to pitch us into deep depression. Emotional, spiritual and physical pain turn us inward until we are literally consumed by self: self-pity, self-righteousness, self-hatred, self-centeredness—everything but self-control.

Jonah learned that the hell of self could be a far worse hell than the bottom of the sea or the belly of a big fish. In fact, when faced with sure and certain death in the depths of the waters, he turned his face to God and cried out with true devotion to his Creator. But in the hell of self, when things did not go his way and he was feeling petulant, God was far from his thoughts.

Receiving God's Gifts

Jonah was a gifted man, one God had used to prophesy to King Jeroboam II concerning the restoration of land to Israel (2 Kings 14:25). God had singled him out and used him to build up His kingdom. Jonah had the gift of prophecy, but his heart did not yet beat as one with God's.

God's gifts do not change our hearts. Only confession, forgiveness and repentance can accomplish this incredible change as we yield ourselves to God's will. In 1 Corinthians chapter 12

212

Paul describes speaking in tongues, interpretation of tongues, prophecy, divine knowledge, divine wisdom, faith, healing, miracles and the discerning of other spirits as gifts given and directed for use by the Holy Spirit. All of these gifts can bring marvelous renewal and restoration to the lives of God's children. But, as Paul went on to say in his famous "love chapter," 1 Corinthians 13, they are outward signs of an inner and invisible quality that God tells us is far more important—love.

Love was clearly the quality that was missing in Jonah's attitude toward the Ninevites. God used him anyway because He wanted to accomplish a larger purpose, and He will use us and others for His larger purposes if we will be obedient. But the benefits for those of us entrusted with the gifts are sadly shallow if they are not undergirded with love. Saint Paul says gifts minus love sound like clanging cymbals and sounding gongs, and we gain nothing (13:1–3).

So even if we are used mightily by God, even if we have prayed for many who are healed, even if we see miracles in our ministries and have the faith to move mountains, we must always seek the source of love, Jesus Christ Himself. Only by spending daily, intimate time with Him will we learn how to love. Only by immersing ourselves in His Word can we understand love. Only by praising and worshiping Him for no other reason than that He is God can we begin to experience love.

Defining Love Aright

What is love? Many individuals who have had no earthly model of godly love in their lives are at a loss to comprehend it. They may have learned to manipulate others to get their needs met, and, confusing the deviously earned response they receive for real love, find it less than satisfying. Some have sought physical intimacy, grasping a temporary emotional fix and mistakenly calling it love. Numerous men and women are downright suspicious of love because of their past experiences, believing it to be too demanding and destructive.

Love is not easy to define. You know it when you see it. You know it when you experience it. You know it when it flows through you, but it is not easily captured. It took Saint Paul a whole chapter of the Bible to tell us what it is. He described love as patient,

213

kind, not envious, not boastful, not proud, not rude, not self-seeking, not easily angered. He said love keeps no record of wrong-doings, does not delight in evil, rejoices with truth, protects, trusts, always hopes, always perseveres and never fails.

Do you understand now why I say outright that Jonah did not carry the gift of prophecy to the Ninevites with love? It is easy to measure his life against the standard God has set. But sometimes it is not as easy to measure our own. To get an accurate measurement of love in our lives we need to look, not within our hearts, but straight up to Jesus, the One who knows our hearts better than we know them ourselves. He will reveal to us the areas of our lives that are love-starved, love-deficient. And He is eager to share with us His limitless resources of love.

Imaging Love

As you begin your quest to receive more of God's love into your being, begin by taking time alone, in quietness, to see God as your heavenly Father. Ask Him to anoint your holy imagination to see Him in a loving, nurturing way. Give yourself permission to be a little child, walking, maybe even running, up to Him to get to know Him better.

If you fear Him, He who embodies love will be patient and kind. Since He is not easily angered, keeps no record of wrongs and does not delight in evil, you can tell Him how you feel.

Remember, because He is love, He will always protect you, trust you and persevere for you. Let yourself crawl up into His lap. Feel yourself relax in His strong, cherishing embrace. Perhaps you need to explore His face, feel His hands, let your ear hear the beat of His heart against you. Little by little, be aware of letting more and more of your full weight down on His lap, relaxing in His presence. I guarantee you that God will not be the first one to move!

You are His beloved and He delights to have you come to Him as a little child.

Perhaps it is new for you to see your Father God in this way. God's Word is full of imagery of His fatherly and motherly nurture toward us.

"As a mother comforts her child, so will I comfort you. . . ."
Isaiah 66:13

"See, I have engraved you on the palms of my hands. . . ."
Isaiah 49:16

And Jesus cried out passionately to the Pharisees:

"How often I have longed to gather your children together, as a hen gathers her chicks under her wings. . . ."
Luke 13:34

Perhaps it is difficult for you to use your imagination for such holy intimacy. Even though you may have cleansed your imagination just ten days ago, you may still be plagued with unholy images as you begin to picture your heavenly Father in this way. This does not mean nothing happened when you asked God for cleansing. Because of the world in which we live, we all need to cleanse our minds, hearts and imaginations regularly. Eventually we will monitor our intake with more discipline as we get used to the refreshment and freedom of the cleansed condition in which we can experience more and more of God's presence.

Standing before the Cross

Let us draw near to God with a sincere heart in full assurance of faith, having our hearts sprinkled to cleanse us from a guilty conscience and having our bodies washed with pure water.
Hebrews 10:22

1. If you had trouble seeing God, your Father, and sitting on His lap, ask Him to cleanse your imagination. Then try using your holy imagination again.
2. In your prayer journal write out Saint Paul's definition of love from 1 Corinthians 13. Use it as a standard of measurement in each relationship that comes to your mind. If you find love missing, ask the source of love, Jesus, to fill the empty place where you need love most.
3. Be sure to include yourself in your list of relationships that need to be covered with love. You cannot love your neighbor with godly love if you do not know how to love yourself with God's love, too. Read Luke 10:27, inserting the appropriate names.

Day 32

The Vine and the Worm

GOD CONDUCTED A SPIRITUAL THERAPY SESSION WITH JONAH AS HE SAT AT the edge of Nineveh waiting to see how God would act toward that repentant city. Jonah thought he had removed himself from the pressure under which he had been operating. He thought he could be an observant bystander for a period while he nursed his terminal case of self-pity. He was disappointed with God, confused and angry. He wanted to be alone where he could entertain all the destructive emotions coming up in his heart.

When we give in to our obsession with self, we look just like Jonah. We isolate ourselves so no one can interfere, try to talk us into a more rational approach to a situation or (heaven forbid!) pray for us. It is easy for this kind of behavior to develop into a full-blown depression.

Jonah had never really understood the true depths of God's love. He had tasted it at times, and he had talked about it, but he had defined it too narrowly, confining it to a space far smaller than the magnitude of God. God's therapy for Jonah was a tangible illustration of how much greater God's love was and is than what Jonah was willing to contain.

The Divine Therapy

God almost seemed to be playing right into Jonah's neurosis by pampering him with a shady vine, giving him comfort in his petulance. Jonah, still occupied with self, was only happy not to suffer from the day's intense heat. Then God sent the worm to eat the vine, causing it to wither and die. He also sent a scorching east wind and a bright sun, causing such intense desert weather conditions that Jonah felt faint, as if he were going to die. Now the conditions were right for God to reach Jonah's heart. He had set up a scenario that would speak to His distraught servant in an unmistakable way.

"Do you have a right to be angry about the vine?" came God's simple question.

All of Jonah's indignation, anger, disappointment, discouragement, sense of failure, confusion and anxiety erupted in his response.

"I do. I am angry enough to die."

Letting the Symbol Lead the Way

God has presented the vine and the worm to Jonah as a symbolic situation capturing the essence of his problem: that Jonah has not looked past himself, his home and his country to see God's limitless love. God is showing Jonah in a graphic way that until he expands his perception of who God is, his self-worth will diminish.

Over and over I pray with men and women who are stuck in their own self-pity, unable to see the larger picture of how they got where they are. They continue to focus exclusively on the present problem—their "vine and worm"—and completely ignore God's presence, which is available to show them the true source of their pain. Only when we face the true source of our pain and name it for what it is can our healing begin. Only when we are willing to take that pain to the foot of the cross and hand it to Jesus can we be set free, once and for all, from its effects.

Lydia's Story

A woman I will call Lydia had entered into numerous lesbian relationships seeking female affirmation to make up for the inadequacies she felt as a woman. Directing her anger toward her mother as the source of her problems, she talked at length about how her mother had never understood her, how she seemed to find fault with Lydia's appearance and everything she did. Lydia's anger toward her mother had become obsessive, but I could discern no glaring sin or obvious neglect in the relationship.

217

In prayer we asked God to reveal a symbolic event that would pinpoint the root of Lydia's self-hatred, neediness and depression. God brought immediately to her memory a specific evening when, as a young teenager, she was sitting on the sofa with her father watching television. Her mother was sitting in a chair across the room. Two of her girlfriends came to the front door and when they entered the room her father, showing off, grabbed her, pinned her under his body on the sofa and began kissing her on the mouth.

One friend cried out, "Mr. _____, what are you doing?"

He raised his body, leered at the assembled group and said, "Making love to my daughter."

Lydia was humiliated and embarrassed and tried to hide her shame by acting as if her father's actions were a big joke. No one in her family ever mentioned the incident again, and Lydia had not thought of it in years. It was a despicable thing for a father to do to a daughter even in jest, but it was an isolated, albeit bizarre, occurrence.

Now, as Lydia recalled the event, God showed her that down deep in her heart she had disassociated herself from her mother, her model and link to the true feminine. Why? Because her mother, who was in the room, had refused to defend her, protect her or explain to her friends that nothing had really happened. Her mother's stunned silence spoke "acceptance" of the act to a young teenager.

Because Lydia had cut herself off at that point from her mother's affirmation she began to be attracted to the feminine in other women. In her twenties she finally began to act out her neediness, desperately seeking feminine affirmation and, at the same time, despising herself for needing it.

To be set free, Lydia had to forgive both her father and her mother, and confess her sinful behavior to God. The memory of that incident with her father became her symbol, the "vine and worm" God used to bring a remarkable healing in her life.

Larry's Story

Larry (not his real name) was a middle-aged, successful businessman who had struggled with and overcome problems with alcohol and financial bankruptcy. His marriage, which had been

218

shaky, now appeared to be on solid ground, and he was making a sizable contribution to his church and community.

But Larry continued to struggle with a sense of failure he could not shake. He wavered in and out of mild depression and negativism. Many strong Christian friends prayed with him regularly, encouraging and affirming him, but Larry could not seem to maintain a positive attitude for long.

The "vine and worm" God brought into Larry's life to show him an important truth about himself was comprised of two memories from his childhood.

One was from his early years, when his mother refused to cut his hair and persisted in dressing him in girl's clothing, pretending that her second son was the little girl she had longed for so desperately.

The other painful memory occurred when he was about twelve years old. Several boys at the private school he attended teased him unmercifully about his appearance, and one day during recess on the playground, they stripped him down to his underwear, handcuffed him to the goal posts on the football field and left him there when the bell rang.

As he held up both these memories to the light of Jesus, Larry saw that his innate sense of failure, one he had almost willed to be played out to the hilt in his adulthood, had its foundations in vivid impressions others made on him in his early years. Although Larry was in every sense masculine through and through, with no temptations toward homosexuality, he had been made to feel like a failure early in his life for being born a male instead of the desired female. His sense of failure to "be" was reinforced later on when the boys teased him for physical traits he could help no more than he could change his gender.

Larry had to forgive his parents and the boys who had tormented him. In the process, he even went back to the site of the place where he had been so humiliated and asked Jesus to resymbolize the place and the event for him in the light of God's healing power.

Marian's Story

Marian (not her real name) found complete release from her longtime distrust of men and God while kneeling at the altar in a church she visited not long ago, one far more formal than her regular place of worship. When she was invited to come to the altar, kneel and receive the bread and wine of holy Communion as the priest offered them to each communicant, she first felt reluctant. When she finally went to the altar and knelt there, waiting, she sensed panic about receiving the body and blood of Christ from this man, the priest. The panic seemed irrational, but she realized she was actually afraid of the priest coming toward her with the bread. Not knowing if she should run or stay, she allowed the priest to place the bread in her hand.

As she ate the body of Christ, Marian recalled the rejection she once felt from a minister whom she had trusted implicitly. He had wounded her without cause, and in that wounding she had felt God the Father Himself rejecting her as well.

Marian realized that as she anticipated the priest at the altar giving her bread, she also anticipated his reprimand and rejection. Immediately she made the connection to her attitude concerning intimacy with God the Father: She had always distanced herself from Him to avoid the reprimand she felt would eventually come.

This important revelation renewed and strengthened Marian's relationship with God, the source of all her healing. She had experienced *anamnesis,* a Greek word used to explain the theology of the holy Communion. According to Leanne Payne in her book *Restoring the Christian Soul,* anamnesis

> denotes bringing forward into the present an event from out of the past, and like our Lord's statement "This is My Body, this is My Blood," it is not merely an act of psychological remembrance.

Marian was so excited by her restoration to the Father that she burst into tears of joy as she returned to her pew, unable to contain her newfound freedom with her God.

Receiving God's Therapy

Lydia's "healing of memories," Larry's "resymbolized childhood" and Marian's "anamnesis" are ways in which God often drops a "vine and worm" in our midst so He can uncover misconceptions, often lifelong ones, that keep us from the wholeness we seek. Openness and vulnerability to God's ability to redeem are the keys. When we decide we do not want or need what God has to offer, we cut ourselves off from that for which we are starving. When we decide our condition is beyond God's ability to act, we shut the door in His face.

Are you willing to allow the pain to surface, to let the memories return to your conscious mind? Do you know that the Master Therapist is willing to work with you for as long as it takes, and that you can release all that does not belong in your heart at the cross in the Body of our Lord Jesus Christ? Answering "yes" to both questions will take you farther on the journey to wholeness than you have ever thought possible.

Standing before the Cross

Bear in mind that our Lord's patience means salvation.
2 Peter 3:15

1. When you are in real need, do you tend to isolate yourself from those who would be willing to help you? Are you willing to spend time with Jesus today, asking Him to show you when and where that pattern was established in your life? As memories surface, be sure to keep the image of the cross firmly before you.
2. Write all that Jesus shows you in your prayer journal.

Region 6
Coming into Freedom
from the Bondages of My Past

BASED ON THE EXPERIENCES OF MOSES, AS FOUND IN THE
BOOK OF EXODUS

Day 33

Nothing Is Impossible

DO YOU FEEL HOPELESSLY TRAPPED BY "FATE" BECAUSE OF THE FAMILY INTO which you were born, circumstances of which you have involuntarily been a part, a difficult physical characteristic or a string of bad choices? Do you feel as if a death sentence hangs over your head? How can you overcome such impossible "odds"? How can you become whole with so many strikes against you?

For the next few days we are going to spend time with God, asking Him to untangle our complicated pasts and redeem the destructive patterns of behavior that have been part of our history. To do this we need to become well-acquainted with a hero from the Old Testament—Moses. His life will illustrate amply many of the excuses we hold up to God.

Let's look at Moses' family history. Jacob, the Hebrew patriarch, had migrated into Egypt with seventy members of his family to escape famine in Canaan (Genesis 46). Because of God's favor toward them through Jacob's son Joseph, an official in Egypt, the Hebrews not only survived, but were granted good health and a huge increase in population: From a family of seventy they grew to a people of hundreds of thousands in only 430 years.

Once the memory of Joseph's importance faded, the Hebrews were enslaved by the Egyptians (Exodus 1:1–14). Their labor became increasingly important to their masters in the areas of commerce and industry, but the Egyptians also feared the Hebrews' numbers and physical strength. Healthy and hard-working, the Hebrew women gave birth easily, and their children survived childbirth and infancy better than those of the Egyptians (Exodus 1:19). It is not surprising that the Hebrews' prolific strength caused Pharaoh to want them closely controlled. As Moses came on the scene, the Egyptian ruler had become so concerned that he issued a command: All newborn Hebrew males were to be put to death to curtail the burgeoning population of their race (Exodus 1:22).

Moses' Story

Through no fault of his own, therefore, Moses was born into a horrible kind of bondage. The innocent child of a devout Hebrew couple, Jochebed and Amram, Moses had a death sentence on his head from the moment he drew his first breath.

Moses had an older sister, Miriam, and an older brother, Aaron, whose births had preceded the Pharaoh's death sentence. Jochebed desperately wanted to save her new baby's life, so with the help of her family she hid Moses for three months. Unable to keep her secret any longer (and most certainly with God's inspiration) she devised an ingenious plan to save her son. She wrapped him in his baby blanket, carefully placed him in a hand-made basket of papyrus and clay and, undoubtedly praying prayers of blessing and protection, set him afloat in the Nile River. She assigned Miriam the task of running along the shore, keeping the baby in sight until she could know how God would provide for him.

Miriam, raised by religious Hebrews, had been taught of God's mercy to His people, of His divine providence and protection for those who trusted Him. I am sure that as she watched through the bulrushes she prayed for little Moses to be delivered from those who wished to kill him.

How frightened Miriam must have been when the basket floated right into the area where the royal family did their wash! Her breath must have stopped as she secretly watched Pharaoh's daughter herself discover the treasure in the river.

Was Pharaoh's daughter childless? Was she praying to her own gods for a child? Was she asking for her own miracle?

Whatever the circumstances of her heart, God was in control. As soon as she saw Moses, the royal princess felt a surge of love

226

for him. Overwhelmed by maternal instincts she decided to take baby Moses into the royal palace to raise him as her own child. (See Exodus 2:1–10.)

Divine wisdom prompted Miriam to approach the princess and offer to find a Hebrew woman to be the baby's wet nurse. Thus God provided a miraculous way for Jochebed to nurse and care for her own child, to see him raised with every advantage and protection and at the same time to be able to teach him the ways of his own people and the one true God.

Overwhelming Odds

Only by a true miracle of God could all the circumstances of Moses' remarkable salvation from certain death have been accomplished. It was a "sure fact" that he would die as an infant, yet he lived. It was a "sure fact" that if he happened to survive he would be a slave in Pharaoh's service; yet he grew up within the walls of the royal palace, loved and cared for by the royal princess, educated by the royal tutors and privy to the most intimate knowledge of the cultural and business affairs of the Egyptian kingdom. It was a "sure fact" that if he could gain access into the royal family he would have to disclaim his Hebrew heritage and practice the pagan worship of the Egyptians. Yet he was cared for by his own birth mother, who instilled in him the true worship of God, how to hear His voice, how to sacrifice to Him in pleasing ways and how to become a man after His own heart.

Lindsay's Story

Some time ago I met a twenty-two-year-old I will call Lindsay. She told me a story she had heard many times in her life. It went like this:

At Lindsay's birth her paternal grandmother had come to the home to declare that from that day on her son, his wife and their new baby girl would no longer be part of the family. They were disinherited, shamed, no longer recognized as family members. They were to be thought of as dead. Neither Lindsay nor her parents ever saw the grandmother again.

The little family moved to another town and struggled to make a new life. Other children were born. The mother and father attempted to live normally, but the grandmother's death sentence hung over their heads. Affection for each other ceased. No touching, no affirmation, no love passed between family members. Lindsay suffered greatly from her parents' passivity and coldness.

Lindsay forced herself to be outgoing and personable, and few people suspected the insecurities, unstable emotions and deep confusion that lurked in her heart. She either avoided close relationships altogether or greatly envied individuals who seemed to possess the very things she desired so deeply. She became a lovely-looking yet broken, lonely young woman. She followed the pattern set by her family, and although she struggled to be free, she resigned herself to a life with no security.

When Lindsay came for healing prayer she was seeking a place in full-time mission work. Never having felt adequate, she thought more and more commitment would give her the "place" she so desperately desired. She shoved her personal needs out of sight in order to give the impression that she was more committed to serving God than anyone else. But when I looked with God's eyes deep into her heart, I saw a miserable young woman.

The Healing Power of Symbol and Memory

When we asked God to bring up the one memory that would allow Him the opportunity to minister healing in Lindsay's life, He immediately showed her the day of her birth, the day of her paternal grandmother's visit. Lindsay "saw" the curse that had been placed on her family as a long, black snake coming into her even as her grandmother spoke, coiling around her heart and growing with her as she matured. She had no doubt that this evil woman's curse was the source of her lifelong struggles with inadequacy, no true sense of being and a constant feeling of unworthiness.

As Lindsay realized the hideous truth of what had happened she began to hyperventilate; her heart raced and she was heaving physically. I asked her to name the snake she saw in the Spirit. What did she think it represented? Immediately she said it was a spirit of hatred so tightly wound around her she could not get free. Its primary target was her own soul. She coughed and choked as though the snake would certainly take her life.

I told Lindsay that the only way she could successfully get rid of the snake was to forgive her grandmother in Jesus' name. She could not do so in her own power or compassion, for she had neither in sufficient quantities. Rather, the holy power of Jesus Christ who lived within her would make the forgiveness possible. This in no way would condone what her grandmother had done or excuse the years of heartache and evil that had come as a result of her actions. But it would free Lindsay from the effects of that evil so she could become the young woman God had always intended her to be.

Lindsay literally choked on the words, but she got them out: "In Jesus' name I forgive my grandmother. In His power I forgive her for all the evil she inflicted on my family."

I made the sign of the cross on Lindsay's forehead with holy oil (blessed for healing by the prayers of the Church) and pronounced her forgiven and set free from her grandmother and all the evil her grandmother represented, according to her confession (1 John 1:9).

I then told Lindsay that now, in the name of Jesus, she could renounce the curse placed on her and on her family. Neither unforgiveness nor sin bound her to the curse, and it had no place in the life of a forgiven child of God.

Literally gasping for breath, Lindsay screamed out the words, "I renounce the curse of my grandmother in Jesus' name!" As she did, she "saw" the snake's long, black coils being pulled up out of her by a divine hand. She made physical motions to "help Him get it all up and out," and when it was gone she knew it. She relaxed in my arms, began to breathe normally and regained a healthy color. I then took holy water (blessed and prayed over with the ancient prayers of the Church) and washed her clean from the evil that had attempted to consume her. It was a powerful symbol and reminder of the baptismal waters that had given her new life. We prayed for the new life of the Holy Spirit to enter her, especially every place where hatred had formerly dwelt.

We saw a miraculous transformation in Lindsay within only a few moments. This was, after all, a major deliverance from a lifetime of evil spoken over a family. Lindsay felt "normal" for the first time in her life, and said over and over, "I am free! I am free!"

Her whole demeanor changed and within her heart a remarkable transformation occurred. She was now free to become the woman God had been calling her to be all her life.

God's Divine Plan

What were the "odds" of this miracle happening to Lindsay? Even if she had recognized her grandmother's evil, could she have changed her own heart? Even if she had desired to be set free from the curse over her family, could she have done it on her own? Every part of this incredible healing was according to God's divine plan.

God was remarkably in control of Moses' life, and against all odds saved him from the curse of the bondage and the death sentence to which he was born. God was also in control of Lindsay's life, despite the curse of death and "nonbeing" her grandmother intended.

And God is in control of your life. He is not willing to give up on you until His will is accomplished, even if, according to the world's "odds," that is highly unlikely!

There is no bondage from our past that God cannot and will not redeem. Many of us have not yet dared to realize the freedom God has for us. Do you feel like "circumstances will never change," "people are always going to be the way they are," "memories will always be there to haunt and taunt" or "scars of the past never heal"? Does your life struggle seem impossible? Ask God this week for a miracle in your heart. If you do not have the faith to pray for yourself, then pray this prayer with me:

> Lord Jesus, I am desperate. I cannot even put words to all that is wrong inside me. But I ask You to give me a beginning place to start the healing. I will not try to tackle it all at once. I will wait for You to deal with each situation and problem as You will. I will spend time with You each day so I can begin to hear Your voice and know it is You speaking, not my own unhealed heart.
>
> Lord, I will give You as long as it takes to make me whole. I acknowledge that You and You alone can allow me to be the person You created me to be, the person I want to be with all my heart. I ask for a miracle of Your love to come inside me so I can respond

to You as You direct. I believe this miracle will happen and I am excited about what You and I are going to accomplish together! I pray this in Jesus' name, Amen.

Coming into Freedom

"The LORD does not look at the things man looks at. Man looks at the outward appearance, but the LORD looks at the heart."

1 Samuel 16:7

1. If, after praying the above prayer, you experience thoughts, memories or vivid impressions, write them in your prayer journal. Even if the thoughts are cloudy or incomplete, write them down and ask God to fill in the blanks for you as you sit in His presence. Do not strive. The object is to be in His presence, not to get a clear answer.
2. In your journal, list any impossible situation, circumstances or people in your life on which you have given up—even if you believe they are "sure facts." Give each one to Jesus for safekeeping. They are now no longer just your problems: They are also His.

Day 34

An Encounter with Holiness

INTO EACH OF OUR LIVES COMES ONE PARTICULAR "AHA" MOMENT WHEN we know we have come face to face with the living God, when we encounter holiness. When that happens, we know we can neither deny His existence nor continue to live untouched by the encounter.

For many of us such an encounter will come in this lifetime; for the rest it will surely come in the afterlife. Unfortunately this time of "reckoning" often comes only after we have so damaged our souls that we are desperate for help.

Moses was desperate when he had his encounter with holiness.

Under royal tutelage Moses had grown into a responsible young man. He had been given some degree of supervision over the Hebrew slaves, but his heart was always tender toward his own people, whom his birth mother had taught him to love and respect.

It is possible that Moses' adopted mother (who was most likely Queen Hatshepsut) tried to insist that Moses be made Pharaoh. God did not allow this, for Moses certainly would have had to renounce the religion of the Hebrews. We know he never forsook the deep respect for the holiness of the one true God that had surrounded his life since his conception.

One day, perhaps while Moses was supervising some Hebrew slaves at work, he observed an Egyptian beating a Hebrew. Deep rage rose up within him at all the injustices committed against his people, and in a fit of anger he killed the Egyptian. Thinking no one saw his deed, he hid the man's body in the sand.

232

The next day as Moses walked among the slave laborers he observed two Hebrew slaves fighting each other. He questioned them about their dispute, but they resented his intrusion. They also told him they had seen him kill the Egyptian, and asked if he was now going to kill them as well.

Moses panicked when he realized his act had been discovered. The Pharaoh was told, and he put a death warrant on Moses' head. Moses could do nothing but flee the country, so he went to live in exile in the desert of Midian (Exodus 2:11–15).

While he was there, now in bondage to his impetuous past, Moses had his face-to-face encounter with the holiness of God (Exodus 3:1–6). In the middle of an ordinary day, while doing an ordinary task (watching sheep for the father of the woman he had married after arriving in Midian), Moses observed from a distance that a common bush on the side of Mount Horeb was ablaze, but was not being consumed by the fire. It was a most unusual sight, so Moses went closer to have a look. Then he heard God's voice:

"Moses! Moses!"

"Here I am," answered Moses.

"Do not come any closer," God told him. "Take off your sandals, for the place where you are standing is holy ground. I am the God of your father, the God of Abraham, the God of Isaac and the God of Jacob."

Moses knew then that he had encountered the true living God, the same God his mother had told him about as she nursed him. He removed his shoes and stood barefoot in the awesome presence of the God of his fathers.

Moses knew that to be barefoot was the sign of slavery. Hebrew slaves wore no shoes, and Moses would have made the connection right away: God was the supreme Master of all creation and in His presence all were as slaves to His authority.

Moses saw a powerful symbol that day in the bush that burned, but was not destroyed. He, too, could be purified, purged, cleansed by the fire of God, but not destroyed.

The Burning Bush in Your Life

Look at Isaiah 43. Realize that the same God who spoke to Moses is speaking to you about how He desires to purify your past.

"Fear not, for I have redeemed you; I have summoned you by name; you are mine. When you pass through the waters, I will be with you; and when you pass through the rivers, they will not sweep over you. When you walk through the fire, you will not be burned; the flames will not set you ablaze. . . . You are precious and honored in my sight, and . . . I love you."

Isaiah 43:1–4

Why will the bush blaze and not be consumed? Why will I pass through waters and not be swept away? How will I walk through fire and not be burned? How can I be cast down and not forsaken? Grievously tempted, but not destroyed? How can my past be so despicable and yet not damage me beyond repair?

Because God Himself is in the midst of all these circumstances and situations!

Where God is, is sacred. When we encounter God, we take off our shoes in humility before Him as Moses did, humbly acknowledging we are mere slaves in comparison to His majesty.

The book of Numbers tells us why Moses knew to do this: "Moses was a very humble man, more humble than anyone else on the face of the earth" (12:3).

If we do not learn to stand humbly before our God, even—and especially—in the glaring face of our sinful past, we will be consumed by the world, the flesh and the devil. Humility will help us break free from bondages that would hold us to the past.

A Word from the Fire

My friend Clay McLean taught about the power of forgiveness one night at an out-of-town church. Tired after a long day, he was more than ready to get to his hotel at the end of the meeting. But a determined, angry-looking woman blocked his exit from the building.

"Reverend McLean," she said, "if you knew the circumstances of my childhood, the way my stepfather and my brothers systematically raped me every night of my life from about age eight until I could move out of the house at about age fifteen, you would never ask me to forgive them. How dare you suggest such a thing?"

Clay said that in his fatigue he humbly gave himself entirely to the power of the Spirit. The following reply came from his heart.

"Yes, ma'am, but if you don't forgive them in the power of Jesus, they will continue to rape you every day of your life."

That night the woman forgave her stepfather and brothers and was set free from her past.

This is how we can live through heartbreaking tragedy and not be consumed. God brings His holy presence into the midst of the ordinary and stands with us, redeeming the impossible, healing the destroyed, blessing the broken.

In the midst of such a circumstance the holiness of God spoke to Moses, calling him to lead the most important mission of his life, the exodus of his people out of Egypt. In the midst of our own brokenness we must look for God's holiness to appear to us, giving us the plan for our own salvation and the exodus from our own destructive circumstances.

Coming into Freedom

Humble yourselves before the Lord, and he will lift you up.
James 4:10

1. Have you been tempted to "clean up your act" before you allow God to be present in your life? Do you feel you must be more "presentable to God" before He will speak to you or redeem your mistakes?

   If so, confess your pride before Him and humbly ask Him to forgive you. State your willingness to allow Him to burn in your heart, believing that the fire will purify and not consume you.

2. In what ways have you refused God access to the painful parts of your past? By refusing to forgive those who have wounded you? By believing that time would heal the past? By seeking other sources of comfort that provided only temporary relief?

   Write in your prayer journal any methods you have tried to use to make your past bearable. Ask God to show you which ones will endure the burning flames of His presence.

Day 35

Renouncing Idol Gods

A YOUNG WOMAN CRIES OUT THAT SHE HAS NEVER BEEN ABLE TO HAVE satisfying sexual relations with her husband. She has labeled herself "frigid." How does she get help?

A young man bemoans the fact that even as a Christian he is unable to overcome driving temptations to indulge in pornography and compulsive masturbation. He feels unable and unworthy to continue in the full-time Christian work to which he once felt called. What is his answer?

These are real-life situations, not isolated, but repeated in many, many lives. As honest Christians seek healing prayer for such problems, they often evidence total discouragement and the belief that there seems to be an answer for every other child of God, but not for them. They hoped by fasting and private prayer to overcome the terrible weights they carry. Finally, humbling themselves in desperation, they confess their deep secrets to trusted Christian friends, hoping for a one-time prayer of deliverance, or at the least a modicum of understanding. They feel like Christian freaks, and no one seems to talk about their particular problems.

Today we will talk about the diseased fantasy life, the preoccupation with self to the point that healthy relationships with others deteriorate and the all-consuming preoccupation with sex that holds numerous Christians in bondage to idol gods.

The History of the Problem

These are age-old problems, and even our hero, Moses, ran smack dab into them.

Moses had led the Hebrews out of Egypt, through the Red Sea and into the desert in preparation for entering the Promised Land of Canaan. But as they approached Canaan they encountered powerful adversaries among the pagan tribes. Not all of them wanted to fight the Hebrews; some wanted to seduce them into following their tribal religions. These, by far, were the most dangerous. They looked peaceable, they acted friendly and they offered hospitality. But their outward appearance was deceptive and seductive in the extreme.

Through Moses God told the Hebrews, His chosen ones, that they were to have no other gods but Him (see Exodus 20:3–4). He was acutely aware of the dangers inherent in the pagan religions His people would encounter, so He warned them far in advance to stay away from all forms of religion except for the one true religion He had instituted. His presence would provide adequately for them in every way; they would lack nothing.

Yet even as Moses went up on Mount Sinai to receive words from God that would become His people's standards of living and wholeness (what we now know as the Ten Commandments), his Hebrew brothers and sisters waiting below in the desert were rebelling against God. While God was telling Moses on the mountain, "Do not make any gods to be alongside me; do not make for yourselves gods of silver or gods of gold" (Exodus 20:23), the Hebrews were already disobeying.

At that same moment in the desert valley the people, growing tired of waiting for Moses to come down from the mountain, told Aaron, Moses' brother, "Come, make us gods who will go before us."

And Aaron, taking his cue from the pagan worshipers of Baal and Ashtoreth, gave the Hebrews permission to take all the gold jewelry the Egyptians had given them, to melt it down and to cast an idol in the form of a calf. He then told them to build an altar in front of the calf and allowed them to indulge in their revelry as they had seen the pagans do!

The Implications

The new idol was not a harmless, Disney-eyed creature. It was a direct adaptation of Baal worship; the Baal worshipers had successfully seduced the Hebrews. They served a god who was known as the "lord possessor," or, more commonly and obscenely, "the god of the hole." They also served his consort, Ashtoreth, the fertility goddess and "great mother of the earth." Worshiping nature and the creature rather than the Creator quickly led the followers of Baal to the worship of the procreative parts of the creature. In so doing they identified themselves with the procreative nature of their god and goddess and with that of all nature.

The early pagans followed a lengthy fertility ritual. First, the ruler of a tribe celebrated the rites of spring by having sexual intercourse with the earth, symbolizing his people's hopes for the fertility of the earth, and thus, abundant crops. Then young virgins were chosen to symbolize the earth by receiving the seed of the carnal priests in temple ceremonies. Every other man and woman was enjoined to imitate the ritual with the male and female prostitutes of the temple. When children were born from these couplings they were offered as "holy" sacrifices to the god Molech (the other side of Baal), and were thrown into fires or off cliffs or into a river. Modern excavations have uncovered graveyards filled with pottery vessels containing bones of millions of tiny infants sacrificed to the gods. These are always located adjacent to the temple ruins.

The golden calf, therefore, was a well-known pagan symbol of the fertility cult, fashioned with a distended phallus. The golden calf also implied an invitation to participate in the sexual orgies that constituted the worship of Baal and Ashtoreth.

Fashioning the calf was an abomination to the Lord, a direct compromise of good and evil, as if God would not care.

A Modern Baal and Ashtoreth

The god of sexual orgy still holds court even in modern, "enlightened" society. He may not be worshiped by the name of "Baal" and he may not be fashioned into tangible idols. But he is lifted up among modern people in unmistakable ways and offered homage and sacrifice today, even as in ancient times.

The seemingly innocent initiation many men undergo to enter the fellowship of the Masonic Lodge, for example, is in reality an enticement into deeper and deeper spiritual confusion, exacerbated by the overlapping of Christian symbols, pagan symbols and symbols with strong sexual overtones. In Great Britain, where this movement was birthed, we have ministered to many men who have felt led to renounce their Masonic vows, and particularly the vows of giving their firstborn sons to the Lodge. Although this may have seemed to be merely a rite of passage to the initiates, the god Baal/Molech took these vows seriously.

Only after observing one tragedy after another, ruining the lives of eldest sons in Masonic families, did some of these Christian men make the connection between the vows they had made and the destructive effects on their families. Much of the Masonic ritual in its higher degree comes not from Scripture, as initiates are led to believe, but from an eclectic mixture of Christian and pagan symbol which opens the door, not to God, but to the prince of darkness.

The worship of and preoccupation with the procreative parts of God's creatures is prevalent today as never before. Some cable television stations and many magazines are full of sexual idolatry. Pornography has become accepted in our society as a "viable option for those who want to indulge." Compulsive masturbation, which always accompanies pornography, is a way of life for many. Our teenagers view R-rated movies as standard fare. Song lyrics and video scenes portray acts that would have been considered X-rated obscenities twenty years ago.

Young children who are exposed to primetime television have seen the sex act performed many times by the time they are four or five. Lifestyle is determined by what kind of sexual activity a person prefers. Incest and sexual abuse run rampant. Our society's sexual mores have become so loose that a couple on their first date may have sexual intercourse before they learn each other's last names! Yet incidents of reported rape have increased dramatically, demonstrating graphically that sex has moved past lust and turned to violence in the lives of many disturbed individuals.

Marriage vows are no longer taken seriously and are often thought to be unnecessary, even by prominent, well-respected figures in our society. Modern-day heroes are frequently admired because of their ability to attract multiple sexual partners. Because of the frequency of sexual contact outside monogamous marriage, venereal disease and AIDS are real threats to all of society. Unwanted children, the "by-products" of this glut of sexual activity, are disposed of by the millions every year through a legal procedure known as abortion.

Even in some parts of the Church we read of increasing movements toward embracing ancient forms of goddess worship. Not only are liturgies being written for the worship of female deities, but prominent theologians are attempting to shape God into a primarily feminine presence. Although God embodies the feminine attributes of nurturing, responding, intuiting, sensing, perceiving and receiving, these in no way overshadow the masculine attributes of His character.

God, the One who initiates, brings order out of chaos, organizes, presses through difficulties, sets boundaries, defines and constructs, is the eternal Masculine. It is to the true masculine of God that all creation responds. It is the strong masculine voice of love that blesses us, His creation, calls us forth and makes us whole.

To relate to "our Mother who art in heaven" is to deny the necessity of being in relationship with a Father who affirms us in our God-given potential and orders our lives to obtain wholeness.

Let's face it: We live in a society that serves Baal, Ashtoreth and Molech as surely as the pagan Canaanites did!

What Is the Answer?

In the midst of all this sexual freedom how could a young woman like the one I mentioned earlier fear that she is sexually "frigid"? Why do her body and emotions not respond to her husband's embrace?

Over and over I have asked women like her to tell me about their husband's sexual practices during and even before their marriages. I also ask them to tell me about the sexual practices of fathers, brothers, uncles, grandfathers and great-grandfathers on both sides of the family. And nearly always I hear sad stories of infidelity, pornography, rape, abortion, misogyny and abuse.

These women shrink from unwelcome, undefined presences in their own marriage beds. Yet inevitably their husbands—and therapists—place the total blame for their frigidity on them, sometimes for years.

I have found, however, that as soon as the husband of one of these women renounces the gods of his fathers or mothers (and perhaps the gods he has served), and asks God and his wife for forgiveness for bringing foreign gods into the marriage, the marriage bed is sanctified. Such honesty on the part of a husband has given many wives a godly release to enjoy the pleasures of marriage as He intended.

Many women, too, need to renounce the idol gods from their family backgrounds or personal histories. The practice of Baal worship can be passed just as easily through the maternal line.

And the young man who cannot shake free from the temptations of pornography and masturbation? He, too, must ask God to show him where there have been patterns of Baal worship in his family line. He must confess, repent and renounce any involvement he or his fathers have had in this kind of activity. Only as he is freed from the influences of a god who would seek to possess his body and soul is he able to relate lovingly to a woman in a healthy and biblical way.

Getting Free at Last

We must all be willing to pray the prayers of renunciation of Baal, Molech and Ashtoreth for ourselves, for our families and for our nations simply because of the time in which we live. Not one of us is immune to the temptations of the evil one. Sexual idolatry is so insidious that some of us are completely ignorant of its consequences until they are lovingly pointed out to us.

God told Gideon, His hand-picked servant, the same thing He is telling us:

> Tear down your father's altar to Baal and cut down the Asherah pole beside it. Then build a proper kind of altar to the LORD your God on the top of this height.
>
> Judges 6:25–26

Coming into Freedom

> "Get rid of the foreign gods you have with you, and purify yourselves and change your clothes."
>
> Genesis 35:2

241

1. List in your prayer journal any evidences of Baal worship you have experienced, observed or heard about in your family (i.e., fornication, adultery, incest, pornography, homosexuality, sexual abuse, ritual abuse, misogyny, abortion, sexual addiction, compulsive masturbation, etc.).
2. If your fathers and mothers have indeed served idol gods through secret societies, lodges, relationships and/or ungodly sexual activity, please pray this prayer with me now:

> In the name of the most holy God, the one true God, I renounce the idol gods of my fathers and the idol goddesses of my ancestors. I renounce you, Baal. I renounce you, Ashtoreth. I renounce you, Molech. I command any evil presence hiding within to manifest itself now in Jesus' name.

If you do see with the eyes of your heart any evil manifestation of idol gods, look closely to see with your spirit what God does with them. God wants to send His holy fire to cleanse you as He cleansed Gideon. Now pray again:

> As You have cleansed me, O Lord God, I thank You. I receive into myself Your holiness, Your beauty, Your purity. I gratefully accept Your washing me clean by the power of Your Holy Spirit.

If you have access to holy water, wash yourself or have a prayer partner, pastor or priest wash you with it. Pray over and sprinkle your home, and especially your bedroom, with the holy water.

As you pray aloud the prayer renouncing Baal and Ashtoreth, the phallic demons may reveal themselves to you. There is no need to fear. Ask God to show you what He does with those demons; see in your heart how He takes care of them.

3. Ask Jesus to come now and cleanse your imagination, filling it with His Holy Spirit to be the receptacle of truth, beauty, goodness, purity, holiness and images of His Presence. Even if you have no holy water with you, you may enjoy taking a shower, symbolic of the cleansing God is doing inside you at this moment. Rejoice under the running water for His cleansing power within you.

Day 36

Breaking Free

NOT EVERY KIND OF BONDAGE THAT HOLDS US IN ITS GRIP IS CATEGORICALLY "evil." We can be slaves to many things that the most sincere Christians consider good, worthwhile, selfless and honorable. We need to know the difference between God's will for us, the expectations imposed by others (even well-meaning ones) and the expectations we impose on ourselves.

That is why I strongly emphasized an intentional time of regularly reading God's Word and practicing His presence when we started this journey some weeks ago. Only in continuing to do so will we become aware of regular, seemingly harmless habits that keep us in bondage to a life far inferior to the abundant one Jesus has for us.

Some of these habits we have acquired have been part of our family's way of doing things for so long that we have never thought to question them. I am not suggesting that you dredge up a lot of "stuff" to examine. Rather, I am encouraging you to ask Jesus to point out areas of your life that inhibit you from being totally free to be the person He is calling you to be. One of those areas may be the subtle bondage of tradition.

A Security Blanket

Tradition offers security to many of us. Home and church traditions may be the only areas of stability left in our lives, and when I (or anyone else) start tampering with them some folks feel threatened, as if I were declaring war! In addition, our traditions may be so ingrained in our personal identities that we literally are afraid to give them up, or let anyone alter them without putting up a terrific struggle.

The tradition of the Church that is rooted in godly principles and symbol is a way we have of connecting with the saints of years gone by and with the goodness of our religious heritage. The ways in which people worship God can become precious traditions, especially if those ways bring us closer to Him. Although God never changes, He constantly nudges us to be transformed by moving closer and closer to His likeness, by moving in His Spirit. Sometimes these changes will involve worshiping in new ways or making room in our corporate and private worship for a more intimate relationship with Him. When we are listening closely to the Spirit, changes will inevitably occur in our liturgies, our architecture and our music. Getting accustomed to these changes, and even to some of the new translations of the Bible, can be difficult and painful.

Traditions in the home often feel equally sacred, and family members sometimes defend them to the death. Just watch the dynamics of newly married couples trying to decide when to open Christmas presents—on Christmas Eve or on Christmas morning? Should they serve ham or lamb on Easter? Which is the "right" kind of dressing for Thanksgiving Day? Is it better to have a big Sunday lunch at home or to go out for dinner after church? When family members hold rigidly to such traditions major arguments, tension and dread may surround these discussions year after year.

Taking the time to be still and listen intentionally to God seems especially difficult for us in this matter of tradition. Yet we need His wisdom to take precedence over any traditions to which we have become overly attached or accustomed in ways that lead to unloving actions. Unfortunately we seldom remember to seek His wisdom until a major conflict occurs. Perhaps premarital counseling should include a lesson in listening prayer about what traditions God would like to establish in the new family with which He is entering into a covenant relationship.

Exposing My Bondage

One of the bondages to family tradition I have faced recently involved a family principle that I not only have been taught all my life, but have passed on to my children as well. It is the principle of "making excuses."

By example and teaching I learned as a child that when someone asks you to do something you do not feel comfortable about doing, you must offer a satisfactory excuse for not doing it, an excuse that is socially acceptable even if it stretches the truth. Never, for example, would I have dreamed of saying to a friend, "No, I'm sorry, I can't do that tonight. I want to stay home." I always felt I should have a "previous engagement" or a "conflict" or "company." Telling the truth seemed to imply that a quiet evening at home was preferable to the other person's company (which it may have been)!

Even when this "excuse-making" got me into trouble I never questioned that making excuses might not please God. It seemed like a nice southern tradition designed to avoid hurting the feelings of others.

When lying became abhorrent to me as I attempted to walk more fully in the Spirit, I quit stretching the truth and making excuses. But I substituted an equally bad tradition: I mistakenly began instead to accommodate other people's agendas, jumping to meet whatever needs or requests they expressed. Many times I intuitively felt I should refuse, but not knowing how to back out gracefully, I would accept. When others' demands collided with my own schedule, I attempted to rationalize that God had arranged the request, that He would take care of all my other commitments and that I was selfish not to want to help or spend time with that person.

Often I felt manipulated. I complained about it, feeling that my life was out of control, and I murmured at God because I could not do all He wanted me to do. Now I was projecting my predicament onto God. And I constantly confessed selfishness.

I even became familiar with teachings on codependency and wondered if this was my problem. But as I lifted this question up to the Lord, I felt assured I was not codependent, although the consequences were similar.

I hit a new learning curve in this area when I came to a desperation point over finishing this book. Over and over, just as I would get in a rhythm of quiet time, listening prayer and journaling, a rhythm absolutely necessary to my writing, an outside request or demand interrupted. Suddenly I felt as if I were juggling fifteen balls in the air and they were all beginning to fall. And yet everything I was juggling seemed important.

How could I possibly refuse to pray with someone whose life was hanging in a spiritual balance? How could I not talk and pray on the phone with a woman whose husband was about to walk out? How could I say no to a wonderful visit from my daughter-in-law and granddaughters? How could I put off a last shopping trip with my son who was going back to college? How could I refuse dinner invitations from friends who for weeks had been trying to get on our schedule? How could I ignore an invitation from my husband to watch the sunset from the end of the pier?

Yet God was telling me to write this book. What was I to do?

Uprooting the Azaleas

During a recent monthly meeting of our church prayer team we paired off; each person was to pray for the other's most immediate need as God brought it to our hearts. My friend Becky prayed with me about my "juggling act" and the discipline of writing. One phrase in her prayer opened up the most powerful image and word from God I had had concerning these problems: "Lord, keep Signa rooted deeply in You."

I immediately remembered in great detail an incident from that very afternoon. We have two large dogs: Holly, a black Labrador retriever, and Sonny, a yellow Labrador retriever. They are lovable, playful, friendly and fairly obedient, but in hot weather they persist in digging large, deep holes in the dirt in which to sleep and stay cool. And one of them routinely found that special spot in my flower bed!

Day after day I had found two azalea bushes, planted last spring, uprooted and tossed beside the deep hole that had become the napping place for one of the Labs. I had fussed at both of them, but I did not want to spank either, for fear I would spank the wrong one. And I could never seem to catch them in the act! So every day I got the shovel, fluffed up my wilted azaleas, replanted and watered them and piled pine straw around them. Then I tried to invent a new deterrent to the dogs' pastime.

But that afternoon I had caught Holly digging up my azaleas! She got the end of my flyswatter on her rear and a good scolding besides. I took one look at those poor, pitiful azaleas and knew they were not going to survive another replanting. No matter how hard I had tried to save them, their roots were dried out from overexposure.

The incident flashed vividly in my mind while Becky prayed and I began to laugh. To God, I looked like one of my pitiful azalea bushes! He had lovingly planted, watered, nourished and tended me. Deep roots went to the source of my nourishment. I was becoming healthy, I was growing, and I was going to flower and bear fruit. But I was allowing circumstances and people to uproot me constantly, lifting me out of the environment in which God had placed me. And the constant exposure was wilting me!

The next day I began to talk to God about this image. I asked Him to show me how to keep my roots well watered and covered by Him, and yet not isolate myself from my loved ones and those who needed my help. He took me to a less-than-well-known part of the story of Moses.

Do you remember when Moses welcomed his father-in-law, Jethro, into the Hebrews' camp in the desert? Jethro had accompanied Moses' wife and children there from Midian, and he was interested in all God had accomplished through Moses' obedience to His word. Moses told him about the defeat of Pharaoh and the Egyptians, about all the hardships the Hebrews had endured in the desert, about the miracles of provision and about the defeat they had brought upon the Amalekites. Moses had given himself completely into the hand of God and his life was bearing much fruit. Jethro was so moved he brought sacrifices to God and worshiped Him there in the desert with the Hebrew leaders.

But the next day Jethro sat and watched objectively as Moses went about one of his normal activities, that of serving from morning until evening as judge for the people. The Hebrews brought every problem, large and small, before Moses and awaited his godly decisions. By the end of the day everyone was exhausted. That was when God spoke His wisdom through Jethro.

> "What you are doing is not good," [he told Moses]. "You and these people who come to you will only wear yourselves out. The work is too heavy for you; you cannot handle it alone. Listen now to me and I will give you some advice, and may God be with you."
>
> Exodus 18:17–19

Jethro then told Moses how to delegate authority, how to teach the people to minister to others and how to lighten the load by sharing it.

"If you do this and God so commands," he said, "you will be able to stand the strain, and all these people will go home satisfied" (Exodus 18:23).

Living in Freedom

This was God's message to me: This book is to be my way of teaching others the things God has taught me, of sharing leaves of healing from His Word and His wisdom. The bondage I had been living under, thinking I could not say no to any honest request, was broken as I named it and shook it loose. Being able to pray about each situation as it comes before me, obeying God as He leads and truthfully telling some folks that my first calling right now is to finish the project God has given me has empowered me to accomplish what seemed like an impossible task.

Bondage to our past keeps us from being totally free to say yes to God. This morning as I read the daily devotional from Oswald Chambers' book *My Utmost for His Highest* (Barbour, 1935), I was blessed to find the following:

> Never allow the dividing up of your life in Christ to remain without facing it. Beware of leakage, of the dividing up of your life by the influence of friends or circumstances; beware of anything that is going to split up your oneness with Him and make you see yourself separately. Nothing is so important as to keep right spiritually. The great solution is the simple one—"Come unto Me."

Coming into Freedom

> Though we are slaves, our God has not deserted us in our bondage.
> Ezra 9:9

1. Are you aware of traditions in your church that have caused conflict or division? Are you aware of traditions in your family that have produced pain and hard feelings? Are any of these keeping you from becoming all God is calling you to

be? If so, list them in your prayer journal and lift them individually before God to receive His loving exhortation.

2. Confirm before God today your desire to have your roots firmly established in Him, well covered, watered and nourished by His Spirit. If He shows you any way in which your roots have become exposed to the withering, destructive climate of this world, confess it to Him. Ask Him to perform in you a miracle of growth.

Day 37

The Path of Becoming

ALL OF US ARE BECOMING MORE HEALTH-CONSCIOUS. WE MAY NOT YET BE healthier, but at least we are aware of the consequences of what we eat. We know now that if we eat a lot of fat we are going to be fat. We are beginning to believe the old saying, "You are what you eat."

My mother had a similar saying about relationships. When I was a young teenager she constantly reminded me which kinds of people I should and should not be spending time with. Her adage was, "Any group will eventually be reduced to the lowest common denominator."

God's Word repeatedly tells us the same truth about worship. He has exhorted His people forever about their associations with the false gods of this world. In essence His statement is, "You become what you worship."

Specifically, God recounts the sad events in the wilderness:

"When I found Israel, it was like finding grapes in the desert; when I saw your fathers, it was like seeing the early fruit on the fig tree. But when they came to Baal Peor, they consecrated themselves to that shameful idol and became as vile as the thing they loved."
Hosea 9:10

Another account reads this way:

They followed worthless idols and themselves became worthless.
2 Kings 17:15

The Sin of Envy

One of the most insidious idols we can follow is that of envy. It is a worthless habit and will inevitably lead the envious one into a worthless existence. Envying in another what we lack in ourselves has become a religion in our society. The sin of envy takes absolute control over us, putting us in a bondage over which it is very difficult to exert any power. Giving ourselves over to envy will ultimately destroy us. What may start off as admiration, respect or affection, if not grounded by a healthy spiritual heart, can easily deteriorate into bondage so hideous it takes a major miracle of God to get us free.

Selena's Story

I saw with great sadness the dead look in Selena's face. In her fifties, she looked completely out of touch with her femininity and was so ill at ease she could not look at me as I spoke to her. Her manner was distant but friendly as she asked me apologetically to make time to pray with her. It took little spiritual discernment to see that she was extremely needy.

Selena's appearance was purposely severe: Her haircut and style, her clothing, the set of her features, her gestures and her words presented not a masculine look, but rather an asexual one.

Selena's story was tragic. Her cruel father drank excessively, was unfaithful to her mother and beat her mother repeatedly. Finally her mother gave up—literally gave up. Selena remembers getting out of bed several times at night to see if her mother was still breathing. Terrified she would lose her one source of love, Selena watched her mother retreat further and further into herself until she died when Selena was an adolescent. Selena believed that her father had murdered her mother as surely as if he had stabbed or shot her.

Selena's frantic attempts to grasp the precariously fragile connection with the feminine presence she had once felt with her mother left her so fearful that, when her mother died, Selena let the feminine in herself begin to die as well. She made several short-term attempts to connect with the feminine through lesbian relationships, but finally something deep in her soul, even the desire for life, died. She dreamed about her mother frequently, but when she awakened she realized her mother was dead. So, she felt, was she. In Selena's mind, her father had killed them both.

Selena eventually became a Christian and found a place for herself in full-time Christian work. She studied hard to make herself "worthy" for Christ's service, but had no feeling, no passion for her work; she appeared robot-like in her duties.

Selena came to me for prayer not because of her tragic past and her sense of nonbeing, but because she sensed some foreign emotions springing up within her. She had become so used to functioning without any emotion at all that to "feel" again was in itself a concern. Furthermore, she knew as a Christian that the emotions she was experiencing had no place in her life: strong feelings of hate and envy, violently directed toward one person—her missions supervisor, Krista.

When Selena had met Krista a few months ago, she had felt a frightening ambivalence she did not understand. Krista was a beautiful, extremely feminine woman, gifted and poised, who loved the Lord and was wonderfully adept at calling forth godly gifts in others. Selena began to admire the true feminine in Krista and to desire femininity again for the first time in decades. She was attracted by the way in which the feminine and godly presences merged in Krista. She trusted her, learned a great deal from her and wanted to be like her, but saw no way to do that except *through* her. Consequently if Krista spent time with any other woman, Selena was devastated. She wanted Krista all to herself so she could vicariously enjoy the experience of the true feminine.

At the same time she felt admiration and respect for Krista, Selena hated everything she saw Krista do. She conspired to trip up her supervisor at every turn. She resented the way Krista exercised authority over others, began to pick her apart mentally and resented any time Krista spent with the other trainees.

Not only did Selena feel she could not take the true feminine into herself, but her desire to connect with it through Krista produced another conflict: She felt totally disloyal to her mother's memory for admiring another woman. If she ever became Krista's friend, would she lose the last tenuous claim she had to her mother's identity, the only identity she had ever loved?

252

As a result of this internal struggle, Selena began to hate Krista with a passion. She watched her constantly, envied her and began to think unclean thoughts about her. She wanted (in her own words) to "swallow up" Krista. She told me all this with great shame and in a whispered voice, fearful that someone would overhear.

The Choice

Selena was at a crossroads with two paths ahead of her from which to choose. One path was the path of "becoming"—of loving and blessing all that was good in Krista and learning from it; of seeking the good in Krista for herself and asking God to make it real in her own soul.

The other path was the path of "no longer becoming"—of envying in Krista what she did not find in herself, of wishing Krista did not possess the godly qualities she herself lacked, of wishing she could kill Krista to avoid the torment she felt in her presence.

Sadly, prior to our encounter, Selena had chosen the second path, becoming like that which she had chosen to worship, the memory of her mother. All of her mother's characteristics became hers. She assumed the "victim posture." All that was good and healthy in her began to dry up. She developed many physical symptoms and was in constant pain. She no longer had any healthy emotions. She was slowly dying, as her mother had done so many years before.

We began to teach Selena about what envy does to a person and about how, when we envy another instead of blessing him or her, the very thing we desperately want for ourselves stays beyond our reach. In this state we eventually begin to hate what we want and to hate the person we envy.

To counter her envy, we taught Selena how to see beauty and goodness and bless it in another, calling it forth and rejoicing in it. And we taught her how to listen to the desire of her own heart and give it to God, believing that all good desires come from Him.

After much prayer, confession, repentance and healing of the past, Selena faced her crossroads again. This time she chose the path of "becoming." She went forward at the conference to bless Krista publicly. She chose to love and call forth the gifts in Krista as blessings of God. She chose to pray that God would bless

Krista even more as she ministered to others. She chose to see all good gifts as gifts from God, not special favors for a privileged few.

If Selena continues on her new path of blessing rather than envying she will become all Jesus intended her to be—alive, productive, gifted and beautiful.

Whatever our hearts desire, we will become. If we desire revenge, punishment, retribution or physical satisfaction, it will eventually consume us. If we desire godliness, beauty, truth, gentleness and blessing, they, too, will consume us.

Choose wisely. If you recognize any traces of envy residing in your soul, expose it to the light of Jesus immediately. Choose to travel on the path of "becoming."

Coming into Freedom

> You have made known to me the path of life; you will fill me with joy in your presence, with eternal pleasures at your right hand.
> Psalm 16:11

1. Perhaps you are in Selena's situation, wanting desperately what you see in another. Tell God you repent of your envy and renounce it in the name of Jesus. Receive His forgiveness and be free to become the person He created you to be.

   Begin now to bless the person you have envied. Write out a prayer in your journal asking God to make this person all He created him or her to be. Ask God to call forth this person's gifts, using them for His glory.

2. Perhaps you are in Krista's situation, knowing someone envies you to the point that all Christian fellowship is cut off. Begin to pray for that one to hear from God the truth of his or her own worth and creative giftedness. Choose to put healthy barriers between yourself and the envious one, so he or she can receive healing directly from the Lord. Release this one to God's hands to receive the inner healing needed to become a real person in His Kingdom.

Day 38

Received into Jesus

WHEN BEN, MY YOUNGEST CHILD, WAS ONLY A FEW WEEKS OLD AND THE excitement of just having delivered another baby by natural childbirth was still fresh in my mind, I received a phone call late one night from a friend, whom I will call Julie, who was expecting her first child. She told me she had gone into labor, but her husband was out of town. Would I meet her at the hospital and act as her labor coach?

Younger than I, emotional and excitable, Julie was a member of the church where Conlee and I belonged. We had spent a lot of time together, and had even shared the same baby shower. In some ways I felt that I could have been her mother, and she certainly looked to me and to other women in the church for advice, since her mother did not live nearby.

Julie's pregnancy had already been traumatic, but then, her whole life was traumatic. Her husband, Steve, was good-looking, bright and ambitious, but he was not particularly committed to their marriage. His job kept him away from home for weeks at a time, and he seemed to relish the freedom. When he was at home he was the picture of a faithful, devoted husband, but his long absences were taking a toll on the relationship. A volatile couple, Julie and Steve laughed and loved and played with great passion, but they fought, screamed and tore one another apart with equal intensity. The environment in their home was anything but stable.

Now it was time for Julie's baby to arrive, and Steve was out of the country for an indefinite period of time. In truth, Julie did not know if he would return home at all.

Of course I agreed to coach Julie, and I set off for the hospital for a real adventure, praying all the way.

A good friend of ours was the obstetrician in charge and he had also just delivered my son. Both he and I arrived at the hospital before Julie did, so I filled him in on the state of Julie's household and why she had called me to be her coach. He agreed we would make a good team.

Once Julie arrived, nature took its course and labor progressed normally. Julie and I did our breathing and kept our focal points; everything was textbook perfect.

But when we got into the delivery room for the final stages of labor, the baby's breathing became distressed. The doctor determined that the baby was arriving in a breech position, and Julie panicked. She began to scream and would not hold her focus. I prayed intensely for both mother and child.

Our doctor friend began making preparations to do an emergency cesarean section, but suddenly he stopped and said, "Signa, we're going to clear the room for just a minute. You'll know what to do."

The attending nurses looked startled, but no more startled than I! What was he expecting me to do? I was just there to coach Julie's breathing—and to pray. Of course! God was leading me to pray in a special way for this distressed infant.

I had no idea what I was supposed to pray, so I quieted myself and asked God what to do.

Speak life to the child, He replied in my spirit.

Forcefully I told Julie to concentrate on her baby, to pray for him, to look at me and to agree with what I said. Wide-eyed, she nodded. Then the following words came from my spirit as God gave them to me:

> Little one, there is no need to fear. You are resisting coming into an unsure world where there is no security or peace in your home. But there is One here right now to welcome you with peace and love and safety. Turn yourself toward Him and slide into His arms as He welcomes you with love. Julie and I welcome you with love also, and we will care for you and keep you in Jesus' care. He has strong arms to support you and He will never desert you as long as you live.

I watched in astonishment as the baby turned completely over within Julie's body; both of us saw it with our own eyes, and rejoiced.

I called the doctor back into the room and we witnessed the easiest, quickest delivery he had ever seen. Within fifteen minutes Julie *walked* out of the delivery room carrying her newborn son at her breast. He was asleep in her arms, and in the arms of Jesus.

Healing of Memories

Deep trauma in a home at the time of a child's birth can cause the little one to develop fears and anxieties that take such strong root they may last into adulthood. I have often prayed the same prayer I prayed for Julie's baby over a grown man or woman, asking God to heal the deep-seated, infantile fears still resident in their lives. Time and time again we have offered an individual's painful memories up to Jesus and have witnessed miracles of healing as the ever-present, all-protective arms of Jesus took the "little ones" in His embrace.

Please do not misunderstand me: It is a blessing that cesarean sections and other dramatic measures can save the lives of mothers and babies and avoid severe complications. It is a blessing that children can be treated for all sorts of problems in utero and immediately after birth. But the wonder of medical miracles in no way eradicates the stress, fear and anxiety a newborn may retain from emotional or physical trauma in the womb, the separation from the secure environment of the womb and, all too often, the premature separation from the loving, secure breast and arms of a mother, vital for the establishment of a sense of well-being in the little soul.

Prayers of peace over the deep-seated memories of traumatic birth can bring enormous relief to a troubled soul. The image of Jesus welcoming the new life into the world, perhaps even standing guard over the isolette while treatment is given, or holding the baby in His arms while he or she is separated from mother, can be healing and redemptive.

We cannot change the circumstances that surrounded your conception, time in the womb, birth and first few weeks of life. Yet even if you were conceived through violence, not love, Jesus was there, surrounding you with His love. We cannot re-parent you if your mother or father was not able to give you what you needed.

Yet even if your mother feared having you or tried to abort you, Jesus held you tightly in His hands. Even if you were separated from your mother by illness, her death or adoption, Jesus never left you for a moment. He was there for you. Let Him make those authentic memories of His presence a reality to your heart.

Coming into Freedom

Before I formed you in the womb I knew you, before you were born I set you apart. . . .

Jeremiah 1:5

1. In your prayer journal write out the circumstances of your birth, to the best of your ability.
2. Ask Jesus to show you where He was in each phase of your first hours on this earth. Welcome Him into your memories. Let Him speak words of His peace to you right now and free you from bondage to the circumstances of your birth.

Day 39

An Account of Love

No one is more in awe than I of the incredible ways in which God can remove bondages caused by our inhibitions, our self-consciousness or our feelings of inadequacy, setting us free to become all He is calling us to be. If for no other reason I would stand in awe after observing the lifelong struggles of so many individuals, praying with them and watching God give them liberty to "become" as they learn to collaborate with Him through confession, repentance, forgiveness and obedience.

But I am in awe of His grace and power even more because of what I know He has done in me! Let me share with you just one example: how He liberated me from the bondage of false perceptions of Christian womanhood.

Signa's Story

I was born in the 1940s. I was raised in a strict family. I was surrounded by the traditions of the South. All of these factors, added to my parents' own personal struggles, combined to instill in me, an only child, a guiding "principle": There were certain things a female could never, should never and would never attempt.

I am always amazed when women tell me they grew up hearing "You can be anything you want to be," "There are no limits to what you can achieve" and "Set no boundaries on your desires." From my earliest years I heard statements such as "It's a man's world," "There are certain things women just aren't meant to do" and "A woman is happiest if she knows her place."

The deepest desire of my heart as I grew up was to become an obstetrician. But I was told early on that women did not go to medical school; medicine was not a suitable profession for a woman. My father, in fact, did not want me to pursue a profession at all. He thought it would be best if I found a successful husband to care for me when I graduated from college.

When I mentioned my lifelong dream to my mother a couple of years ago, it was enlightening to discover that she had absolutely no recollection that I had ever wanted to be a doctor. My family's mores were so strong that when my father said it was not appropriate for me to pursue such a career, I evidently did not press the point. The fact that I thought so much about my desire made me assume I must have spoken of it frequently. This realization showed me how much of the true masculine ability to press through a difficult situation and follow a goal had atrophied in my spirit.

As I grew up my father let my mother and me know that he could provide for us adequately; we would not have to work outside the home. All my high school friends got summer jobs; I was not allowed to do so, because my father felt it would reflect on his ability to provide for his child. I cannot remember a time when I was denied anything I wanted, but I had no conception of budgets or financial limits. Although a part of me enjoyed being given money and things whenever I asked for them, I also felt demeaned that I had to ask. I was not allowed to manage money or be responsible for an allowance.

When I went to college to major in French (a nice, safe area in which to get a degree that did not smack of professionalism), my father found an "acceptable" way to give me the spending money I needed. He gave me a checkbook and lots of checks, but never told me how much money was in my account. When I ran out of checks I assumed I was out of money. When I did overdraw (and I have no idea how often this happened), a friend of my father's who worked at the bank called to tell him to put more money in my account. That was my only experience in handling money before I married Conlee.

Once Conlee and I began our life together, my father never once interfered in our marriage with help, advice or criticism. As far as he was concerned, I was now my husband's responsibility.

Because of my limited experience with money and our limited newlywed bank account, all the ingredients were present for matrimonial explosions! When at the end of every month our checking account was overdrawn and Conlee struggled with our shaky finances, every nerve in my body would tense up. My heart would pound. Conlee never yelled at me, never threatened me, never demeaned me in any way, but we did have many "do better" talks. Each time I was convinced he was terribly angry with me and that it was only a matter of time before he would no longer want to be married. Eventually my anxiety was so strong that I ran into the bedroom, slammed the door and got into bed under the covers whenever I saw him pick up the checkbook!

Not until many years later did I realize that I had internalized my father's rigid restrictions about women handling money as an expression of his love. I was certain that if Conlee really loved me he would protect me from handling money, as my father had. And I was certain that when he confronted me about money, even in his gentle way, he was expressing his lack of love.

Submit Yourselves to One Another

When Conlee and I made a serious commitment to Jesus in our tenth year of marriage and established a living relationship with Him, I added new misconceptions about the status of Christian women to my repertoire. I was taught many false ideas about the submission of women to their husbands, and ultimately to all men. I was taught that whether I believed Conlee to be right or wrong I was to obey him in all things. I was taught in our church, as I had been taught at home, that I would find my identity as a fulfilled woman in my husband. In other words, I was encouraged once more to put to death a good mind, to deny my personal ambitions and callings and to enhance the ministries of the men who surrounded me—this time in the name of Jesus.

I truly wanted to please God, so with all my might I bent myself toward Conlee, begging him to define me as a woman, to tell me who I was supposed to be. I had no idea what to do, how to act, how to dress, what to say—and Conlee had no idea what to do with me, either.

At the same time I attempted to find my identity in my role as a mother. My children were wonderful, but they could not define me any more than my husband could. Besides, they constantly grew and changed, and their ideas of who they wanted their mother to be changed, too. What worked one day was wrong the next.

I could find no acceptable outlet for my creative gifts, so they lay, reduced to the dormant, stifled category of "trivia." The exchange of original thoughts and ideas was frowned upon because "women were so easily deceived." I bored quickly of the roles set out for me as a woman in the church, and falsely equated this boredom with unspirituality. I carried a constant, low-grade sense of guilt because I did not fit into the church culture's expected mold.

Here I was a new Christian, with all kinds of overwhelming insight and meaningful information entering my soul as I got to know the Lord and His Word, but I was flailing about in all directions. I had no idea how to receive help from God in this area and then respond creatively to His Holy Spirit.

Because this was such a personally confusing time I put a lot of pressure on Conlee. He admits that at first my "submission" sent him on an ego trip; he got all of my *attention* with no *contention*. But, as many Christian men have discovered, it did not take long before Conlee found it exhausting to make every decision, to be totally responsible for every member of the family, to always be the "voice of God" in the home. And although I gave the outward appearance of submission to my husband, a terrible resentment toward him for not meeting my needs began to grow in my heart. A subtle competition between us challenged the honesty in our relationship. I suppressed thoughts, feelings and ideas because I did not want to risk their being dissected through spiritual examination.

Perhaps you can sense that the first few years of my Christian journey were the most frustrating of my life. I was emerging into freedom in Christ, but was being challenged at every step; every Christian teacher seemed to have a different idea for how I was to "be," which influenced my Bible study as I tried to interpret God's Word in the light of the latest teachings. My prayer life lacked power. I was so double-minded that I tried to be one person in the morning and another in the afternoon, depending on the company I was with.

I was not sure how much longer I could keep treading water. I was very, very tired.

Liberating Love

The answers I was seeking did not come in one word, in one day, or even in one year, but they came! Jesus heard my cries for help and consistently loved me with a liberating love, the same kind of love He has for you. He moved me toward healing and freedom by teaching me several important lessons.

1. *He taught me how to live with a single eye.* That meant to live with one face, the same face, before God, men, women, family, church, friends and self. No longer would I be comfortable "walking alongside myself," analyzing every thought, word and action to make it fit a prescribed role. I was becoming painfully aware that I was a different person at home than I was at church, at a party or with my parents. Jesus was calling me to accountability; He was calling me to be real.
2. *He gave me an enthusiasm for reading His Word.* I realized that although many commentaries and teaching tapes were good, I could learn the most from the Holy Spirit. Each time I sat down with my Bible I asked Him to interpret the Word for me. He began to reveal my hang-ups, but more importantly, He taught me who He had created me to be. He told me I had endearing worth to Him, that He loved me unconditionally, that He had called me for a purpose beyond my own little world, that I had a good mind and that with His help I could overcome all my inadequacies. I began to believe Him.
3. *He taught me to listen to His voice.* I learned I was capable of hearing Him and capable of being responsible for what He told me, and He told me some pretty amazing things, especially about myself. No longer was I to depend unquestioningly on the interpretations of teachers, tapes or books. I learned to trust His words as they came directly to me, not

263

just through my husband or pastor or teacher, and I disciplined myself to write every one of them in my prayer journal.

4. *He showed me that, as a Christian woman empowered by the Holy Spirit, I could be used by Him in healing prayer.* I also learned that if I sensed in my spirit that He wanted me to touch someone with a healing touch, speak a healing word or give a godly exhortation, I did not necessarily have to wait until a male believer heard that word, too. My pattern had been that when I heard God tell me something should be done in a situation I would tell Conlee and urge him to take action. But he began to encourage me to step out in boldness when God prompted me. "God didn't tell me. You speak it! You do it!" he would say.

For some reason, when God pointed out someone in need, I felt paralyzed, but God wanted me to take the initiative in faith. So in the name of Jesus I began, tentatively at first, to lay hands on people and believe they would be healed. I spoke the healing word He gave and believed He would plant it in their hearts. In almost every case I did this not out of any spectacular feeling or sensation of anointing, but in obedience to the still, small voice in my heart that I had learned to recognize as God's.

The process of my "becoming" as a Christian woman has accelerated as God has asked me to step out in ways I could not have imagined. First, He began using Conlee and me in the healing ministry and we were asked to *speak to groups.* I wanted to yield to Conlee, believing that if he spoke the healing word, it would have more impact than if it was spoken by a woman. But Conlee continued to encourage me, to push me forward. Astonished, I started to believe that I, too, could convey truth and see miracles happen when I obeyed the gentlest nudgings from the Holy Spirit.

The second way in which God asked me to step out was to *write this book.* I argued with Him for a long time, battling His direction. I knew this should be a book for all believers struggling toward wholeness, not just a woman's story aimed at female believers. Surely, I told God, it would be accepted more readily if a man wrote it. Besides, I had no credentials to publish a book. Who was I to think anyone would read something I had written? What if the book turned out to be just a mass of simple, subjective ramblings from my prayer journal?

Recognizing Misogyny

Every inadequacy I ever had flew in my face when God called me to write. I became reluctant to ask for prayer, fearing I would be laughed at by those I respected when I told them God wanted me to write a book.

As I dealt with this fear, I slowly realized that I was battling the terrible sin of *misogyny*, which is the Greek word for "the hatred of women." This generational sin had covered my family for a long, long time. My male ancestors had been raised upon this lie. My female ancestors had been victims of it and eventually believed the lie themselves, passing down the generational line the devaluation of the feminine and the putting to death of many creative gifts.

Many parts of the Church have perpetuated the lie. Society has reinforced its grasp. Women who have forced their way out of its clutches have been labeled "militant," "feminist," "rebellious" or have been accused of having "a Jezebel spirit."

Let me say a word about this last accusation. Women seem to make it more than men do, and almost always wrongfully.

Jezebel was the real-life queen of Ahab, a wicked king of Israel. She was an outright pagan who had grown up immersed in the worship of Baal and Ashtoreth. When she married Ahab she was not asked to forsake Baal for the worship of the one true God. Her husband, in fact, not only condoned but endorsed Baal worship, blatantly ordering his servants to fashion golden calves, sacrificing on their altars and appointing priests to serve them.

Jezebel had tremendous influence on her husband, but she was purely pagan and never represented herself in any other way. Contrary to popular opinion, it was *Ahab's sin of compromising good and evil* that God detested, and for which He punished the whole country. This story is vividly recorded in 1 Kings 16–22 and 2 Kings 9.

A woman with a true Jezebel spirit, according to the Old Testament, is openly pagan, denying that the almighty God is the one true God. She bows consistently before other gods, opposes the work of the Lord and puts to death what is born of God. According to the New Testament (see Revelation 2:20–23), a woman with a true Jezebel spirit is in the Church, calling herself a woman of God while leading Christians into sexual immorality and paganism. She compromises good and evil and refuses to repent.

Unfortunately this term has erroneously become a synonym for a woman who resists any authority (godly or ungodly) in the Church or in the home. It is a label thrown about frequently by misogynists, whether men or women.

True release for a woman victimized by misogyny and caught in the web of lies surrounding this sin begins when she listens to God, writes out His words to her and renounces in the name of Jesus the sin of misogyny over herself, her family and the generations to come.

This I did. As a result I experienced the most incredible and complete transforming healing. Three times in just one year God brought me face to face with insurmountable obstacles that had become so much a part of my lifetime bondage to the effects of misogyny that I was unaware they were present. And each time, through much pain, He healed me. One result of those healings is that you are now reading this book.

For the man trapped in the web of the sin of misogyny, perpetrating the sin onto others or hating the true feminine of God in himself, renouncing the sin of misogyny is necessary. Many men who have done this have been amazed to see themselves and their families released to become all God intended. In this freedom, creative giftedness springs forth, love is expressed and received, and fruitfulness in ministry is increased.

To be free from the effects of misogyny, one is free to respond eagerly to God's voice, to intuit His Word, to nurture His people and to worship Him with abandon. One is free to become.

Coming into Freedom

"I will restore you to health and heal your wounds," declares the LORD.
Jeremiah 30:17

1. In what areas of your life, whether you are a man or a woman, has the sin of misogyny affected the way you value yourself? Does it go back through the generations of your family? You may need to pray the following prayer:

   Lord, I renounce the misogyny of my father, grandfathers and great-grandfathers. I renounce the misogyny of my mother, grandmothers and great-grandmothers. I forgive them for putting to death the true feminine in me. I see in You the power to receive, respond, nurture, intuit and embrace what is real.

Lord, I choose to become. I choose to bond with the true feminine, that which I see in You. I choose the identity You have for me. Imprint Your name on me. I choose to live!

2. Take the time to write a brief spiritual account of yourself as a man or as a woman in your prayer journal. Include how you feel about being male or female, and what influences you think have shaped those feelings. Be completely honest, neither condemning nor analyzing the content as you write.
3. If you sense inadequacies, insecurities or fears as you realize the person God made you to be, list them before Him. Invite Him to speak His healing word to you today.
4. On Day 1 of this journey you wrote out your story, your spiritual roots and where they had led you at that point. Go back and read what you wrote forty days ago. Compare it to what you wrote today. Are there major differences? Do you now see God in new ways? Has your trust level increased as you have shared new experiences with Him? Write any discoveries in your prayer journal.

Day 40

Coming Home

YOU AND I HAVE BECOME MORE THAN CASUAL TRAVELING COMPANIONS. We now know each other in intimate ways that were not possible before we shared this journey together.

You know a lot about my life—my sins, my weaknesses, my joys and my victories. And I feel that I know a lot about you, because during the time I have been writing this book I have prayed for you constantly. I do not know your name, but I believe God gave me a real love for you because He assured me that through these words, these healing leaves, you were going to come closer to wholeness than you ever dreamed possible.

As we come to the end of our journey together I sense loss in ending a meaningful relationship. But I also sense a deep anticipation about coming home. It is in celebration of that homecoming that I am praying for you today.

You may recall that Conlee and I named the home God provided for us "Hamewith Cottage," using a Scottish word meaning "a home within" or "a path leading towards home." The home within is the real home, the one each of us wants to return to, a place where we can let down all our weight, relax, be real and be at peace.

This is the kind of home that godly wholeness affords.

As we end our journey, then, let's look at some ways in which we can make both our physical homes and our "hamewith," the home within our spirits, sacred spaces to encourage and enhance our wholeness. We will begin with our wood, stone and mortar dwellings.

268

Making a House a Sacred Space

It is a refreshing experience to walk into a well-appointed home that is smoothly run, naturally organized, peaceful and comfortable. Many of my friends have such homes, and I have worked hard to provide one for my family.

Creating a truly inviting home does not take a large bank account, nor the assistance of an interior decorator. You do not need the talent of an artist, a seamstress or a handyman. It does take deliberate intent on the part of the homemaker, whether male or female.

Perhaps you have never wondered why certain homes feel so invitational. Think for a moment about homes you enter where you feel peace and tranquillity. How is the furniture arranged? Are the colors restful, stimulating, annoying or boring? Are the accessories meaningful and warm, calculated and contrived or carelessly inconsiderate of the needs of those who live and visit there? Do you feel like resting? Do you sense the warmth and personality of the homeowner? Or do you only perch, ill at ease, ready to flit off in a moment? What is it about a house that provides a sense of well-being? What is it about the people who live there?

When we bought "Hamewith Cottage" it was dark, dark, dark, with aged paneled walls, ceilings and floors that gave us the feeling of living in a cave. There were not enough lamps in the whole town to provide enough light in this house as far as I was concerned! I knew it had to be painted.

Everyone but Conlee tried to talk me out of it. Some purists thought it was a crime to paint over all that fine old wood, but they were not going to live in it. I was. So we painted the living room and the dining room walls and cathedral ceiling a sunset peach with white trim. We stripped the aged, orangy, wide-planked pine floors and painted them with a thin white glaze, leaving them a shiny vanilla ice cream color.

We did it all ourselves, but every tired, aching muscle in our bodies responded to seeing our "Hamewith" transformed. I love our home. I walk into it and feel fresh and alive.

As you look at your own home, pay attention to rooms besides the living room, dining room and kitchen. What about the room where you spend the most time and are the most impressionable—your bedroom? It usually takes lowest priority because we rationalize, "No one's going to see it except us. I want to spend our money on a room we will all enjoy." What does this say about your own self-worth and value to those who love you?

After all, you will spend more time sleeping in your bedroom than you will spend awake in any of the others. It is vital that the surroundings that comfort you as you fall asleep and greet you as you awake bring images of godliness, peace and a sense of well-being. Yellow rooms or blue and white ones speak peace to Conlee and me. What colors denote peace and rest for you?

And what about the place where you spend time with God? What colors inspire quietness? Put them where you read, pray, write, paint or do whatever God has gifted you to do. I painted my study a soft, dove gray with white trim, maybe because it reminds me of our church's decor and speaks to me of godly presence. I softened the room with liberal amounts of a large, floral English chintz, and the total effect is one of coziness, a place where I can feel loved and comforted.

Setting Your Home Apart as a Sacred Space

It is human nature to want our physical "nests" clean and organized, but making a house a real spiritual haven, a hamewith, requires something more. Setting it apart as a sacred space by opening it to the Spirit of God invites the holy presence into our midst. One of the best ways to do this is to have a house blessing.

Conlee and I love to participate in house blessings. A house blessing is not necessarily reserved for a new home; often it is intended for an older, much-lived-in home whose owner wants to dedicate it anew to be a temple for the presence of God.

With every move, whether it has been to a rented or purchased residence, we have made it a priority to have a house blessing as soon as possible. Any home feels different after Christian friends have soaked it with a spiritual shower of prayers and blessings.

What does a house blessing involve?

1. Intentionally inviting God to be with us, not just as a guest, but as our most honored family member. Our house blessings have taken many forms. In one home we invited over 100 guests to celebrate God's blessings. In another we had in only a few close friends, and another time we prayed with only our family. But each time we invited God to be present, not just on that occasion, but forever.

2. A holy housecleaning. Some folks like to use the wonderful liturgies available for this purpose (see Appendix). Others let the Spirit lead as they walk through each room of the home with songs, prayers and words of blessing.

We believe strongly in the liberal use of holy water as we ask the Holy Spirit to cleanse each room of any unclean spirits that have found a resting place in any corner of our home or property. When we choose a house or land we are never sure what actions, words or images occurred there. The places where we reside and spend the most time should be set apart by God as hallowed places for our spirits to grow in godly wisdom and strength.

One of the most dramatic holy housecleanings I have witnessed took place a few years ago when the parents of some good friends of ours asked us to join several of their closest friends for a house blessing. The concept was new to them, but several indicators convinced them that their beautiful home was not a spiritually healthy place in which to live.

First, neither the husband nor the wife could remember sleeping through an entire night since they had moved in several years before. They were uneasy in the house, even though it was elegantly furnished and decorated in every detail. To them it felt incomplete, and in an attempt to fill the gap they had placed artifacts and collectibles everywhere.

The second significant indicator was the behavior of the family cat. Not only could she not sleep through the night, either, but she slept at the door of the master bedroom, refusing to enter it. She seemed to be standing guard on the threshold, as though she needed to protect her master and mistress. Sometimes in the middle of the night she howled and appeared intensely disturbed.

The third indicator was that the owners sensed a dark presence in the spacious attic where they had stored many items. These were not suspicious or superstitious people; they were well-educated professionals, not prone to be dramatic or emotional. But every time either of them went to the attic a wave of depression came over them that remained for days.

The disappearing staircase to the attic happened to be in the ceiling of the hall right outside the door to the master bedroom.

It was just under this opening that the cat slept. As we asked a few questions we found that the previous owners had a long history of depression with the tragic result that the beautiful young wife had hanged herself from the rafters of the attic. She left two young children and a grieving, heartsick husband, who sold the house to our friends.

We gathered in the living room that night and prayed for the power of the Holy Spirit to come and guide us in our prayers, cleansing the whole house from darkness and filling it with His light. Then the whole troupe of us took flashlights and holy water and went to the attic. We sprinkled it liberally in the name of Jesus to cleanse every dark and recessed cranny from any unclean spirits of depression, grief or death.

This was not a "ghost-buster" mission. God takes care of the souls of the departed. We were taking up spiritual brooms and mops to get rid of any cobwebs of darkness that remained. We prayed prayers of holiness and light into that space and sang spiritual hymns and songs to lift up the presence of the holy. We walked through every room of the house, one at a time, singing and cleansing and praying for the light of Christ and holiness to pervade it. Finally we gathered around the dining room table where we had placed a goblet of wine and a loaf of bread. There Conlee led us in a holy Eucharist, so that the first meal eaten in this newly blessed home would be the body and blood of our Lord Jesus Christ. Most of us had tears in our eyes as we passed the bread and wine.

The owners of that home had few sleepless nights after that, and the cat rested peacefully on the foot of their large bed from then on.

Polluted Objects

At this point I need to mention a response God may ask you to make as part of a holy housecleaning. I refer to the cleansing or removal of polluted objects.

When Conlee and I first began to take our Christian commitment seriously 25 years ago, one of the first things we were led to do was to search our house for objects that were spiritually unhealthy to have around us. "Innocent" little *objets d'art*—a Buddha, some ankh symbols and some pagan statuary went in the garbage or a garage sale. And we found dozens of books. We had acquired many volumes on the occult, for instance, and they had to go. But what would we do with them? We did not want them in the hands of anyone else, so the only reasonable thing to do was to burn them. "Book burning" has a horrible stigma in our society, but after much prayer God seemed to show us He could redeem many things that were spiritually unhealthy, but that some had to be destroyed. Our responsibility was to listen and obey. As we did, we experienced an increased desire to fill our home with godly images, angels, crucifixes, Christian art and good books.

Early in our Christian walk we ran into one particularly powerful example of an expensive artifact that was spiritually unhealthy for its owner. A dear friend had suffered from deep depression for many years and was finally beginning to find some breakthroughs in her newly formed commitment to Christ. She felt, however, that she had reached a plateau in her spiritual development and, after much prayer, determined that she should have a house blessing.

Our friend asked a sizable group of us to assist her, so we went to her lovely home on the appointed evening. It was a rare example of design by a world-famous architect, and she had filled it with expensive antiques from her world travels.

We sang and worshiped God for some time and then began to ask Him for the specific gift of "discerning other spirits" that we might be made aware of anything in the home that had given depression a foothold in her life. We moved through the house, using holy water (over which we had prayed the ancient prayers of the Church for the exorcism of evil spirits). We prayed over and cleansed some old dolls. We prayed the light of Christ over some relics from pagan temples that we discerned had been used in ways that were not pleasing to God.

Then all of us focused at once on a large, bronze dancing girl balancing a tray in one hand. She filled the massive stone fireplace in the living room. Oriental in nature, she did not have any outstanding features to make us uncomfortable, but everyone there recognized intuitively something evil about this particular work of art.

The owner told us the piece was rare and expensive, one of two that had guarded the entrance to a Hindu temple in India for hundreds of years. She had purchased it at auction in London some years earlier, and was told it was a repository for sacrifices made to Hindu gods as the worshipers entered the temple.

The owner realized that she felt the most depressed and dark when she was in this particular room of her home, and the sacrificial aspect of the object gave particular offense to the Holy Spirit who indwelt those of us who were present. We used holy water and prayed over it, but, unlike some of the other objects, we felt it must leave the house. The owner agreed and had several of the men carry the large statue outside and place it behind the garage. I do not know what happened to it, but the woman experienced a major spiritual breakthrough.

Many well-intentioned Christians will argue that a material, inanimate object cannot contain spirits, and that this business of praying over polluted objects is just so much bunk. I would direct their attention to the most basic example: Jesus' use of the inanimate objects of bread and wine in which to posit His divine presence in the Eucharist (Matthew 26:26–29).

Cleansing and Blessing the Soul

It does not take much effort to apply the spiritual application of all we have talked about today to our "hamewith," our home within. For the last forty days we have been about the cleansing of our souls. They, indeed, are the temples God is restoring, the temples where He longs for His presence to reside.

But when our souls contain the combustible mixture of the godly and the ungodly we will know unrest, turmoil, anxiety, depression and dis-ease. God will not tolerate spiritual compromise.

As you begin to search out and cleanse or remove the hidden, so-familiar-they-are-overlooked aspects of your life that are displeasing to God, you will be amazed at the spiritual release you receive. Remember: Ask God to search out the culprits for you. Never resort to the hideous practice of introspection. And let Him lead you in how to deal with them.

As you are cleansed you will naturally want to fill your soul, your home within, with things that are holy. You will be attracted to good literature. You will begin to listen to music that glorifies

God. You will surround yourself with images of the holy (art, symbol, icons, color and nature).

All this takes time and hard work, but it is not impossible. Little by little you will discover new areas in which both your physical and spiritual homes can be made more spiritually attractive and welcoming. You will have a place both within and without where you will find quiet, rest and peace, a place where you can hear His voice and be strengthened, a place where you can rest your full weight on His lap and stay as long as you like.

You will be experiencing wholeness.

Coming into Freedom

> "If anyone loves me, he will obey my teaching. My Father will love him, and we will come to him and make our home with him."
>
> John 14:23

1. Ask the Lord to help you take a spiritual inventory of your house. What surrounds you that inhibits the work of the Holy Spirit in your everyday life?
2. What does God show you as you pray about how to fill your house with spiritual beauty? You might want to designate a section of your journal for "Ideas on How to Furnish My House Spiritually."
3. Prayerfully walk through each room of your house, asking the Lord to cleanse, bless and point out anything that displeases Him. Pray for His light to enter your home as it enters your soul.

Auf Wiedersehen—Until We Meet Again

The journey to wholeness is lifelong. We walk it with an ever-present God who never tires of helping us overcome our obstacles, of helping us to become.

The joy of the healing process is that in each painful encounter with our past we see more and more of Jesus revealed. And what a wonder He is to behold! As we become more whole, we continually perceive more of Him than ever before because the depths of His love, caring and understanding are unfathomable.

In each new and painful encounter with Him we also learn something about ourselves. And the most wonderful thing is that the more we get to know the persons He created us to be, the more we really like ourselves. It is a great feeling to be comfortable in your own skin, happy with your own personality and mannerisms. Becoming comfortable with ourselves is to know the true healing joy of taking our eyes off ourselves and placing them where they belong—on our Lord.

This is why we tell every church we visit that the ministry of wholeness to each member is the most important tool of evangelism they will ever use. If that seems like a contradiction, let me explain.

Until a person becomes whole, freed from bondages to the past, to sin and to unhealthy images of self, he or she can never effectively reach out from his or her own brokenness to take the message of the Good News to others. Yes, God will use us in the midst of our brokenness, but the power comes in our vulnerability, our admission of our inadequacies and our acknowledgment that we need healing as much as do those to whom we minister.

Over the years, we have seen churches struggle unsuccessfully with one church growth program after another. Yet the church bodies that receive the most amazing results in spiritual growth have simply proclaimed that all their members are needy, and that they are willing to become spiritual hospitals, offering healing to any who come. And they admit themselves as the first "patients."

I hope I have conveyed to you the joy of journeying toward wholeness with others in the Body of Christ. I hope you adopt the life goal of always "becoming": Becoming real. Becoming holy. Becoming whole.

Appendix

Prayers of the Church to Help the Traveler

Use of Holy Water

The use of holy water has been mentioned several times during our journey. If you have not spent time in a sacramental church, this may be new to you. I have included in this appendix the ancient prayers of the Church that we use for the blessing of water for the purpose of cleansing and purifying both persons and things. These prayers, as well as the prayers for the blessing of oil, are taken from *A Manual for Priests* (Society of Saint John the Evangelist, 1978). They are the ones we use in our church, with our prayer team, and personally.

Numbers 8:7 says: "To purify them, do this: Sprinkle the water of cleansing on them." Because we as born-again believers are a royal priesthood, we take our proper places as priests in these blessings and prayers. Praying these prayers in the powerful language in which they have been prayed for hundreds of years gives a special importation of the timelessness of God's healing presence and the continuation of the cleansing power of Jesus Christ as we, alongside the leper, cry, "Lord, if you are willing, you can make me clean" (Matthew 8:2).

Keeping in mind that it is *only* the blood of Jesus that has the power to cleanse us from all unrighteousness, we also acknowledge the significance of the deep spiritual washing with water that God instituted in ancient days among His people. His words to Ezekiel ring in our ears: "I will sprinkle clean water on you, and you will be clean; I will cleanse you from all your impurities and from all your idols" (Ezekiel 36:25).

The first time I heard these powerful prayers of the Church over water was 25 years ago at the house blessing described in Day 40. There was so much godly authority in these prayers that the expectation was great for God to do a mighty work in this woman's house before we even began to walk through it. The use of holy water at all house blessings proves to be a vital means of sanctifying the space for God's purposes for the family who dwells therein.

We encourage churches wanting to bring the healing presence of God more fully into their midst to regularly cleanse their sanctuaries with holy water and confessional prayers.

It has been a great blessing for prayer teams to use holy water in prayer for others, both as a washing symbolic of one's baptismal vows and as a mighty aid in deliverance.

When we travel we always take a small container of holy water with us to use as we pray over the hotel rooms where we will rest. We never know what unholy acts may have been conducted in such spaces, and we invoke the Holy Spirit and His light into our midst to drive out any darkness.

The Blessing of Water

Salt, and pure and clean water, being made ready in the church or sacristy, the priest, vested in surplice and violet stole, shall say,

Versicle: Our help is in the Name of the Lord.
Response: Who hath made heaven and earth.

And immediately he shall begin the exorcism of the salt.

I adjure thee, O creature of salt, by the living God, by the true God, by the holy God, by God who commanded thee to be cast by the prophet Elisha into the water to heal the barrenness therof, that thou become salt exorcised for the health of believers: and do thou bring to all who take of thee soundness of the soul and body, and let all vain imaginations, wickedness, and subtlety of the wiles of the devil, and every unclean spirit fly and depart from every place where thou shalt be sprinkled, adjured by the Name of him, who shall come to judge both the quick and the dead, and the world by fire. AMEN.

Let us pray.

Almighty and everlasting God, we humbly beseech thy great and boundless mercy, that it may please thee of thy lovingkindness to bless and to hallow this creature of salt, which thou hast given for the use of men, let it be to all them that take of it health of mind and body, and let whatsoever shall be touched or sprinkled therewith be free from all uncleanness, and from all assaults of spiritual wickedness. Through Christ our Lord. AMEN.

The Exorcism of the Water

I adjure thee, O creature of water, by the Name of God the Father Almighty, by the Name of Jesus Christ His Son our Lord, and by the power of the Holy Ghost, that thou become water exorcised for putting to flight all the power of the enemy; and do thou avail to cast out and send hence that same enemy with all his apostate angels, by the power of the same our Lord Jesus Christ, who shall come to judge the quick and the dead, and the world by fire. AMEN.

Let us pray.

O God, who for the salvation of mankind hast ordained that the substance of water should be used in one of thy chiefest Sacraments: favorably regard us who call upon thee, and pour the power of thy benediction upon this element, made ready by careful cleansing; that this thy creature, meet for thy mysteries, may receive the effect of divine grace, and so cast out devils, and put sickness to flight, that whatsoever in the dwellings of thy faithful people shall be sprinkled with this water, may be free from all uncleanness, and delivered from all manner of hurt; there let no spirit of pestilence abide, nor any corrupting air; thence let all the wiles of the hidden enemy depart, and if there be aught that layeth snares against the safety or peace of them that dwell in the house, let it fly before the sprinkling of this water, so that the health which they seek through calling upon thy holy Name may be protected against all things that threaten it. Through Christ our Lord. AMEN.

Then the Priest shall cast the salt into the water in the form of a cross, saying,

Be this salt and water mingled together: in the Name of the Father, and of the Son, and of the Holy Ghost. AMEN.

V. The Lord be with you.
R. And with thy spirit.

Let us pray.

O God, who art the Author of unconquered might, the King of the Empire that cannot be overthrown, the ever glorious Conqueror: who dost keep under the strength of the dominion that is against thee; who rulest the raging of the fierce enemy; who dost mightily fight against the wickedness of thy foes; with fear and trembling we entreat thee, O Lord, and we beseech thee graciously to behold this creature of salt and water, mercifully shine upon it, hallow it with the dew of thy lovingkindess: that wheresoever it shall be sprinkled, with the invocation of thy holy Name, all haunting of the unclean spirit may be driven away; far thence let the fear of the venomous serpent be cast; and wheresoever it shall be sprinkled, there let the presence of the Holy Ghost be vouchsafed to all of us who shall ask for thy mercy. Through thy Son Jesus Christ our Lord, who with thee, in the unity of the same Holy Ghost, liveth and reigneth God, world without end. Amen.

Use of Blessed Oil

In our church and on our prayer teams, we use blessed oil to anoint a person with the sign of the cross at the beginning of healing prayer. If the person is a believer, it is a strong reminder of the sealing received at baptism when he or she was "marked as Christ's own forever" with the oil of salvation. This anointing typically follows the immersion in or sprinkling of water. Using the sign of the cross to administer the oil in anointing is also a powerful symbol to us that we carry the cross of Christ. It is by His death that we are healed.

Traditionally the type of oil used is the finest olive oil obtainable. We find that adding just a drop or two of some appropriate essence oil is helpful to reach all the senses. Oil of lavender and oil of cloves seem especially appropriate for their traditional healing and refreshing properties.

The Blessing of Oil

V. Our help is in the Name of the Lord.
R. Who hath made heaven and earth.

The Exorcism of Oil

I adjure thee, O creature of oil, by God the Father Almighty, who made heaven and earth, the sea and all that is therein. Let all the power of the adversary, all the host of the devil, and all haunting and vain imaginations of Satan be cast out, and flee away from this creature of oil; that it may be to all who shall use it health of mind and body, in the Name of God the Father Almighty, and of Jesus Christ his Son our Lord, and of the Holy Spirit the Comforter, for the love of the same our Lord Jesus Christ, who shall come to judge the quick and the dead, and the world by fire. AMEN.

V. O Lord hear my prayer.
R. And let my cry come unto thee.
V. The Lord be with you.
R. And with thy spirit.

Let us pray.

O Lord God Almighty, whom all the hosts of Angels do serve with fear and trembling, and who dost accept their spiritual service, vouchsafe to behold, to bless, and to hallow this creature of oil, which thou hast brought forth from the sap of the olive tree, and with which thou hast commanded the sick to be anointed, that they may receive health, and give thanks unto thee the living and true God: grant, we beseech thee; that all who shall be anointed with this oil which we bless in thy Name, may be set free from all weakness, from all sickness, and from all the craft of the enemy, and let every hostile power be kept away from the work of thine hands, which thou hast redeemed with the precious blood of thy Son, Jesus Christ our Lord. Who with thee, in the unity of the Holy Spirit, liveth and reigneth God, world without end. AMEN.

Prayers for the Blessing of a Home

Whether a home is inhabited by a large, extended group of people or by only one person, a family resides within its walls. The fellowship of God (Father, Son and Holy Spirit) makes up a family unit with the ones who dwell within the home. The head of that home, under the authority of the Lord Jesus Christ, might be a college student, a single mother, working parents with many children, a widow, a couple with an empty nest, or roommates who share the rent.

In order to sanctify or consecrate a living space to the glory of God, there is nothing more meaningful and effective than the special occasion of the blessing of a home. Conlee and I have participated in many house blessings, as well as several blessings of business or office spaces. Blessings have been offered in such places as a sprinkler system plant, a drugstore, a realtor's office, a textbook store, a doctor's office and an engineering firm.

It is a godly occasion when a family or group of friends gathers informally to walk through a home, spontaneously praying blessings and light over the space. As those gathered for the occasion move from room to room, they may be led by the Spirit to offer appropriate prayers, songs, Scripture readings or blessings.

The form offered here for the blessing of a home is a guideline for those who prefer some structure for a starting-off point. This is especially helpful if a large group assembles for the occasion. For each person to have his or her own copy of a liturgical blessing to follow does not hinder the Spirit, but rather gives shape and structure for more freedom in the Spirit. Spontaneous prayers may still be offered following the liturgical prayers in each room.

Our family traditionally asks one of the children to carry a large, lighted Paschal candle into each room, forming a sort of processional, bearing the light of Christ into each corner of the home. These candles, with Christian symbols imprinted on them, are available at most Christian bookstores or from Christian mail order suppliers.

If it is convenient to have someone in authority to celebrate the Lord's Supper, the blessing of a home may end in the dining room as the family of God gathers around the table to share the body and blood of our Lord. This puts the appropriate emphasis on the great symbol of being "at table" together with Him at every meal.

To use water that has been blessed for exorcism and cleansing is an effective symbol and mediator of the sanctifying power of the Holy Spirit, as we invite His presence into our midst to hallow it for His purposes. We sprinkle the blessed water liberally throughout the home and use it to make the sign of the cross on the doorposts and windows in each room. It is especially meaningful for each person of the household to receive an anointing with the holy water and a personal blessing at the conclusion of the service.

If water has not been blessed already, the family may gather in the living room for the prayers over the water.

After the water is blessed, let there be a knock on the front door of the home. If a child is present, he or she might ask, "Who knocks at our door?" As the leader opens the door, he or she reads the words of Jesus, the One entering the home.

Leader: "Here I am! I stand at the door and knock. If anyone hears my voice and opens the door, I will come in and eat with him, and he with me" (Revelation 3:20).

Response (all): Welcome to this home, Lord Jesus.

Leader: "If anyone loves me, he will obey my teaching. My Father will love him, and we will come to him and make our home with him" (John 14:23).

Response: Lord, make this Your home, a place to be filled with Your holy presence.

Leader: Let the mighty power and light of the risen Lord be present in this home to cleanse it from all that is unholy, unclean, and from any trace of darkness and evil that resides within it, in the name of our Lord Jesus Christ. AMEN.

Blessing at the Entrance of the Home

Leader: "When you enter a house, first say, 'Peace to this house'" (Luke 10:5).

Response: May all who enter this home receive the peace of the Lord.

Prayer: Lord Jesus Christ, You are Lord of this home, and as You enter this dwelling, You bring peace and light and holiness with You. If any darkness has entered through this doorway, cleanse it by the anointing of Your presence. May Your healing presence permeate the hearts of all who dwell within these walls, and all who come in and go out these doors. Bless this entrance as a gateway into the refuge of a holy God. May we find solace and refreshment as we enter this home. AMEN.

Blessing in the Living Room or Family Room

Leader: "May those who love You be secure. May there be peace within Your walls. . . . Live in peace with each other" (Psalm 122:6; 1 Thessalonians 4:13).

Response: May each person who enters this room be always aware of the security of Your presence and the peace that passes understanding.

Prayer: Lord Jesus, free the gift of hospitality in our hearts. May the invitation to gather in Your name be always on our lips. Guard our activities in this room by the power of Your Spirit. May we be constantly aware of Your presence with us in this place as we converse, watch television, listen to music or read. If anything in this room is displeasing to You, we ask that You cleanse it by Your Spirit. Pour Your light upon us as we spend time in this space. AMEN.

Blessing in the Study or Library

Leader: "Do not conform any longer to the pattern of this world, but be transformed by the renewing of your mind. Then you will be able to test and approve what God's will is—his good, pleasing and perfect will" (Romans 12:2).

Response: May all who read, work and study in this room be constantly aware that all the treasures of wisdom and knowledge are hidden in Christ Jesus.

Prayer: Lord Jesus, open the riches of Your wisdom to those who seek it in this place. Restore the good of reason along with the hunger for good Christian literature. If any books in this room displease You, shine the light of Your Spirit on them. Cleanse this space from any cynicism, negative thoughts, unbelief and darkness. Teach eternal truth to all who seek You. Inspire each mind to take in all that is true, noble, right, pure, lovely, admirable, excellent and praiseworthy. Guard each mind in this home by Your holy presence. AMEN.

Blessing in the Kitchen

Leader: "Do not work for food that spoils, but for food that endures to eternal life, which the Son of Man will give you. . . . I am the bread of life. He who comes to me will never go hungry, and he who believes in me will never be thirsty" (John 6:27, 35).

Response: May everyone in this family hunger and thirst for the things of God.

Prayer: Lord Jesus, thank You for the bread of life. Increase the hunger in our hearts for Your Word and the things of Your Spirit. Decrease our appetites for the things of this world that keep us from becoming all You created us to be. Give us appetites for those things that bring us health and wholeness. May those who prepare meals for this family do so in love and with joy. Stir up the creative gifts of Your Spirit so that the preparation of each meal may carry the love and significance that would be given to serve You at our table. AMEN.

Blessing in a Workroom

Leader: "Whatever you do,work at it with all your heart, as working for the Lord, not for men, since you know that you will receive an inheritance from the Lord as a reward" (Colossians 3:23–24).

Response: Bless the work of the hands that labor in this room.

Prayer: Lord Jesus, may Your creativity stir the hearts, minds and imaginations of all who work and labor in this place. May each task that is accomplished, whether large or small, bring honor and glory to You. May the fruit of workmanship be an expression of Your grace to those who labor. Let those who work in this room find their identities in You and not in the work of their hands. Give rest and re-creation to those who offer their creativity back to You. AMEN.

Blessing in a Bedroom

Leader: "I will lie down and sleep in peace, for you alone, O LORD, make me dwell in safety" (Psalm 4:8).

Response: Guide us waking, O Lord, and guard us sleeping, that awake we may watch with Christ, and asleep we may rest in peace.

Prayer: Lord Jesus, speak to Your servants even as they sleep. Speak to them in the language of godly dreams and visions. Let rest that comes only from You penetrate even to their bones. May Your angels watch over those who sleep. Cleanse this room from any hidden darkness that may have entered through words or actions. Let the healing light of Your Spirit be a nightlight, and the canopy of Your glory a blanket on those who rest in this bed. Renew and refresh as You lay them down to sleep. AMEN.

Blessing for a Guest Room

Leader: "Share with God's people who are in need. Practice hospitality" (Romans 12:13).

Response: May we give freely to others from the storehouse of what You have given us.

Prayer: Lord Jesus, as guests visit this home, may they sense the welcoming presence of Your Holy Spirit. May each one feel honored and respected, a special part of Your creation. Make each family member sensitive to the needs of those You send here, and equip this family to lead them to You, the One who meets all our needs and the desires of our hearts. Give this family a holy boldness to proclaim Your goodness and Your saving grace. May this home be a shelter for the weary and a glow of warmth for the cold of heart. AMEN.

Blessing in a Child's Room

Leader: "I tell you the truth, unless you change and become like little children, you will never enter the kingdom of heaven. Therefore, whoever humbles himself like this child is the greatest in the kingdom of heaven" (Matthew 18:3–4).

Response: Let us celebrate the joy of childhood and the freedom to come to You in complete trust.

Prayer: Lord Jesus, bless the child who sleeps and plays in this room. May *his* heart be open to You though imagination, wonder and joy. Let Your angels watch over *him* as *he* sleeps and may *he* hear Your lullabies when *he* is distressed. Guard *his* mind and protect *his* body in all *he* does. May *his* toys and games direct *him* toward the holy things of life and away from worldy pursuits. Lead *him* into a deep, personal relationship with You. AMEN.

Blessing in a Bathroom

Leader: "Do you not know that your bodies are members of Christ himself?" (1 Corinthians 6:15).

Response: May all who use this bathroom be reminded constantly that they are the supreme workmanship of their heavenly Creator, the crown of His creation.

Prayer: Lord Jesus, let everyone who tends to the necessary maintenance of the wondrous work of the physical body be in awe of the ways in which he is fearfully and wonderfully made. Give grace to the members of this family to bless their bodies aright, to use them as You intended, to love and not despise them, to tenderly care for and not abuse them. May we have the wisdom, until we are clothed eternally in glory with You in heaven, to care for ourselves, Your creation, with godly respect and honor. AMEN.

Blessing for a Deck, Patio, Terrace or Garden

Leader: "You will be like a well-watered garden, like a spring whose waters never fail" (Isaiah 58:11).

Response: May the times spent in this outdoor area be reminders of the beauty of Your creation and the fruitfulness You call forth.

Prayer: Lord Jesus, let all who come to this place, either with company or in solitude, be refreshed by the sweet Spirit of Your presence. May each one who comes hear Your voice, walk with You, sit by Your side and be renewed. Bless the hands who plant here and increase the yield of their labors. Let Your glory blossom forth in the plantings, both in the dormant times and in the times of increase. May the heavens declare the glory of Your name in this place. AMEN.

Blessing in the Dining Room or Eating Area

Leader: "I have food to eat that you know nothing about. . . . My food . . . is to do the will of him who sent me and to finish his work" (John 4:32, 34).

Response: May we be content with the daily bread You provide for us.

Prayer: Lord Jesus, feed us with Your manna. Fill us to overflowing with the food that satisfies. Thank You for Your provision. At every meal be present with this family. Birth in us the great Christian symbol of being "at table" with one another. Release the flow of healthy, affirming conversation at every meal. Give a meaningful place to each member of the family around the table. Prepare us constantly for the great banquet we will share with You at the Marriage Feast of the Lamb. AMEN.

After the House Blessing

Holy Communion may follow the blessing of the home.

It is appropriate to ask the Lord to bless some meaningful Christian symbol to adorn the home permanently as a reminder of this occasion. An anointing with holy water and a blessing may be said over each member of the family. The following benediction and blessing may be offered by the leader:

"Now fear the LORD and serve him with all faithfulness. Throw away the gods your forefathers worshiped . . . and serve the LORD. But if serving the LORD seems undesirable to you, then choose for yourselves this day whom you will serve, whether the gods your forefathers served . . . or the gods . . . in whose land you are living. But as for me and my household, we will serve the LORD" (Joshua 24:14–15).

"May the God of peace, who through the blood of the eternal covenant brought back from the dead our Lord Jesus, that great Shepherd of the sheep, equip you with everything good for doing his will, and may he work in us what is pleasing to him, through Jesus Christ, to whom be glory for ever and ever. Amen" (Hebrews 13:20–21).